THE NEWS IN AMERICA

The Library of Congress Series in
American Civilization
Edited by Ralph Henry Gabriel

THE NEWS
IN AMERICA

Frank Luther Mott

HARVARD UNIVERSITY PRESS · CAMBRIDGE · MASSACHUSETTS
· MCMLV ·

To

RALPH D. CASEY

SCHOLAR, COUNSELOR, FRIEND

Preface

This book deals with the American scene, but it is offered to its readers in full awareness that our own problems are part of a world situation. Mass communication is a global phenomenon, with multiple political, economic, and social aspects. Slightly less than one-fourth of the daily newspapers of the world are published in the United States. The need for news is universal; and many of the factors involved in gathering, processing, and distributing it are common to most of the peoples and nations of the world.

In this essay I have attempted to define and describe news in the United States, and the way it is assembled, edited, and disseminated. I have tried to resist following bypaths, however alluring. The news is associated more or less closely with so many interesting outlooks and prospects in our world of communication that it is not always easy to keep faithfully to the main road, but the news itself furnishes a broad enough subject for such a modest volume as this.

I have not intended this book as a controversial tract; I think it is primarily a piece of exposition. But the news, like all dynamic elements in our contemporary civilization, is the subject of much debate; and I shall be surprised (and a little disappointed) if some readers are not moved to strong disagreement with some of the points of view that are maintained in these chapters and some of the conclusions that are reached. It may be as well to state definitely at the outset one of the central positions of the argument which will be found in the following pages.

I believe that the leading critics of our news system are ill-advised in giving so much attention to the fact that the number of our newspapers is decreasing — a trend which has little or no effect upon the copious distribution of reliable news and virtually no relation to the real abuses of news handling in America. Besides, that decrease results from the operation of economic laws which would be about as hard to repeal as the schedule of tides at the Bay of Fundy.

What we should concern ourselves with is the wide dissemination of the idea that news is a set of counters in a "game" by which the people are to be excited at any cost. One of the chief theses of this volume is that the great fault of our whole system of reporting and editing is an overemphasis on the so-called "soft" news of relatively unimportant things, and a corresponding unwillingness on the part of many information agencies to accept the responsibility for teaching readers and hearers and viewers to accept "hard" news of real significance.

But we must not anticipate further.

It is impossible to name here the many persons, institutions, and agencies which have supplied ideas and data for this study. Many busy newspapermen, radio directors, bureau chiefs, and others have taken the time to reply to questions. Perhaps outstanding among those to whom I owe special thanks are Paul Mickelson, of the New York office of the Associated Press, and Jack Shelley, of Station WHO, Des Moines. I am grateful to Dr. Ralph D. Casey, director of the School of Journalism, University of Minnesota, and Dr. Earl F. English, dean of the School of Journalism, University of Missouri, for reading the manuscript and offering many helpful suggestions.

FRANK LUTHER MOTT

University of Missouri

CONTENTS

1 News-Hunger 1

2 Feeding the News-Hungry 9

3 What's the News? 22

4 News as History 33

5 Speed: The News as Timely Report 41

6 News as Sensation 48

7 The Human-Interest Story as News 58

8 Objective News *versus* Qualified Report 67

9 Local News 88

10 Domestic News and the News Services 97

11 News of Government 105

12 Foreign News 122

13 No. 50, Rockefeller Plaza 131

14 The "Daily Tribune" Goes to Press 140

15 WZZZ Airs the News 148

16 The Form of News 156

17 News Controls 173

18 To Lead or to Follow 199

19 The Responsibilities of the Reader 205

20 Looking toward the Future 214

    Notes 219

    Index 227

THE NEWS IN AMERICA

CHAPTER ONE

News-Hunger

News-hunger is fundamental in human nature. It is characteristic of social man, whether he is conscious of it or not. The
basic desires are those for food, shelter, and sex expression; after
these are satisfied, other desires crowd forward — for social life,
for recognition among one's fellows, for new experience and adventure. These latter desires are greatly stimulated by information,
or news, about others. Especially exciting are the adventure stories
about struggle of all kinds — with the elements, with wild animals,
with other tribes.

So it is now; so it has been from the beginning. Doubtless the
most primitive ancestors of modern man squatted in a ring in a
murky cave as Ug told them about the slaying of a lion or a fight
with the tree-men. As they chewed on bones and roots, they
paused to interject grunts of encouragement for the narrator, for
was not Ug their spinner of tales, apt at gathering rumor and hear-
say wherever he went, and weaving all into a web of words? And
so Ug and his colleagues of the cave and tepee and igloo and
cliff-dwelling were the newsmen of those primitive groups — the
enterprising reporters of the cave.

The ancient Egyptian papyrus tales, as collected by W. Flinders
Petrie, some of which possibly go back to 4000 B.C., show a good
journalistic sense of what was interesting to an audience, and a
gift for the exciting and sensational. Thus two types of oral communication developed together — the imaginative narrative and
the factual story, the embellished tale and the faithful recital of
fact. Both developed, of course, in response to the desires of their
audience, and often they are hard to separate. But the former was
designed more for amusement, was on a higher aesthetic level,
and might, by repetition, attain some permanence; while the latter
met a more immediate need, was sometimes quite essential to
very existence, could be communicated by everyone, and was generally ephemeral.

One may catch echoes of the circulation of news among the ancients. In the Book of Genesis, in the Hebrew Scriptures, we are told that when Joseph's brothers came down into Egypt to see him, "the report thereof was heard in Pharaoh's house, saying, Joseph's brethren are come." This is among the earliest recorded instances of news of family visiting — a type of reporting not unknown today, especially in community newspapers.

The ancient Greeks, with their insatiable democratic curiosity about affairs, were especially fond of news.[1] In his First Philippic, Demosthenes observed, "It is the greatest pleasure of the Athenians to wander through the streets asking, What is the news?"

The Romans were similarly news-hungry, and Tacitus once wrote something about the Romans that sounds much like what Demosthenes said about the Athenians: he called Rome *sermonum avida et nihil reticente* — greedy for talk and never quiet. About the time of the beginning of the Republic, the Romans developed written newsletters, which continued from Rome as a center for a thousand years, or until the fall of the Western Empire. At its height, the Roman newsletter was a great institution, helping to abate the hunger for news of those Romans who had to reside for a time far from the world's capital, that great city, their home. To abate indeed, but never to satisfy that hunger; for example, when Cicero was in Cilicia as proconsul there, he complained to his friend Caelius that the newsletters he received contained too much sports news (combats of the gladiators) but not enough of that political news so important to the proconsul.

From early times, the Romans at home were served some news in official proclamations posted on the whitened bulletin board called *album*, which was under the direction of the Pontifex Maximus. But it was Julius Caesar who, on assuming his consulship in January of 59 B.C., immediately caused the writing and posting of a rather extensive daily news bulletin called *acta*, or record of events.[2] This has come to be called the *acta diurna*, or daily record, though Latin writers more frequently refer to it as *acta populi*, or people's record. It was indeed a service for the people — as precisely designed to satisfy a popular hunger as were the later *panem et circenses*. At first there was much about Senate proceedings in the *acta*, Caesar having special reasons for turning the light of publicity in that direction; but eventually the curia shared space in this forerunner of the newspaper with a great variety of news — that of the law courts, whose decisions were important in the contents of the *acta* from the beginning; war news, as Caesar's Gallic campaigns developed, and later other movements of Roman arms; and an extraordinary miscellany, as births, marriages, and deaths, family scandals and divorces, murders and other crimes, as well as omens and prodigies and monstrosities. These things were rather badly written in a sad jumble by reporters called *actuarii*, posted daily, read by the populace, and copied down by those who served Romans far from home with their newsletters.

For the newsletter business continued to flourish. Journalists appeared who, mustering a group of slaves who could write — buying or hiring them — stood before them on a raised dais and dictated the news of the day, which was thus turned out by these *amanuenses* in an "edition" for a number of subscribers. Newsletters continued to be used throughout the Middle Ages, chiefly to convey business and political news between the various cities of Europe. Venice became a center for them; but there were professional *nouvellistes*, *zeitungsschreiber*, and newsletter-writers in all the large cities. The Fugger brothers, of Augsburg, with large commercial interests all over the continent, received many of these newsletters in the fifteenth and sixteenth centuries; and today the Fugger collection of such material in the National Library in Vienna is the greatest repository of newsletters in existence. The Fuggers became one of the wealthiest mercantile and banking families in the world, not only by boldness and shrewdness, but also by being well informed; for them, as for hundreds of other men who were engaged in business and politics, news was an absolute necessity.

Since the need for news becomes sharper and more insistent in times of crisis, war has always been a great whetter of the news appetite. The first German pamphlets of printed news, in the sixteenth century, were most often devoted to stories of battles and threats of dangers. The first English news-sheets came into being in response to the desire for news of the Thirty Years' War. Wars and disasters always cause a "boom" in news. During the

first year of the American Civil War, Oliver Wendell Holmes
wrote an article for the *Atlantic Monthly* in which he said:

> Bread and the Newspaper — this is the new version of the *Panem
> et Circenses* of the Roman populace. . . . We must have something
> to eat and the newspapers to read. Everything else we can give up. . . .
> The newspaper is as imperious as a Russian Ukase; it will be had
> and it will be read. To this all else must give place.

There are thus degrees and gradations of news-hunger, ranging
from that which is based on mere idle curiosity to that which
derives from agonies of personal anxiety. There are also differences of news-hunger which are based more on reasoning and less
on the feelings: some phases of the desire for news may be
recognized as much more *important*, in the scale of social values,
than others.

There is the desire for information about how other people
live and act, not in extraordinary situations, but in common life.
This news-hunger is met most adequately by what, in modern
journalism, we have learned to call the "human-interest story."
How high in the scale you place the desire for such news will
perhaps depend on your evaluation of that common life of which
it treats.

There is the desire for sensation in the news — for whatever
thrills, surprises, or shocks. The social value of such news depends
less on its quality as sensation than on the importance of the
events and conditions reported. Wars and disasters are undeniably important; they are also sensational. Great political
contests, and indeed most stories of conflict, furnish news that
thrills, surprises, or shocks. On the other hand, the desire for
sensationalism for its own sake, as sometimes fulfilled in news
of sex and crime, must be placed low in the scale.

There is also, in this news-hunger we have been discussing,
often a desire for self-improvement. This is a zeal for the
acquisition of knowledge about what are conceived to be the
important things that are going on in the world. It is what the
serious reader or listener feels as he picks up his newspaper or
turns his radio dial. He may be impelled by an aspiration to
become an informed man, either for his own satisfaction, or for

recognition among his fellows, or for both. And back of all this, consciously or unconsciously, all readers hope to gain from a knowledge of the immediate past some insight into the immediate future. This desire for aid in prediction will be discussed in a later chapter.

But in a democratic society there is a special reason for the feeling of the people about the necessity of serious news. Wherever the ultimate decisions depend upon the will of the people, it is obviously necessary, if those decisions are to be made intelligently, that they should be based upon adequate popular knowledge of events and conditions. Nobody has ever expressed this fundamental principle of democracy better than Thomas Jefferson. In 1787 Jefferson wrote a letter to Edward Carrington about a recent popular uprising in Massachusetts against the courts and other supposed abuses, led by Daniel Shays. One sentence from this letter has often been quoted, but let us read the context with some care:

The people are the only censors of their governors: and even their errors will tend to keep these to the true principles of their institution. To punish these errors too severely would be to suppress the only safeguard of the public liberty. The way to prevent these irregular interpositions of the people is to give them full information of their affairs through the channel of the public papers, and to contrive that those papers should penetrate the whole mass of the people. The basis of our governments being the opinion of the people, the first object should be to keep that right; and were it left to me to decide whether we should have a government without newspapers, or newspapers without a government, I should not hesitate a moment to prefer the latter. But I should mean that every man should receive those papers, and be capable of reading them. . . . Cherish, therefore, the spirit of our people, and keep alive their attention. Do not be too severe upon their errors, but reclaim them by enlightening them.

We do not need to elaborate here upon Jefferson's theories of government. We are concerned only with the doctrine which he expressed again and again regarding the essential nature of the service of news to the democratic system. It was after he retired from the Presidency that he put the doctrine into a maxim of fourteen words: "Where the press is free, and every man able to read, all is safe."

This has the terseness of an aphorism, and deserves acceptance as a fundamental tenet of the democratic system. Of course, there are today other "channels" of news and information. Jefferson himself, in 1816, probably had in mind not only newspapers, but pamphlets; today he would have to include also radio and television broadcasts, motion pictures, magazines, and topical books.

Such was the Jeffersonian doctrine of the necessity of news and information in a democracy. It was a doctrine severely tested by the scurrilous and vicious journalism of the period. Jefferson suffered more than any other American President from abuse by the newspapers, and he said some very bitter things in retaliation. Yet throughout his life he maintained his testimony to the essential service of the press in a democracy. Shortly before his death, the aged statesman and philosopher took up his pen and wrote with trembling hand to his faithful correspondent in France, M. Coray, that "the press . . . is also the best instrument for enlightening the mind of man, and improving him as a rational, moral, and social being."

It is, of course, the general acceptance of the doctrine so well expressed by Jefferson which has made journalism in the great democratic nations superior to that of other countries in quantity, in freedom of utterance, and in the scope of its news. In the United States, at least, the communication agencies have become a true Fourth Estate of democratic government.

In seventeenth-century England, the three "estates of the realm" were royalty, lords, and commons; but later they were designated as the lords spiritual and the lords temporal, who sat in the House of Lords, and the commons, who were represented in the other house of Parliament. These three "estates" came to be recognized as comprising the English government, but writers and orators would occasionally refer to other powerful factors in the English body politic, such as the Army, as "a fourth estate." Apparently the first to use this designation for the press was Macaulay, who, writing an essay on Hallam's *Constitutional History* in 1828, observed:

The gallery in which the reporters sit has become a fourth estate of the realm. The publication of the parliamentary debates, a practice which seemed to the most liberal statesmen of the old school full of danger to the great safeguards of public liberty, is now regarded by many persons as a safeguard tantamount, and more than tantamount, to all the rest together.

A few years later Carlyle was using the term in referring to the "able editors" for whom he had such an admiration; and in 1840, in his lecture on "The Hero as Man of Letters," he dramatically ascribed the *bon mot* to Edmund Burke. The paragraph is well worth rereading:

Witenagemote, old Parliament, was a great thing. The affairs of the nation were there deliberated and decided; what we were to *do* as a nation. But does not, though the name Parliament subsists, the parliamentary debate go on now, everywhere and at all times, in a far more comprehensive way, *out* of Parliament altogether? Burke said there were Three Estates in Parliament; but, in the Reporters' Gallery yonder, there sat a *Fourth Estate* more important than they all. It is not a figure of speech, or a witty saying; it is a literal fact — very momentous to us in these times. Literature is our Parliament too. Printing, which comes necessarily out of writing, I say often, is equivalent to Democracy: invent Writing, Democracy is inevitable.

All this is interesting as a footnote to Macaulay and Carlyle. Or to the history of the English Parliament, for it will be noted that what the invention of the term "Fourth Estate" did was to indicate the importance of the press as distributor of the news of Parliamentary debates.

But in the United States the expression has taken on wider meaning; it refers to the public press, without reference to the special reporting of Congress or acts of government. It is apt, moreover, because of the tripartite division of the United States government. If we transfer the old designation "estates" to the three divisions of our government — executive, legislative, and judicial — then we may add in truth and actuality a fourth "estate" consisting of the agencies of communication. And whether or not this estate is "more than tantamount" to the others, as Macaulay, the great Whig, asserted, it is without the slightest doubt *essential* to any government which rests on the will of the people.

This transcendent importance of news and information in a democracy is deeply felt by the reading and listening public.

It is not that they stand up and beat their breasts and shout, "We have a passion for news because we are citizens of a country we love!" But, beginning with the time of the American Revolution, when democratic participation in public affairs became the outstanding feature of our political system, that participation has been made possible through the newspaper, the pamphlet, and public speaking. Later these agencies were reinforced by the motion picture, the topical book, and the radio. Through the years the tradition that the people should look to the communication agencies for knowledge of public affairs, and thereby make them their own affairs, has persisted and strengthened. It is this tradition, ingrained in the thinking of the common citizen, which has made Americans so deeply news-conscious and constantly news-hungry.

It cannot be denied that some citizens take their responsibilities too lightly. On the whole, it is evident that the contemporary American is less serious and more distracted by a many-faceted society than were his forefathers. We give too large a proportion of our attention to the comics in the newspapers and the gag-shows on the radio. God knows we need emotional escapes in these days, but our news appetite is directed too much toward the spicy dishes and too little toward the heavier and more nourishing foods. Newspapers and magazines have always given the public a fairly accurate response to its desires, and the press of the first third of the nineteenth century, for example, certainly gave its readers a much plainer as well as heavier fare than does the press of the middle of the twentieth century. Yet, even today, with a readership far broader and less homogeneous, the demands of the more earnest readers and listeners are evidenced by many columns of carefully informative news in the papers and many hours of serious reports on the radio.

For demand is always answered by supply, and any discussion of news must begin with an inquiry into the phenomenon of news-hunger. What we get from any and all of our news media is a fairly direct response to the demand of the people, as it is understood by the managers of those media. Through the various channels of communication flow the millions of words which the news-hunger of the people requires.

Of course, all this does not relieve the newsmen — all the managers and workers in communication agencies — from tremendous responsibilities of their own, which they must realize and face. They cannot escape their obligation as guides and interpreters. They cannot point to the basest elements of their public and say, "They wanted chaff and slops," and thus alibi their failures. The man whom Carlyle exalts by the term "able editor" is a leader, a preceptor, a teacher who, as Henry Adams said, "affects eternity; he cannot tell where his influence stops."

But fundamentally, and in the long run, it is the people who make the news what it is. Their news-hungers must be satisfied.

CHAPTER TWO

Feeding the News-Hungry

The broad base of the demand for news — coming from people of all levels of intelligence, interests, and tastes — is matched by a broad base of news supply.

We often think of the news as under the control of the metropolitan daily newspapers, but these great papers by no means monopolize the distribution of our current intelligence. There are good reasons indeed for questioning whether they are even the most important factor in that vast operation.

Let us take a look at the media of news distribution which are active in the United States at the mid-twentieth century. We shall disregard, for the present, the middlemen who supply the suppliers in our complicated news industry, and limit our survey to the agencies and processes which feed the news directly to the people. We shall also disregard for the present those media which deal with information which, though it may contain reference to recent events, is scarcely to be classified as news, such as the sermons of the clergy, classroom lectures, stump speeches (formal oral propaganda), and books in general.

We must begin our survey of actual news dissemination in America by directing attention to the informal and noncommercial

circulation of news among the people. This comes chiefly by word
of mouth, though personal correspondence plays some part in it.
The writer of these pages remembers hearing his grandfather
tell of receiving the news of the assassination of Lincoln from
a man who came riding horseback along a country road, and
then hurrying home to tell his wife and family. As a boy at a
county fair one afternoon in September, 1901, the grandson
caught the tragic news of the assassination of President McKinley,
which was passing rapidly from one person to another in a crowd
of farmers and townspeople. Today radio flashes often bring us
our first intelligence of major news-breaks; but few of us listen
constantly to the radio, and our first information about such
matters is likely to come from the excited exclamations of some
acquaintance. "Have you heard? . . . The radio says . . ." And
aside from information of great importance, there are innumerable
little items of news which we pick up on the street, on busses
and streetcars and subway trains, in barrooms and barbershops,
at bridge parties, at trade union meetings, at business conferences,
in clubrooms. Women's clubs and men's service clubs are centers
for newsmongering, not only in speeches and programs but also
in the conversation of members.

But much of the news thus circulated is mere gossip and rumor.
Part, but not all, of it is reckless and irresponsible. It is a mélange
of news and comment and background stuff and jokes and
propaganda and chatter. But it is tremendously important. As a
basis for the molding of opinion there is probably nothing more
effective than conversation with a friend whom one considers
well informed and well balanced.

But your friend doubtless got at least a part of his information
from the press — what used to be called "the public prints."
And of all printed news media, the newspaper has, of course,
the premier position. We call it a newspaper because its chief
function in our journalism has been to publish the news, and it
reaches our population in a near approach to saturation. Newspaper circulation has increased much faster than population in
recent decades. It has required more than fifty years for the last
doubling of the population of the United States, but the aggregate
circulation of American dailies has doubled in the last thirty

years. Americans are keeping up their reputation as assiduous readers of newspapers; and the hope of Thomas Jefferson, which he expressed in his famous letter to Edward Carrington, has come pretty close to fulfillment: "But I should mean that every man should receive those papers, and be capable of reading them." And even before the adoption of the Nineteenth Amendment, we could have written it "every man and woman."

It should be recognized that newspapers carry news not only in their regular news columns, but in other departments as well. News is often found in the editorial columns; indeed, many editorials are informative rather than argumentative, and almost all are supposed to have a "news peg." Syndicated columns, so important in the modern newspaper, may be devoted chiefly to comment; but, like the editorials, they contain a vast deal of information, and some of them are almost wholly given to news. The type of thoughtful article sometimes referred to as an "editorial feature" usually has high news value.

What is called "feature" material, because it is not regarded as either "straight news" or comment, often has a strong news angle. Frequently features are so closely related to straight reporting that we call them "news features."

And advertising, too, has great news value. James Gordon Bennett was one of the first to recognize this. Soon after he started his *New York Herald* in 1835, he threw out all the annual advertisements which ran throughout the year without alteration, filling the "ad" columns of those days, and demanded that advertisers in the *Herald* change their notices daily, thus providing fresh and interesting matter (news) for his readers. When *PM* was conducted as an "adless" paper, it recognized the news value of some kinds of advertising by devoting a department to interesting offers of New York's retail stores; but that was not enough, and beyond doubt *PM's* failure was due in a considerable degree to the fact that it did not satisfy the need of most readers for advertising news as well as the regular news and comment. The fact is that many readers take quite as much interest in the advertising columns as in those devoted to "straight" news. Careful studies of reader interest have shown that the rate of readership of women in Sunday papers is higher for the news of department-store offerings than for anything else except the columns of women's styles and the roto and comic sections. Men's readership of department-store advertising is also high. A summary of 138 studies of reader-interest which have been made by the Advertising Research Foundation since 1940 for daily papers all over the country was published in January, 1951; it shows a remarkable increase in interest in advertising, which now compares favorably with that in news and editorial features. Classified advertising, for example, with its fresh and usable news, scored in the prewar period 32 per cent for men and 38 per cent for women; in the war years 40 per cent and 48 per cent, and in the postwar period 44 per cent and 48 per cent.

Now, if we are to understand the status of newspapers as the purveyors of the latest information about current affairs, we shall have to set up some categories. The curse of our discussions of newspapers has been our habit of generalizing about them. Newspapers differ so much in so many respects — size, field, policy, etc. — that sweeping and inclusive statements about them are untrustworthy. Indeed, it may be said that the only generalization about newspapers that is really safe is that no generalization about them is safe.

Most prominent of newspaper categories is the one which includes the metropolitan dailies. At mid-century 229 dailies were published in the 106 American cities of over 100,000 population. Or if you prefer to reserve the term "metropolitan" for cities of over 200,000, there are, by such definition, 128 "metropolitan" dailies.[3]

The circulation of these city papers is not wholly limited to the metropolitan areas in which they are published, for they often compete with the local dailies which serve smaller cities many miles distant, and with weeklies in the rural sections. New York city papers, for example, have some circulation in a large part of New England, New York, New Jersey, and Pennsylvania, and sections at greater distances. Many Washington newsstands provide not only local papers but those from New York and Baltimore. Some great newspapers have considerable mail circulation; the *New York Times* and the *Christian Science Monitor* have extensive daily distribution by mail throughout the nation. Many metropolitan papers have great regional circulations. Chicago papers cover not only Illinois, but much of Michigan, Indiana, Iowa, and Wisconsin. The circulation of the *Des Moines Register* far exceeds the population of its home city, and the paper is delivered by trucks all over Iowa. The *Kansas City Star* has long been notable for wide regional distribution. Sunday papers nearly always have an even larger distance-circulation than the daily editions.

So it goes throughout the nation. The point to be remembered is that the big papers break into the small fields. Although Sandusky, Ohio, now has only one paper — the *Register-Star-News*, result of multiple consolidations — the city has Toledo and Cleveland papers practically on its doorsteps; and the news that is served to it is not limited to what the *Register-Star-News* prints.

Conversely, the areas staked out by the great metropolitan papers are disputed in every town of a few thousand population by one or more small-city dailies. This type of newspaper nearly always carries a wire service. If it is in sharp competition with a metropolitan paper which provides a large amount of national and international news, it will use a shorter wire report and rely largely on local news, in which the big paper cannot compete. Though it is thus more local in interest than its big-city brothers, it carries the most important state news, an abbreviated Washington and national report, and leading stories of world events. The small-city daily, often neglected by students and critics of our communication system, closely integrated with its home community and more thoroughly read than the big papers, is an effective agency in bringing the news to the American people and a powerful opinion maker.

Also competitors of the great metropolitan papers are the suburban dailies, many of which have attained prosperity and editorial excellence in the lion's mouth. Like the small-city dailies, they are able to work more closely with their immediate communities than are their big rivals.

Small-city and suburban dailies numbered 1551 in 1950, in comparison with the 229 metropolitan papers; and they provided approximately one-third of the aggregate circulation of American daily newspapers. But let us not neglect another non-metropolitan sector of the American press — the weeklies.

There are about ten thousand weekly, semiweekly, and tri-weekly newspapers in the United States. Nearly all of these are community papers — what we used to call "country weeklies." The former is the better term, for not only do these papers make a specialty of community service, but many of the towns in which they are published are above the status of country villages. While the census includes inhabitants of towns of 2500 or under in its enumeration of rural population, a considerable proportion of these weeklies are published in towns of 2500 to 5000. Thus the community weeklies serve not only the nearly sixty million persons (about 44 per cent of the total population) who are classified as rural, but about five million more — which brings the total up to almost half the people of the United States.

For these folk the home weekly furnishes local news, an adver-tising medium, leadership, and in general a central point for the integration of the activities of a community which includes the town of publication and the outlying area or trade territory. As a purveyor of news, it is commonly in competition with a neighboring weekly or two, a small-city daily, and at least one metropolitan paper. The dailies may be delivered in town and country by truck and carrier. Besides this competition, the weekly may have a "contemporary" in its own town, for the inevitable economic pressures toward consolidation have left a good many two-newspaper towns and villages, and even a few with three papers. In addition, there may be a free-distribution advertising sheet, which "regular" publishers in both town and small city usually regard as the pest of the "legitimate" newspaper business.

When rural free delivery was instituted by the Post Office Department in 1897, it was believed by many to sound the death knell of the country weekly because it would bring the dailies to the farmhouses. It did do that, and since then the dailies' own trucks have done the same thing more promptly; but daily competition did not kill the weekly. The home paper, more definitely localized, not only lived but prospered. What this paper does is to supplement the various news agencies which serve its community — the big daily, the small daily, the city radio, the news-magazine — with something those media cannot furnish: a record of local enterprises and events. Moreover, the impact of politics and national and international events on the local community is duly recorded and discussed in the weekly, with potent influence on the thinking and opinion of readers. But we must defer to Chapter IX further commentary on the weekly papers.

There is one other large and varied class of newspapers which must be mentioned — the specialized papers, adapted to certain groups of readers. Among them are the foreign-language press, not as large as it was in the days of vast immigration quotas, but still published in some thirty languages. There also is a group of nearly three hundred labor papers, chiefly organs of particular unions. Over a hundred weekly newspapers are issued by and for Negroes. Industries and trades have their own newspapers, such as the *Women's Wear Daily*, of New York. Organizations of many kinds — religious, educational, industrial, etc. — issue papers which contribute to the universal flow of news.

Supplementing the newspaper and in some respects competing with it is the weekly news-magazine. This is usually regarded as a new development in American journalism, and it is true that the pattern set by *Time*, when it was founded in 1923, was different from that of its forerunners. *Niles' Register* (1811–1849), *Frank Leslie's Illustrated Newspaper* (1855–1922), *Harper's Weekly* (1857–1916), and the *Literary Digest* (1890–1938) were, however, distinguished weekly news-magazines of the past. The *Pathfinder*, founded in 1894 as a news digest for schools, has broadened its audience in recent years. But it was *Time* which, omitting the literary miscellany which had been included in most of its forerunners, brought the news-magazine into full flower. A little later came *Newsweek*, the *United States News*, the compendium *Facts on File*, more recently *Quick*, the capsule news-magazine, and so on.

The news-magazines now have a circulation that carries them into every state and county, every city and town, and nearly every village and rural route. Such prosperity testifies to a widespread approval of certain techniques: orderly weekly news summaries, an interesting and often acute style of presentation,

and a free-wheeling commentary which supplies liberal interpretation. Alert, though by no means infallible, editorship directs
a widely distributed corps of correspondents, many of them
part-time newsmen who have their eyes open for both news and
feature material. The news-magazines employ the regular
telegraphic news services, besides having their own foreign and
domestic correspondents.

The picture magazines must not be neglected in a census of
news media. *Life* and *Look* do not pretend to cover the whole
news scene, but their leading picture stories are nearly always
news reports. The large circulation of these magazines makes
them an important factor in the dissemination of the news in every
part of America. Also such weekly journals of comment and
opinion as the *Nation*, the *New Republic*, the *Reporter*, and the
New Yorker play their own considerable parts in the spread of
the news throughout the country.

Today monthly magazines give rather less attention to news
as such than formerly. Our eighteenth-century magazines always
had regular departments of news, and this custom persisted for
a long time. When *Harper's* was begun in 1850, for example, it
had a "Monthly Record of Current Events," edited by Henry J.
Raymond, who was soon to become editor and one of the trio
of founders of the *New York Times*. Today both *Harper's* and the
Atlantic are in much closer touch with public affairs than they
were in their earlier lives, but they prefer to leave the recapitula-
tion of current events to other agencies. This may be said to be
the usual policy today not only of the general monthlies but of the
great weeklies — the *Saturday Evening Post* and *Collier's*.

An extraordinary spate of class periodicals is issued in the
United States — thousands of them — more than ever get into
catalogues or directories. They serve various movements, classes,
industries, professions, trades, institutions, organizations, arts,
hobbies, governmental agencies, etc. A large proportion of them
contain more or less news. *Broadcasting*, for instance, brings us
the news of the radio industry; *Publisher's Weekly*, of book publishing; *Engineering News-Record*, of the various fields of
engineering; *Printer's Ink*, of advertising; *Editor & Publisher*, of
the newspaper world, and so on to great length. *Business Week*,

of wider scope, is in many respects a news-magazine. The religious periodicals all contain much news; at least two of them have adopted the news-magazine form — *The Living Church* and *Presbyterian Life*.

One other class of news periodicals must be mentioned, if only to list it. These are the "confidential" letters, prepared chiefly for businessmen, and sold at a high subscription price. They specialize in appraisals of trends and predictions in the economic field.

But printed news does not end with newspapers and periodicals. It includes many pamphlets and books, as well as posters, broadsides, and flysheets of all kinds.

We have come into a new age of pamphleteering. Anyone with a crackpot idea and a hundred-dollar bill can get out a little pamphlet and thereafter consider himself as a molder of public opinion. Also, some of the best and noblest plans for curing the ills of an old world and providing the program for a new one are often presented in a modest pamphlet or brochure. To mention only one series, the *Public Affairs Pamphlets* have made a real contribution to American information. And all kinds of reports, studies, essays, addresses, propaganda, offers, and so on come to the desk of a busy man, the door of a housewife, or the mailbox of a farmer. All this is very democratic; it is the essence of free speech and free press. Let everybody be heard. And in much of this mass of printed matter there is some news content; brochures, pamphlets, bulletins, and mailing pieces in general add measurably to the total flow of news.

More topical books are published today than ever before. We call them by that name because they deal with the topics of the time; and this gives them a close relation to the news, even when they do not contain actual news reports. Also, such books often increase the desire of the reader for the more significantly important news, and thus have a good effect on newspaper and radio.

When radio newscasting first came over the horizon, it seemed to some publishers such a horrific apparition that they had to triple their allowance of stomach-ulcer pills. On becoming better acquainted with it, they found it less frightful; and not a few of them went so far as to adopt it into the family. As a matter of fact, radio broadcasting represents merely one more new technology for doing what the newspaper has been doing for some three centuries. The newspaper's functions are, succinctly stated, to publish news, comment, features, and advertising. That is what radio does, using transmitters instead of presses, except that in the case of radio, features are placed first in the list. Thus the activity of newspaper publishers in buying radio stations or setting them up is similar to what they have done in newspaper consolidation. But there is this important difference: whereas one paper usually perishes in a consolidation, the newspaper and the radio station continue to operate side by side.

In whatever hands, radio was bound to do great things in the news field. In the first place, the speed of the radio report was inevitably superior to that of any other medium. This was important chiefly in relation to the news of highly important events, and especially the first bulletins of the reports on such events. These are the "flashes" that used to sell the newspaper "extras" which radio has virtually driven from the streets. In the second place, it is obvious that somewhat less effort — both mental and physical — is required to listen to the radio than to read a newspaper. The Lazarsfeld studies have indicated that "preference" of radio news over that of the newspaper increases at the lower cultural levels as well as at the lower age levels, but even on the higher levels almost 43 per cent "prefer" radio news. Of course, by no means all of this radio "preference" can be written off as due to lack of ability or willingness to exert oneself in order to focus attention. Probably much of it is due to a third factor, the superior dramatic quality of radio news presentation. Lazarsfeld suggests a fourth factor when he presents the Katz analysis of content in Cincinnati newspapers and radio news programs, showing that radio featured crime and disasters relatively more than the press. But it also gave a larger proportion of its news time to international news than the press gave of its news space.[4]

Certainly the radio, like the newspaper, has become virtually a universal medium of communication in the United States. With a receiving set for every two persons in our total population, and some to spare, the supply may be said to approach saturation. And the news steadily increases its popularity as a radio feature; news, commentators, and special events, considered as one category, top the list in the distribution of time on evening network programs. Surveys of evening program preferences place news highest for all levels of age and education. In short, radio news penetrates and permeates the whole of the United States.

While government and national news, together with international relations, are emphasized in the network programs, the wire services furnish more general news to the radio stations, and local staffs gather the home news. Many stations have as many as twenty newscasts a day, lasting from three to thirty minutes each.

Television has made a spectacular entry into the world of news dissemination by its success in telecasts of special events. Although TV is limited, at this writing, to urban centers, it has achieved immense popularity and it will soon cover the country completely. The inauguration of President Truman on January 20, 1949, is said to have been witnessed by ten million persons — more than the sum of those who witnessed the inauguration of all other presidents from Washington to Roosevelt. The meetings of the Assembly of the United Nations have been brought into the living rooms of millions of homes. The hearings of the Kefauver Committee on crime excited a large video audience, and the San Francisco treaty conference had many ardent followers. Records were broken with General MacArthur's appearance before the joint session of Congress, for which there were an estimated thirty million viewers. TV put a new face on national political campaigns in 1952. However, at the present writing, sports dominate TV special events; perhaps they always will. There is presently a rapid development in station news shows and panel interviews, while the newsreels have found an important place in all TV shows.

Special events have long provided material for the newsreels of the motion picture theaters. While these shows have given us plenty of sports, they have not been lacking in more serious news coverage. Documentary films, notably the great "March of Time" series, have been valuable. Newsreels have brought to all movie screens in the land, from Rockefeller Center to Smith's Corners, a sense of intimate relationship with leading events and personalities of the world. To this contribution we must add the great

and increasing number of documentary and educational films
shown to schools and clubs the country over.

The list of the leading agencies of news-dissemination which
we have set forth and briefly discussed [5] should make it clear (if
it was not obvious in the first place) that no agency, no group,
no project or operation, has a monopoly, in the country at large
or in any place, in the distribution of news. There are many and
grave dangers in the various controls of news, which we shall
have to discuss later; but a monopoly of the flow of news into
any given locality is not one of them. That flow is too various and
vital, too closely connected with all our habits of living and
thinking and speaking, to be controlled, even superficially, by
anything short of a dictatorship.

A writer in the *Atlantic Monthly*, shortly after the consolidation
of the *New York Sun* with the *World-Telegram*, discussed "The
Monopoly of News," making the following striking remarks:

> Accurate news is not merely a prime necessity in a representative
> democracy: it is *the* prime necessity. Nothing takes precedence over it.
> But when any article is a necessity and when that article cannot
> be supplied except by an immense organization at vast expense, the
> business of purveying it becomes a natural monopoly. Communication
> is such a necessity.

What the writer means here is not "communication," but the
daily newspaper business in any great city. He is dismayed, as
we all are, by the death of a great newspaper. But no New York
paper, nor all of them, nor all the metropolitan dailies in the
land represent American communication. Indeed, American
news communication could get along without any newspapers;
and who knows, in these days of fast technological changes, if we
shall not soon be getting along without the newspaper as we
know it now?

But publicists have got into the habit of talking as though the
news were all in the custody of great metropolitan dailies. The
commission on Freedom of the Press, set up under a private grant
in 1942 to study the problems and performance of the press,
takes the same astigmatic view in its report entitled *A Free
and Responsible Press*. Discussing the "giant units" of the press,
it says: "Their control over the various ways of reaching the ear

of America is such that, if they do not publish ideas which differ from their own, those ideas will never reach the ear of America." The "giant units" are important, and need watching, but they do not control the total flow of news or comment in America. We shall not solve the problems in this field unless we try to understand realistically what the American system of communication is, in all its complexity, variety, and vigor.

In its number for August, 1947, *Fortune* presented an interesting little survey of how the news comes to Paducah, Kentucky. This is a one-daily town of forty thousand. The daily paper has a weekday circulation of about 24,000, nearly half of it within the city, and a small weekly has 1500. Paducah has two radio stations, one of them owned by the newspaper. The *Louisville Courier-Journal* has a daily circulation there of 1400, and 2400 on Sunday. Newspapers from Chicago, St. Louis, Memphis, and New York come in to the number of 428 daily and 2770 on Sunday. The great picture weeklies circulate 1968 copies in Paducah, the news magazines 429, and the great general weeklies 1769. Monthly magazines send in 13,037 copies. The public library has 110 magazines in its reading room, and circulates about ten thousand books a month. There are four movie theaters, all under one management; all of them show newsreels. There are four service clubs, many women's clubs and lodges, and other organizations galore. Such are some of the chief agencies for the distribution of news in one small city.

There we have it in a single case study. Paducah differs from the metropolis on the one hand and from the rural town on the other, but it is not a bad microcosm of the United States in its representation of news communication. Its story helps to bring to focus some of the various elements through which news is supplied in response to the ceaseless demand of a great news-hungry people.

CHAPTER THREE

What's the News?

Many professors, publicists, and press-men have tried their hands at definitions of the word *news*, and sometimes with amusing results. There was, for example, the ingenious fellow who observed that the word was an anagram, made up of initials of the four major points of the compass — north, east, west, and south — and that it must therefore be defined as happenings in all directions. This naive theory of the origin of the word has actually had a considerable acceptance, and was set forth in an early edition of Haydn's dictionary.

Of course, the word originally meant simply new things, novelties; but recent reports of events were new things, and in the sixteenth century *newes* came into common use for *tidings*. Thus we have it in Lord Berners' translation of *Froissart's Chronicles* in 1523: when the Duke of Lancaster heard some bad reports from France, "he was right pensyue and sore troubled with those newes." At that time *newes* meant recent reports of events or situations, and that is still the primary or generic meaning of the word today.

In the interest of sound thinking about the news, it is well to keep in mind this basic meaning. News is always a report. The event itself is not news. When we say the election of a President is "big news," we are speaking figuratively; we are employing what the rhetoricians call synecdoche, that is, reference to the material instead of the thing from which it is made. The American news agencies commonly make up lists each December of what they call the "biggest stories of the year," when what they mean is the most newsworthy events of the year. Such figures of speech are defensible and serviceable, but they should not cause us to forget that news itself is not an event or condition or idea, but the report of such a matter.

The one quality of the report which is necessary in order to make it "news" is timeliness. In other words, news must be new.

As we shall see, this truism embodied in the generic definition persists as an essential in the working definitions of news as it is understood by editors and reporters on modern newspapers. For editors eventually took over the news and defined it for themselves and their readers.

We did not need anything more than the simple, generic definition so long as news was anybody's business, and everybody's; but when professional newsmen appeared in the seventeenth century, people began to think of "newes" in terms of what Nicholas Bourne, Nathaniel Butter, and William Archer printed in London, or George Veseler and Broer Jonson in Amsterdam. The first English newspaper was called *Corante, or Weekely Newes*. For more than a hundred years, it was common usage to refer to a news-sheet as "the newes," so that a man might refer to his "copy of the news," meaning his copy of the current newspaper. Thus the popular concept of what news was came more and more to be formed upon what news was printed.

With this development, the editor assumed a special suzerainty over the news. He decided what was news and what was not. This was not as arbitrary or as absolute an authority as it seemed. The editor was, professionally, in charge of the news, but his control over it was limited sharply by several factors.

Space in the newspaper is always restricted. The first American newspaper, *Publick Occurrences*, contained 5300 words, all told; it could all be printed in half a page of a modern newspaper. But the modern metropolitan newspaper of sixty-four large pages is no more able to publish any considerable proportion of the news reports from all the states in the Union and all the countries of the world than was Ben Harris' tiny sheet. The slogan of the *New York Times*, "All the News That's Fit to Print," is more a sentiment than a fact. The slogan originated in the years when Ochs set his newspaper off sharply from the "yellow journalism" of morbid sensationalism which flowered so nauseously during the competition between the *World* and *Journal* at the turn of the century. The *Times* had two slogans: "It Does Not Soil the Breakfast Cloth" and "All the News That's Fit to Print." The emphasis was on the matter of fitness, not comprehensiveness.

The modern news field is so vast that an editor's first task is one of selection. He becomes a specialist in news values. But he is less a dictator than a compromiser of interests.

Second only to space limitations are those imposed by the availability of news reports. News was meager in the early years of the American press, not because important events did not occur, but because the papers had no adequate reports. Mathew Carey in 1785 wrote in his *Pennsylvania Evening Herald* that

the European news is all, all equally flat, equally insipid. Hard indeed is the lot of the poor Printer! obliged to furnish out his bill of fare, at all events; he must run through piles of papers, glean an article or two amidst heaps of trash, and yet be liable to the charge of stupidity and dulness.

This was in the years when papers received as "exchanges" were an editor's chief reliance. Modern communication has developed only in the last hundred years. But even now, with extraordinarily efficient news-gathering agencies at work, the iron curtains, wars, censorships, and the recalcitrance of sources of information set up many barriers to the free circulation of news.

Moreover, much of the news that is procurable is not usable because it is not of high interest to a given paper's audience. Thus the internal affairs of Chile or a meeting of the Arkansas legislature would reach the columns of the *Baltimore Sun* only in rare instances. They may be important to many thousands of people, but the telegraph editor of the *Sun* has to decide whether they are interesting to his readers.

This imposes the third limitation on news — that of reader interest or disinterest. An editor is, in a considerable degree, the servant of his readers. He is not their slave, and (as we shall try to make clear later) he has responsibilities as a guide and public teacher; but he has to select news, in the main, which he believes his readers want. Unless he can satisfy their desires fairly well, his paper will soon be out of business and he will be out of a job. A good editor is supposed to have a "sixth sense" for news — that is, for knowing what will interest his readers. Some of them have such a sense because they are, by backgrounds and training, a part of the group for which they work, and themselves participate in the ideas, feelings, and interests of their audience. Others of them, through intense study and long experience, have learned to know and understand their readers. Still others have what they think of as an instinct for news; they guess, and if they are lucky they guess right.

These editors with a sixth sense for news have been loath, in some cases, to accept modern methods of measuring readers' interests. Helped on by the advertisers, however, such methods have achieved wide acceptance. George Gallup, working out his doctorate at the State University of Iowa, devised a system whereby interviewers, armed with copies of a given issue of a newspaper, obtained statements from readers of that issue as to exactly what they had read and what they had skipped over; then it was only a clerical task to correlate the information obtained and figure out just what items and what types of news were actually being read. Given a proper sample of readers as respondents, and careful techniques in interviewing, this is a valuable means of supplanting editorial guesswork with facts, though, of course, it does not tell what people might have read if they had been offered something else. Used on many papers (142 in the *Continuing Studies* by 1952) over several years, it has provided useful guidance.

And there are still further limitations on the work of the editors of the news. There are certain controls, pressures, and prejudices, sometimes obvious, sometimes subtle and devious. These will be discussed more fully later, but they must be mentioned here in order to complete our description of the practical background which the newspaperman has when he attempts to define "news." Many of these controls and pressures are not at all sinister. All are a part of the intricately complex pattern in which the editor must work.

When the newsman, then, who is professionally in charge of the gathering, the processing, and the distribution of the news, defines this thing with which he deals, he is thinking of *what he prints*. He is not thinking of all recent reports throughout the habitable globe, or of the *fama* of Virgil's famous passage, or of anything unsuited to his columns; the reports which he recognizes as news are severely limited by the actual conditions of the newspaper.

Thus we have such definitions as that of W. C. Jarnagin, one-time editor of the *Des Moines Capital*: "News is anything that happens in which people are interested." "News is whatever your readers want to know about," wrote a former editor of the *Kansas City Star*. "Anything that enough people want to read is news, provided it does not violate the canons of good taste or the laws of libel," wrote J. J. Schindler, of the *St. Paul Dispatch*, in *Collier's* famous symposium, of March 18, 1911. These are the authentic voices of busy news editors. Or hear Arthur MacEwen, whom W. R. Hearst made editor of the *San Francisco Examiner* when he first took it over: "News is anything that makes a reader say, 'Gee whiz!'" And finally, note the perfect editorial-type definition: "News is whatever a good editor chooses to print."

One expects a definition to be neat and carefully circumscribed. But in view of the extreme diversity of those human beings who edit newspapers, this kind of definition is anything but tidy. Gerald W. Johnson, at the end of his excellent essay, *What Is News*, published by Knopf in 1926, wrote:

the news in which an intelligent [newspaper] man will find most satisfaction is the sort of news which, while it may contribute little to his financial well-being, will test his professional capacity in its presentation; and the severest test of that capacity comes in stripping away the ambiguities and obscurities that have enshrouded some important truth and making it understood by a world in which ignorance, carelessness, and stupidity are far more common than keen delight in the battle of ideas.

That, though, is a definition of the best news. In general practice, news is what is in the newspapers; and newspapers are what newspapermen make them. It is a depressing reflection, rather a terrible reflection. But it is true.

Mr. Johnson was confessedly writing as a newspaperman. Tidy or not, his is the pragmatic definition of news, though we have to keep in mind always that the newspaperman himself is not a dictator, but works under the limitations which have just been reviewed.

What goes on in the editor's head as he tries to evaluate the reports that come in to him, as he makes his choices and processes his material? What criteria does he use in this evaluation? There is general agreement that the "importance" of news (that is, its importance for use in the newspaper) is commonly measured by at least four tests: timeliness, prominence, proximity, and probable consequence.

Timeliness is always one of the editor's chief measuring-sticks. The most recent development or detail of a running story must always take priority. Yesterday's news is no longer "important." This repeats an essential of the simple generic definition of news.

The prominence of the persons involved in a report affords another test. Anything the President of the United States does makes "important" news. The reputation of a movie star may be factitious, but Hollywood personalities and names become so well known that their activities often make "must" stories for the newspapers. Most of us are hero-worshipers at heart, and we want to know how the great ones live. It is true that the newspaper plays a large part in developing a prominence which it must then exploit, as that of a Lindbergh, a Di Maggio, a Capone; but there must have been a dynamic activity which made the personality newsworthy in the first place. Nor can we shrug off the validity of the popular feeling that prominence equals importance; the potency of prominence for good or ill is not to be denied.

Proximity is a third criterion. The news of a paper's home city is of first importance to that paper's audience, and even the largest American newspapers are to a considerable extent local. In spite of modern developments in fast transportation and communication, we have no national newspapers in the United States as they have in some other countries, notably in England. Such a paper is by no means impossible for the future, in view of inventions and technologies presently on the horizon; but thus far the vast scope of our country has prevented such a development. Anyway, readers are primarily interested in their neighbors and their own affairs. Isolationism may be on the wane, but it will be a long time before a massacre in Allahabad will interest the readers of the *Memphis Commercial Appeal* as much as would a bond issue for a new water system in Memphis.

The fourth test which the editor uses to determine what news is important for his paper is probable consequence — the expected or possible effect on his readers of a given event or condition.

A congressional debate on a new tax law, the spread of a polio epidemic, a market crash: such events make front-page news, of course. A war overseas in which our nation is engaged, or likely to be engaged, changes the meaning of "proximity": its probable consequences bring it close to all readers.

Editors are, in general, with due allowances for slight divergences in emphasis, pretty surely guided by these four criteria — timeliness, prominence, proximity, and probable consequence. If a story ranks high in these four qualities, it is regarded as important to the reader, and therefore "big news" and a "must" for the newspaper. That the qualities are not actually equal in real importance seems fairly obvious, but that is a question we must postpone for the moment.

Here we must go on to point out that the editor has a second set of tests by which he evaluates the multitudinous happenings of the day. These are tests by types of subject matter which are known to be interesting, and they are founded on well-known feelings and curiosities of the reader. A sex story, for example, will ordinarily draw quick interest. An incident dealing with a large sum of money is likely to attract interest, especially if it is dramatized or associated with persons. Other sure-fire matters in the news are bitter or violent conflict, suspense, disaster, horror, unusualness, appeal to sympathy or pity, romance, "human interest" bits of common life, children, animals. These are interest-provoking factors commonly named in such an enumeration, but we might prolong the list until we have named all the objects of popular curiosity. Indeed, these "elements of reader interest," as MacDougall calls them, might well be arranged in a schedule based on the fundamental human emotions.

Journalism founded on a rule-of-thumb such as the foregoing list suggests is subject to many abuses. Before we criticize news reporting based on such concepts of popular interest, however, let us remind ourselves that (a) it is a proper function of the newsman to serve his public, (b) if he does not do so he will be forced by economic means to give place to someone who will, and (c) by and large, and in the long run, the people are likely to be right and sound in their interests, emotions, and desires. The high-brow berates *demos* too glibly. It is too easy, for example, for the sophisticate to condemn the use of the romance motif as "corny," for the altruist to lambaste the money theme in news as sordid, or for the tender-minded to object to the element of horror in many reports. It is too easy for H. A. Overstreet to allow his aversions to lead him into such a generalization as: "The newspaper has found its vested interest in catastrophe" (*The Mature Mind*, page 108). Of course catastrophes, of which war is the greatest, must be recorded in the newspapers. Reports of mine disasters, destructive fires, and railroad and airplane wrecks point toward investigations and reforms. Popular interest in such things is certainly not wholly morbid, and often useful. Shrillness of faultfinding dies down when we study the basis of such news and try to understand its roots in human needs.

Scolding subsides, perhaps; but there is still plenty of room left for sober and serious thinking about what the newsman is doing with the news in the mid-twentieth century. We have seen how, long ago, naturally and perforce, he took over the definition of news and the news pattern. He has defined it on the run, under the strain of quick decisions, on the edge of a deadline, in the midst of action and noise and multiple pressures. He has made it, day by day, what it is, and has then rationalized the process. Mostly by trial and error, he has approximated the wishes and needs of his public.

The great danger in such a process is that there should be too little sound and philosophical thinking about the aims and responsibilities of journalism by the men who are making it. The reporter has too often taken over from his teachers in the newsroom the idea that certain elements of interest, such as we have listed above, form an informal code — the unwritten but accepted rules of the "newspaper game," without much thinking or much wise guidance. He finds a game with such rules exciting and absorbing, and has little opportunity or inclination, in the midst of action and the pressures of competition, to give thought to his obligation of professional service to society.

The lowest and yellowest journalism is that which accepts newspaper work as a game in which a set of obvious "elements of interest" are the counters, and sees no significances in news beyond those immediate emotional appeals. A money-sex story is always a "good" story to the ill-trained and short-sighted reporter who works in such a tradition, especially if there is also an element of unusualness and perhaps some suspense. Indeed a story involving all these factors — a sex-romance built around an heiress to a vast fortune, with a violent contest for her dubious favors through the use of unusual weapons by the suitors, with the outcome of it all in suspense, and with appeals to sympathy, a dash of horror, and something about a pet animal — such a story would seem to such a reporter to deserve an eight-column, front-page banner. Fantastic manipulation of "elements of interest," such as this, have not been lacking in certain sections of the American press. Jazz it up; fake it; make it exciting at whatever cost! Anything to make the reader say, "Gee whiz!" Such myopic and overemphatic use of a small group of themes believed to be exciting to the reader is disgraceful, and makes thoughtful readers question the extent to which aiming at popular interests may be justified.

It comes down to a question of importance in news. There is an obvious importance in the "elements of interest" which the editor is quick to see and to seize upon; their proper use is legitimate and necessary. Though crude overplay of them is silly and outrageous, they always have been and doubtless always will be recognized and used by good newsmen.

But there is another kind of importance in news which is not so immediately obvious. This other kind we shall call, here and in later pages, "significant importance."

It will be helpful in this connection to note Wilbur Schramm's doctrine of immediate and delayed rewards in reading the news, which is itself based on the work of E. L. Thorndike and other psychologists. Schramm says that readers and listeners take their news of crime, accidents and disasters, sports, and human interest for immediate "pleasure reward"; while news of public affairs, economic and social problems, science, and education is generally read for a delayed reward of general preparedness and information.[6]

For example, the reader of sports stories, which are based on interest in conflict, receives an immediate reward in the stimulation of his emotions, though he knows that the Dodgers' victory yesterday has no more than an ephemeral interest for him, though he may forget the very name of Ezzard Charles next year, and though the clowning of the wrestlers on the TV screen means less in his life than the good dinner he has just eaten. But he finds such news easy and diverting, and he forms a taste for it. His attitude is somewhat the same toward most crime stories, news of disasters, Hollywood sex scandals, and so on — the news that centers upon the elements of interest which we have been discussing. These stories bring out his personal partisanship, his shared experience, a quick stimulation of his emotions; he likes them, and therefore the editor of his newspaper and the director of his newscasts know that they are "important."

But there are other kinds of news which are based less on exciting conditions and events. They may involve conflict, as nearly everything in the world does, but not yet open and violent conflict. They deal with matters which may ultimately have vital and tremendous consequences to every reader, but which at the present moment do not seem highly interesting because the situation has not "broken," to use the newsman's term. They have not yet reached the stage of what Walter Lippmann, in his book *Public Opinion*, calls "overt news"; they have not yet come clearly out into the open arena of conflict between recognized leaders, of bitter fight, shock of battle, and frenzied propaganda. And yet these stories may even now be recognizably behind the "overt news," looming up as background, and far more significantly important than most of the thousand little happenings and private scandals and baseball scores that fill so many newspaper columns.

It will be recognized by the patient reader of this chapter (whom we hopefully conceive of as possessing an analytical turn of mind) that this delayed-reward news stands a much better chance of getting into the newspaper or on the air through the first set of editorial tests which we discussed — timeliness, prominence, proximity, and probable consequence — than it does through the criteria of the "elements of interest." Indeed, the test of probable consequence is virtually a measurement of significant importance. Of course, the two categories of immediate-reward news and delayed-reward news are not as sharply defined or mutually exclusive as they may at first seem. But, in general, it must be perceived that the editor works under a double standard: he has to decide what news he will print, on the one hand, because his readers demand it for the easy reading which brings immediate responses, and what he will select, on the other hand, because he thinks it may, in the long run, affect the lives and fortunes of his readers. He has to apportion his news space between the important and the significantly important.

Arthur Hays Sulzberger, publisher of the *New York Times*, speaking on "The Responsibilities of Maturity" at the University of Missouri in 1950, said:

> We have two choices. We can report, and define, and explain, in honest perspective, the great issues which are now before the nation and the world; or we can ignore and minimize these issues and divert our readers to less important, but no doubt more entertaining, matters. My vote goes for the paper that informs.

This is a problem of which thinking newsmen are well aware. They have come to use the terms "hard news" and "soft news." "Hard news" refers to the less exciting and more analytical stories of public affairs, economics, social problems, science, etc.; and "soft news" is that which any editor immediately recognizes as interesting to his readers and therefore "important" for his paper. The two terms represent the double standard of news evaluation with which editors must cope.[7]

The chief fault and failure of American journalism today — and this applies to all media of information — is the disproportionate space and emphasis given to the obviously interesting news of immediate reward ("soft news") at the expense of the significantly important news of situations and events which have not yet reached the stage of being exciting for the casual reader ("hard news"). The divided responsibility for this failure is not easy to place with fairness to all; it is basically that of the reader, but publishers, editors, and news-gatherers cannot escape their share of it.

This is a matter for later chapters, and must await a fuller discussion of the nature of news. Let us now proceed to examine certain great concepts of news which have developed in the journalism of the past, and see how and in what degree they have become fixed in the modern pattern.

CHAPTER FOUR

News as History

The three reasons which Benjamin Harris gave for the establishment of the first American newspaper are worthy of our careful attention. Let us consider them in detail.

"First, *That* Memorable Occurrents of Divine Providence *may not be neglected or forgotten, as they too often are.*" It must be understood that "providence" had a specialized meaning in the language of the times. Increase Mather defines it:

> Such Divine judgements, tempests, floods, earthquakes, thunders as are unusual, strange apparitions, or whatever else shall happen that is prodigious, witchcrafts, diabolical possessions, remarkable judgements upon noted sinners, eminent deliverances, and answers of prayer, are to be reckoned among illustrious [illustrative] providences.

This definition appears in the introduction to Mather's popular collection of *Illustrious Providences*, which he brought together in order to explain (with some approach to scientific method) the ways of God to man. Ben Harris was a pious man, and he agreed with the New England clergy that these remarkable occurrences illustrating the divine will should not be forgotten, but ought to be recorded. Rather than gather them in a book, as Mather had, Harris would bring them together in his newspaper; but the purpose was the same: both men designed to make records of these providences.

Incidentally, it may be noted that this idea of the newspaper as a kind of diary of the Lord's doings did not die out with the Puritans. James Parton wrote in the *North American Review* in 1866: "The skilled and faithful journalist, recording with exactness and power the thing that has come to pass, is Providence addressing men." And in another famous review of the midcentury we are told of a certain Baptist clergyman that, "a newspaper having been brought into the room, he held out his hand to receive it, saying, 'Be kind enough to let me have it a few minutes, till I see how the Supreme Being is governing the world.'" And Charles A.

Dana, one of the most famous of American editors, had a facile reply to those who objected to the crime news in the *New York Sun*: "I have always felt that whatever the Divine Providence permitted to occur I was not too proud to report." [8]

But to return to Ben Harris: we are interested in his statement mainly because it emphasizes his conviction that there should be a *record in print* of "Memorable Occurrents of Divine Providence" so they should not be forgotten. He goes on:

"Secondly, *That people every where may better understand the Circumstances of Publique Affairs, both abroad and at home; which may not only direct their* Thoughts *at all times, but at some times also to assist their* Businesses *and* Negotiations." Here we have an emphasis upon probable consequence — one of the modern editor's tests of important news. Some of Harris' news might have a direct effect on the "businesses and negotiations" of his readers. And then our first editor names a final purpose of his paper:

"Thirdly, *That some thing may be done towards the Curing, or at least the* Charming, *of that* Spirit of Lying, *which prevails amongst us.*" This states the principle, so commonly attested by the early news-sheets, that news, when left to oral rumor, is by nature inaccurate and untrustworthy, but when set down in a printed paper, is much more likely to be reliable. In his own paper, Harris promises, "*nothing shall be entered but what we have reason to believe is true.*" Here again is emphasis on the importance of a printed record — set down in black and white.

An even more striking example of the concept of news as a record is to be found in the editorial policy of the second American newspaper, John Campbell's *Boston News-Letter*. For fifteen years, this tiny paper, less than the size of a sheet of modern letter-paper, printed on both sides, was the only newspaper in the Colonies.

In those years about six weeks were ordinarily required for a ship to sail from Liverpool to Boston, bringing the news from home for which the Colonists hungered. These reports from England were thus old when they arrived, but not stale; they were fresh news in Boston when the ships came in. But Campbell did not get out an extra when a ship arrived with the news from home. He plodded along with his little two-page weekly; and, impressed with his responsibility to furnish an orderly record, he did not even try to print the latest news available, but doled it out in proper chronological order in his tiny weekly budgets. Soon it began to pile up on him, but this did not move him from his stern Scotch determination to keep what he called his "thread of occurrences"; eventually he got more than a year behind in his news and had to increase his issue to four pages in an effort to catch up. In short, John Campbell conceived of his news as a continuous record, and of himself as the historian of important affairs.

The only trouble was that Campbell's news came near to being ancient history. His successor as editor of the *News-Letter*, Bartholomew Green, had a better feeling for timeliness in the news; but even he commonly referred to his reports from England as a "History of the Publick Affairs." This respect for the record as such was shared by most Colonial editors; and for this reason the Colonial journals published many state papers, especially addresses of Parliament to the King, royal proclamations, and so on. Later, addresses of assemblies to the royal governors, schedules of grievances, and such documents often filled the first pages of eight-page papers. They seem dull today, but our forefathers read them with interest. They were official, and they were part of the public record.

This concept of the news as history has persisted. Until the middle of the nineteenth century, it was especially notable in the Washington papers, which were devoted largely to the proceedings of Congress and the various departments of the national government; such journals as the *National Intelligencer* and the *Washington Globe* were distinctively record papers. For more than a hundred years the biennial message of the President to Congress was considered a news-break of the first magnitude, and nearly all papers carried it in full. That tradition ended because of a change not in the editorial attitude toward the record, but in the use and status of executive messages.

Today this record, or history, concept has an important place in newspapers. It is found in the documentation of which the *New York Times* is the leading exemplar; the first Pulitzer Prize for "meritorious public service" went to the *Times* in 1918 "for the publication of official reports, documents, and speeches relating to the World War." But many other papers are not far behind the *Times* in the publication of such material. In many cases a speech by the leader of one of the great parties is printed in full even by papers of the opposing party, for the sake of the record.

As has been pointed out, the newspaper editor has a kind of custodianship of the news — or he did before the radio editor appeared, to divide responsibilities with him. But there is a third agency involved in forming news and publishing it to the world — an agency much older than radio, since it has been more or less active for two hundred years and more. This agency is the magazine. Though it has been far less important than the newspaper in shaping and defining news, in the publication of records of current events with the aim of permanent preservation it has a distinctive importance; and this aim has affected the standards and form of its news articles.

Obviously, a chief shortcoming of the newspaper as a permanent historical record is its format. The early gazettes, with their small page-size and rag-paper stock suitable for binding, were not so bad; but when competition in large-size pages brought in the "blanket sheets" in the first half of the nineteenth century, binding was difficult and shelving almost impossible. Later the mechanical wood pulp which furnished the paper stock was unsuited to preservation. A few journals resorted to small rag-paper editions for library binding, and the *New York Times* instrumented such an edition with an index which has proved a boon to researchers. Only in recent years have we had a device — the microfilm — which has made many newspaper files easily accessible in libraries.

But magazines have not known this story of frustration. They have been commonly bound for library shelves. Moreover, historians and other students have used them with more confidence because their weekly or monthly publication has afforded them more time for checking facts, and their articles have often been written with more attention to literary form.

The first two magazines in the Colonies were Franklin's *General Magazine* and Bradford's *American Magazine*, both dated January, 1741, and both issued in Philadelphia. The former had a department headed "Historical Chronicle" and another, "Brief Historical and Chronological Notes"; the latter set up in its "Plan of the Undertaking," the publication of "An Account of the publick Affairs transacted in His Majesty's Colonies" as its chief aim. The custom of magazine departments devoted to records of the month's news continued for more than a hundred years — well beyond the middle of the nineteenth century.

The weekly news-magazine has been much more important in its effect on the presentation of news than the monthly. Its acceptability in this field depends today largely on its handling of events as history. It is far behind the radio and the newspaper in timeliness and in intimacy with its audience; but if it presents a more orderly record, sifts the irrelevant and ephemeral from the important, uses the additional editorial time at its command for checking facts, and religiously abstains from confusing facts with opinion, then it has a valid place as a current historian. Lest the name "historian" should seem to be an insult to *Time* and *Newsweek*, we hasten to make an observation or two about the relations of history and journalism.

We have been using the term "history" rather loosely. History, of course, is the record of the past. But how long past? The newspaper is sometimes described as the historian of the present; and yet, in a sense, there is no such thing as the present. The tick of your watch, once heard, belongs to the past. Thomas Carlyle was fond of the metaphor which made the present a narrow precipice between great chasms which were the two eternities — the past and the future. It is a common thought, and an old one. "Many witty authors," wrote Addison in the *Spectator*, "compare the present time to an isthmus or narrow neck of land that rises in the midst of an ocean immeasurably diffused on either side of it." It is a narrow isthmus indeed, a sharp precipice. By the time the linotypes are devouring copy, the events detailed belong to the past. Newspapers try to keep the illusion of the present by the tense of the verbs in their headlines, but in the story itself they give up pretending and yield to the preterite.

But the newsman is really more interested in the future than he is in either the present or the past; and this is true because it is in the future that the *reader's* interest chiefly lies. Semanticist Korzybski taught us that what we need most in language is predictive reliability: that is what we all desperately desire, and that is what we require from the inferences and generalizations which form and activiate our thinking and speaking. In short, what we demand from news (besides sheer amusement) is some reliable knowledge about the future. Now, there is no doubt that the very desperation of this dire need for some glimpse into that darkness which is the future, throughout man's entire history, has made him an easy victim of false prophets, diviners, sorcerers, and all manner of quacks. So it is today, and there is certainly too much easy prophecy — too much "I predict" charlatanry — in the papers and on the radio. Yet we have to admit that basically what we ask of the news is some data for reliable inferences about the future.

And much the same thing may be said of history. Our chief requirement of the historian is that he furnish us with facts and ideas from the older past which may help us in dealing with the future, just as we demand from the newsman predictive aid based on the recent past.

Moreover, the techniques of the historian and the practices of the newsman have much in common. Digging out the facts about General Scott's campaign for the Presidency in 1852 is similar, *mutatis mutandis*, to learning the truth about General Eisenhower's campaign in 1952: the same checking of facts, the same choosing of significant angles for emphasis, the same use of color, are needed in one as in the other. Just as the good journalist thinks of himself as writing responsibly for the record, so many a historian thinks of himself as a journalist. Thus H. G. Wells, receiving an honorary degree from the Sorbonne for his *Outline of History*, said, "First and foremost I am a journalist"; and Carlyle wrote, "Histories are a kind of distilled newspapers."

Historians have not always had so much respect for newspapers. Early American scholars in this field, recognizing the partisanship and the hurried composition of the journals, commonly disregarded them as sources for their own studies. Perhaps the success of John Bach McMaster's *History of the People of the United States*, the first volume of which was published in 1883, and which was founded largely on a study of old newspaper files, had more influence than any other factor in pointing the way to the discriminating use of "the public prints" in the writing of history. It is certain that the method can be abused; it is equally certain that it can be of the utmost value if used with judgment and studied skill.

In view of what has been said about the similarities in the work of journalist and historian, it should be pointed out that there are at least two very marked differences.

In the first place, despite exceptions, news is essentially recent and timely, while history belongs to the more distant past. The gap tends to close with some of the slower news media, on the one hand, or a hurried history of a war or other episode just finished, on the other; but it remains as the obvious and chief difference between history and journalism.

The second distinction has to do with careful scholarship. We know that some histories have been written with less research than some newspaper series, and that newspaper writers and editors have sometimes been scholars of distinction; but the fact remains that historical writing has been far more generally characterized by scholarship and careful composition than has news reporting. In one of the Bromley Lectures on Journalism at Yale University in 1908, Colonel George Harvey pontificated: "Journalism can never be history; its unceasing activities deprive it of the advantages of scientific inquiry." Never, Colonel Harvey? Well, hardly ever, the Colonel would say. It is true that newsmen, hurried and harried, work under more difficult conditions than historians; yet the best of what they produce will, of course, compare favorably with careful studies and good writing in any field.

Finally, let us consider some of the requirements of journalistic work performed according to the news-as-history concept.

Reliability, which is the chief requisite of news for the record, depends upon three factors — the honesty of the news source, the professional competence of the reporter, and the care of the editors, copyreaders, proofreaders, and printers who process the news story.

Informed, candid, and fair news sources are obviously of the first importance; and they are doubly valuable if they allow them-

selves to be quoted directly. Quotations credited only to anonymous "reliable sources" may be little more than guesses. One
recalls the "gag" recorded by the late Chet Shafer, inspired country correspondent of Three Rivers, Michigan: he tells us that the
town's worst punster, who happens also to be a confirmed reader
of the classics, once observed that Ulysses, on his return from his
odyssey, was the first to advise that his information, while not
guaranteed, was obtained from Circes he believed to be reliable.

But if the reader has confidence in the reporter whose name
"by-lines" the story, or in the wire agency whose logotype appears
in the date line, he may be willing to accept the hidden identity
of an informant. After all, the reporter is the paramount per-
former in the process. As William Rockhill Nelson once declared,
"The reporter is the essential man on the newspaper. He is the
big toad in the puddle." Intelligence, character, good academic
and practical backgrounds, keenness and energy: such are the
qualities and training necessary to the competent reporter in
these days. Given such reporters, the battle is more than half
won; without them, it is much more than half lost.

Of course, bad editing can ruin a reporter's good work, and
bad processing can make it ridiculous. Here again, intelligence
and training are of the essence. Much will be said hereafter about
editorial controls and about pressures of various kinds upon the
handling of the news. Nor should we forget the proofreaders and
the printers, who, without the utmost care, can easily make thousands of mistakes in any issue of a daily paper.

Indeed, when one reflects upon the multitude of pitfalls in the
gathering, writing, and processing of the news, the comparative
reliability of the general output seems a miracle. It could never
be attained without the intelligence, training, and devotion of all
who are concerned in the process. The plain fact is that American
news workers are, in general, both highly skilled workers and
honest men. Certainly the best of our news-gathering is done in
the established American tradition of getting the facts fully, setting them down fairly, and processing them carefully — for the
record.

This is especially true of the serious stories — those which are
designed not for idle amusement but for information of signif-

icant matters. This is "hard" news. "Soft" news furnishes a record, to be sure, of popular interests, curiosities, and diversions of the day; but the record of a great people's progress, its economic and political crises, and its proper culture is written in those more significantly important news stories which belong to a fine tradition of American journalism.

News is not written directly for the historians of the future, but for the readers of today's paper; yet many a trained and responsible writer, pounding out the results of expert investigation in succinct and orderly form, has the feeling that here is something for the record — here is something of value and importance. Such a writer, though he would not be guilty of a comparable literary flourish, could well adopt the motto which old Hezekiah Niles took from Shakespeare for his *Weekly Register* — a speech of Queen Katherine in *Henry VIII*:

> . . . I wish no other herald,
> No other speaker of my living actions
> To keep mine honour from corruption,
> But such an honest chronicler . . .

This consciousness of writing for the record lies behind much of our best newspaper work. Stories so produced will furnish future historians with materials of great value, to be sure; but they also bring to the columns of our newspapers contributions of a high order for the thoughtful consideration of intelligent readers today.

CHAPTER FIVE

Speed: The News as Timely Report

One cannot understand the development of modern news without some knowledge of the history of speed. Speed in communication, speed in the production of paper and printed matter, and speed in distribution were responsible for most of the changes which, in the two decades between 1830 and 1850, transformed the deliberate news of our forefathers into what seemed a miracle of immediacy; later developments in mechanics and electronics have made minutes and seconds, instead of days and hours, the units of measurement in modern communication.

In primitive times there was some use of smoke and flash signaling for rapid communication, followed later by flag messages and pigeon posts; but these were then little more than sporadic devices employed for military purposes. The fact is that for tens of thousands of years speed of ordinary communication was limited by the rate of travel of the horse on land and the sailing ship on water. In the early beginnings of modern Europe there was some use of pigeons, semaphores, and heliography in news communication; but it was not until comparatively recent times — a little over a century ago — that the sudden irruption into the American scene of the steam railroad, the transatlantic steamship, and the telegraph revolutionized communication.

The increased tempo which steam and electricity provided for industry and society in general was one of the most important factors in the development of American life in the nineteenth century. That tempo was both cause and result of the "industrial revolution," and served to make a vigorous and imaginative people more eager and impatient than those of any other nation. Journalism, usually an index to the total life of the people, tells the story of this impatient activity.

The status of news suddenly underwent a startling change. In the old days, news had been merely a new report; it might be a report in Philadelphia of something that had happened in Boston two weeks before, or a New York report of a two-months-old event in Europe. It had taken the story of such a major news-break as the Battle of Lexington four days to reach New York and six weeks to reach Savannah, Georgia. But the steamship and telegraph now changed all that. With Liverpool less than two weeks from Boston, and Washington only minutes away from New York and other eastern cities, the eagerness of the people for recency in their news began to be matched by feverish competition in speed of communication on the part of the newspapers. News was now by way of becoming not merely a new

report but a new report of things that had newly happened —
which was a very different matter.

Pony expresses to the Far West, railway expresses in the East,
frantic extension of telegraph systems as fast as workmen could
stick poles in the ground to carry the inadequate wires — these
were the signs of the opening of an era characterized by a new
kind of news. Rush the news! Ten days from California! One
week from Europe! By magnetic telegraph from Washington!
"Scoop," "beat," "flash," "extra" were terms which came into the
journalistic jargon to give names to the frenzy of competition in
news speed. Then with the coming of the first successful Atlantic
cable in 1866, the *New York Herald's* familiar heading "One
Week Later From Europe" gave place to "Telegraphic News
From All Over the World."

This seemed to all observers to be the ultimate in fast news
service. But we know now that it was not, for in World War I,
Marconi's "wireless" system played an important rôle; and in our
own generation radio and television have stepped up once more
the tempo of the news. By its ability to get early news "flashes"
of important events into American homes, radio has set new
standards of speed in reporting; and television has on occasion
furnished a startling immediacy as well as intimacy to news
reports.

And pictures, which once had to wait upon the slow processes
of wood engraving, and which, when photography and chemical
etching had shortened that operation, had still to submit to the
delays of transport by railway, and later by plane, were finally
adapted to transmission by telegraph in 1924.

The result of this continuous and climacteric process of doubling and redoubling speed of communication in all its departments is to make it possible for the people to be served with
immediate news. In the United States especially, where news
collection and distribution are comparatively untrammeled, and
where the press and the people have a tradition of the fastest possible service of information, news flies with almost incredible
swiftness.

To what effect? Is this frenetic eagerness for immediate news
important, or is it merely evidence of a childish impatience?

Things happen very quickly in this modern world. The long marches of the columns of Alexander took years to perform; today incomparably larger armies are moved half around the world in a few weeks or days. Our government must be informed immediately of important events the world over; and if the people of a democracy are to be censors of their government, they too must be immediately informed. Swift intelligence for the people is certainly important.

But it seems clear that we tend to make too much of a fetish of immediate news. The tremendous exertion required to "beat the world" often involves a sacrifice of accuracy and good reporting. Indeed, the standard excuse for slipshod reporting is the hurry necessary for getting news on the press or on the air; and it is plain to the candid student of our journalism that many of its sins are committed in the name of speed. The better editors do not hesitate to hold stories up for checking and rechecking, even at the risk of a "beat"; and the rewards of trustworthiness which their caution gains for their papers more than offset the occasional loss of an exclusive early story. A well-known managing editor once said, "Speed is the only thing a newspaper has to sell." That is not true: the newspaper has many other things to sell — among them truth and accuracy and reliability.

It also has good writing to sell. One of the most challenging chapters in Lincoln Steffens' great *Autobiography* (Harcourt, Brace) tells of his experiences as city editor of the *New York Commercial Advertiser* in the late nineties. He writes thus about his reporters:

They were not held accountable for news beats; Lachausee and I, with the city news service of the Associated Press, could take care that we were not beaten. My young writers were expected to beat the other papers only in the way in which they presented the news. The flash of a murder would come in. I did not rush a man out to get the news first. Lachaussee would write a short bulletin for the next edition, while I would call up, say, Cahan; I would ask him to sit down, and then, without any urge, tell him quietly what to do.

"Here, Cahan, is a report that a man has murdered his wife — a rather bloody, hacked-up crime. We don't care about that. But there's a story in it. That man loved that woman well enough once to marry her, and now he has hated her enough to cut her all to pieces. If you can find out just what happened between that wedding day and this murder, you will have a novel for yourself and a short story for me. Go on now, take your time, and get this tragedy, as a tragedy."

Was it a hardship for the *Commercial Advertiser*'s readers to be forced to wait a day or two for Abraham Cahan's story of this murder, even though it was more carefully written, showed a better sense of values, and was more "literary" than the hodgepodge that might have been served up immediately? Does immediacy mean more to readers than careful investigation and good writing? The answer probably depends upon both the type of news event covered and the class of readers aimed at. Evidently readers of the *Commercial Advertiser* liked what they were getting, for the paper prospered during Steffens' tenure.

There are some indications today that many readers are willing to wait a few days or a week for certain kinds of news reports. That attitude is evidenced by the increasing popularity of the week-end summary in Sunday papers, and the prosperity of the weekly news-magazines. The considerable long-distance mail circulations of papers like the *New York Times* and *Christian Science Monitor* seem to indicate a willingness on the part of many readers to wait a day or two to read the news served up the way they like it.

The axiom that news becomes stale as soon as it is once published may be questioned. That is a very old tradition. In 1625, four years after the first news-sheets appeared in England, the English playwright Ben Jonson produced a play called *Staple of News*, the first satire on journalism in the English language; and in it appeared this line: "When Newes is printed, it leaves, Sir, to be Newes." At first thought, this seems sound doctrine today. But let us take a second thought. Perhaps the "color" stories, the "folo" stories, the "roundups" are not news in the same sense that the first "flash" is; but there is no doubt that such later reporting has large and attentive readership. The fact that most radio listeners, hearing a "flash" on the air, wish to read about it later in the papers brought to their doors serves to point up the fact that something more than mere immediacy is wanted.

Did you ever allow papers to pile up at home when you were away on vacation, and then read them on your return? Of course, you found much news that was stale, but you also found many of the best and most meaningful stories just as fresh as they were when they were printed. The writer of these pages has gone through files of Dana's *New York Sun* of the 1870's and found the stories written by the old master's "bright young men" as scintillating as they seemed to readers eighty years ago. Dana used to boast: "The *Sun's* news is the freshest, most interesting, and sprightliest current"; and now, when it is no longer current, it is still fresh, interesting, and sprightly. Good writing, like good wine, improves with age.

And yet, after all the abuses of reckless haste and all the values of good writing are noted, speed in news-gathering remains a paramount consideration. After all the discounts are taken, timeliness remains a chief quality of good reporting. It is, indeed, the essence of our generic and basic definition of "news." Speed is a part of the very life of the good newsman. Timeliness is in his blood. The quick, shrewd mind; the sure mastery of effective techniques; the ability to get the news and transmit it without fumbling or garbling, accurately and fairly — these are marks of a great reporter.

The amount of good, readable, succinct copy which a good reporter can actually write under pressure is extraordinary. Stories of some of the giants of the past are familiar. Henry J. Raymond, founding editor of the *New York Times*, wrote out, in his very legible script, copy for no less than sixteen columns in less than half a day when Daniel Webster died on October 24, 1852. Whitelaw Reid, who later succeeded Greeley as editor of the *New York Tribune*, wrote for the *Cincinnati Gazette* a fourteen-column story of the Battle of Gettysburg, all of it penned within sight of the fighting. Any good reporter today can sit down at his typewriter and produce a column or more of excellent copy "on top of" a deadline. Working under such pressure simply makes him call upon all his reserves of nervous energy; and the result, if the newsman is really good, is a better story than one written in more comfortable circumstances.

The race against the deadline is one thing; the race against competition is another. Certainly the latter is an unavoidable part of the news business. Sometimes the enthusiasm for "scoops" seems a little naive and schoolboyish, and it surely is not the most important thing in journalism; but there is probably not a newspaper or radio newsroom in the country that does not prize at least an occasional exploit of this kind, while some are constantly straining for them.

The temptation cannot be resisted to quote here the account written by James Creelman concerning the activities of the young W. R. Hearst at the attack on El Caney Hill during the Spanish-American War. Creelman, a reporter for the *New York Journal*, was an ardent admirer of his employer, Mr. Hearst. In his autobiographical book, *On the Great Highway*, Creelman tells how he himself was wounded in the battle, and carried to the rear. Then:

Some one knelt in the grass beside me and put his hand on my fevered head. Opening my eyes, I saw Mr. Hearst, the proprietor of the *New York Journal*, a straw hat with a bright ribbon on his head, a revolver at his belt, and a pencil and notebook in his hand. The man who had provoked the war had come to see the result with his own eyes, and, finding one of his correspondents prostrate, was doing the work himself. Slowly he took down my story of the fight. Again and again the tinging of Mauser bullets interrupted, but he seemed unmoved. The battle had to be reported somehow.

"I'm sorry you're hurt, but" — and his face was radiant with enthusiasm — "wasn't it a splendid fight? We must beat every paper in the world! "

All of this seems a little theatrical, like a scene out of a musical comedy; but it was serious business.

In Italy under Mussolini there were never any news beats, because government dictated not only what news should be printed but its precise position in the papers. And so it is in Stalin's Russia. But whenever a press is free and competitive, there will be striving for "beats." So long as such competition does not operate as a preventive of accurate, full, and fair reporting of the facts, we can only applaud it. But the young newsman, in his evening prayer, should begin by asking the Lord to make him an accurate reporter, should follow that supplication by asking to be made an industrious hunter after the news and a skillful writer of it, and only at the end of his petition should he ask for a beat on his competitor, the *Clarion*.

Speed is not everything, or even the most important thing, in handling the news; but it is essential. Speed is not inconsistent with accuracy; indeed, they complement each other as two of the chief qualities of good reporting.

CHAPTER SIX

News as Sensation

It is the fashion to castigate "sensationalism" in the news and to refer to the "sensation-monger" as some species of particularly slimy reptile. But as a matter of actual fact, you and I *want* sensation in our news, as does everyone else, including the critics. It would be a torpid and spiritless reader indeed — a cold fish, a vegetable — who would pass by everything sensational in his newspaper to read only that which, important or not, afforded the very lowest degree of emotional stimulation.

Virtually all readers like news from which they "get a kick." That is a good phrase, representing accurately what sensational news does. Any news is sensational which stimulates the minds and emotions of readers by shock, surprise, or unusual interest. In other words, all exciting news is sensational.

Exciting news is easy to read. It is "soft" news. Readers "eat it up," and editors know it is "sure fire." It is the essence of sensationalism that it always affords immediate reward to the reader, though it may also offer a further delayed reward if the news is of more or less permanent value to the individual. That is, sensational news often has its "hard" side: it may be significantly important, as reports of wars, international decisions, the death of a President, the account of a national party convention.

Of course, what is sensational for one reader may not be so for another — as the news of the death of an intimate friend. The stock-market reports and the "Help Wanted" column may be very dull for you, but to the speculator and job-hunter they may be truly sensational. Indeed, everything in the news is essentially sensational in some degree, since if it were so dull as not to "excite" interest, it would not even reach the stage of report, to say nothing of getting into print or on the air.

We ought to understand this broad base of sensationalism in the news, but we must also recognize that what the critics condemn and excoriate is not the merely interesting or mildly stirring news, but that which is calculated to be highly exciting, thrilling, and stimulating for most readers. In this sense, the more violent contests are generally sensational, whether in war, politics, sports, or social intercourse; so are disasters, horrors, most crime and sex incidents, and many human-interest stories. In this discussion, we shall call this "high," or "violent," sensationalism. It is the overemphasis on this high sensationalism in the news and the appeal to morbid interests which are more properly subject to severe criticism.[9]

There is a common misapprehension about the history of sensationalism. Trace the written word as far back as we can, we find it used to record the shocking, the thrilling, the exciting incidents. The Hebrew Scriptures, the Egyptian papyrus stories, ancient Greek literature: all resound with sensationalism. The oldest printed news pamphlets — the German *Einblattdrücken* — were published mainly to record disasters of nature or war, the threats to mankind offered by the appearance of comets or invaders, and the occurrence of curious monstrosities. The earliest newspapers were filled with such things.

The fact that our own early newspapers gave so large a proportion of their space to such delayed-reward news as official documents (as was pointed out in our review of the use of the history concept in news) has often blinded students to the fact that early American editors had a great liking for the boldly and baldly sensational. The first American newspaper, *Publick Occurrences*, contained plenty of sensational items; indeed, it was a little story of the sexual misbehavior of the French king, together with an item about atrocities committed by the Indian allies of the Massachusetts government, which caused the authorities to forbid further issues of the paper. Dull John Campbell, editor of the second American newspaper, the *Boston News-Letter*, devoted about half of his tenth issue to a detailed account of the hanging of six pirates on the banks of the Charles River near Boston. Stories of hangings were common in eighteenth-century papers, with the addresses from the scaffold, the prayers of the ministers (sometimes highly sensational), and details of the actual execution. Sensational also were many stories of the "special providences" referred to in an earlier chapter.

War stories are usually highly sensational, and those of the American Revolution were no exception. After the conflict ended, crime and sex news tended to increase in the papers; and there were more stories than ever before of murders, trials for seduction, piracies, hangings. Fisher Ames, a well-known statesman and *censor morum* of the period, wrote an essay for the *New England Palladium* in 1801 which condemns, too sweepingly indeed, the growing taste for sensations. His comments are worth quoting at length:

It seems as if newspaper wares were made to suit a market, as much as any other. The starers, and wonderers, and gapers, engross a very large share of the attention of all the sons of the type. Extraordinary events multiply upon us surprisingly . . .

Is this a reasonable taste? or is it monstrous and worthy of ridicule? Is the history of Newgate the only one worth reading? Are oddities only to be hunted? . . .

Some of the shocking articles in the paper raise simple, and very simple, wonder; some, terrour; and some, horrour and disgust. Now what instruction is there in these endless wonders? Who is the wiser or happier for reading the accounts of them? On the contrary, do they not shock tender minds, and addle shallow brains? They make a thousand old maids, and eight or ten thousand booby boys, afraid to go to bed alone. . . . Yet there seems to be a sort of rivalship among printers, who shall have the most wonders, and the strangest and most horrible crimes. . . .

Now, Messrs. Printers, I pray the whole honourable craft, to banish as many murders, and horrid accidents, and monstrous births and prodigies from their gazettes, as their readers will permit them; and by degrees, to coax them back to contemplate life and manners; to consider common events with some common sense; and to study nature, where she can be known, rather than in those of her ways where she really is, or is represented to be, inexplicable.

Strange events are facts, and as such should be mentioned, but with brevity and in a cursory manner. They afford no ground for popular reasoning or instruction; and, therefore, the horrid details, that make each particular hair stiffen and stand upright in the reader's head, ought not to be given. Sensible printers and sensible readers will think that way of mentioning them the best, that impresses them least on the public attention, and that hurries them on the most swiftly to be forgotten.

Thus Fisher Ames. His cogent observations are quoted here partly to illustrate an early type of the criticism of the news, and partly to point up the prevalence of sensation in American papers of the decades following the Revolution. We shall discuss some of the points he raises later in this chapter. For the present let us note that Ames's protests and those of his fellow-critics apparently had little effect; it was a matter, as Ames recognized, of serving public taste, and only a minority of editors ("printers," as Ames called them) had much interest in reforming the popular taste. And so it went, up to the advent of the penny papers in the 1830's.

Enter on cue, the villain of the piece, wearing a toothy smile beneath his black mustache. His name is Morbid Sensationalism, but he also goes by the name of Sensation for Sensation's Sake — a name with as many "s's" as a snake's hiss. He has been on stage, as we have seen, in the prologue, but he now advances to fanfare. He is ready to seize the lady and make off with the family's gold.

To drop the figure (which is becoming tiresome, and was not too good in the first place), the penny papers of the 1830's, designed for the masses, made a successful bid for large circulations through police court reports and murder stories. Then in 1836, James Gordon Bennett introduced in the *New York Herald* the technique of all-out "play" (later called "hippodroming") of a sex-murder trial, and some other papers were quick to follow. This was, indeed, high sensationalism. But many moral censors were shocked, and that gave the *Herald's* newspaper rivals their chance to lead what has been called a "moral war" against Bennett. There was much flinging about of abusive terms, in the fashion of that "golden age" of journalism — such as "obscene vagabond," "licentious nuisance," "moral pestilence," and "ribald depravity." Though one may suspect that the main animus behind this "war" was envy of the *Herald's* prosperity, there was undoubtedly also some sense of outraged decency; indeed a reading of the *Herald* and its contemporaries indicates that there was actually a rallying of moral forces against a decidedly morbid sensationalism.

What is morbid sensationalism? It is, clearly, an unwholesome, unhealthful excitement. But what is unhealthful for me may be just what the doctor ordered for you; what is unwholesome for an adolescent girl would make no dent in the psyche of a reasonably tough-minded bond-salesman. Sensationalism in any phase is difficult to study because of this subjectivity in its effect, though it would seem that morbidity in sensational news, especially, ought to be studied. Sweeping statements about the harmfulness of crime and sex news, and the extent of such matter in the papers, are common; they are usually impressionistic and untrustworthy.

Kingsbury and Hart, in a suggestive study of the ethics of representative newspapers, devised a "spectrum analysis of sensationalism in the news" in which they gave the "sex-money line of interest" the highest sensational value. Apparently many of their sex-money stories also included crime. Their method was basically impressionistic, but they made an interesting contribution in a series of "spectra" showing graphically the differences in "sensationalism" among great metropolitan newspapers. Rarely has the stupidity of sweeping generalizations about American newspapers been better illustrated. The profile graphs showed highly "socialized" interests at the top, and in the "spectrum" of the *Christian Science Monitor* these jutted far out, while the profile became slimmer as it descended to a vanishing point in the highly sensational subject matter. The profile of the *New York Mirror*, the Hearst tabloid, on the other hand, jutted far out at the bottom and slimmed toward the top, so that it was virtually the *Monitor* profile turned upside down.[10]

Much of our crime news is highly sensational, and one of the commonest criticisms of the American press for the past hundred and fifty years has been levied against its stories of crime and criminals. There have been many space-measuring studies designed to discover what proportion of the American newspaper's columns are dedicated to crime, and their results always surprise us with small percentages — in the common run of papers, less than 2 per cent; and even in a confessedly sensational sheet, under 7 per cent. Curtis D. MacDougall's comprehensive and eclectic chapter, "News of Anti-Sociability," in his *Newsroom Problems and Policies*, gives some of these figures. But space is only one factor in the "play" given a story. Position, headlines, and objectivity as opposed to emotional appeal in writing are probably even more important than space.

Three ruling principles emerge out of the welter of the long debate over crime reports in the news.

First, the suppression of crime news would be dishonest. It would amount to a distortion of the news-scene which would violate the primary obligation of an editor to present fairly the events of the world in order that his readers may know what is going on. Agnes Repplier put the matter perfectly in an essay in the *Commonweal* a good many years ago, and every line of the following passage will bear careful reading. As will be noted, Miss Repplier was writing in reply to a statement of the policy of the *Christian Science Monitor* against the printing of any crime news in that paper:

There is a great deal to be said in favor of expurgated news, and only one objection to be urged against it — the life so indicated is not the life about us; the world so described is not the world we live in. It is pleasant to dwell with the *Monitor* upon "every event, material, intellectual, and spiritual, which has its bearing upon the ascent of man"; but man is not ascending in a straight line, beautiful and exhilarating to behold. His progress is so impeded that it is a trifle hard at times to know if he is going up or down. He was stumbling along in this fashion when Plutarch unkindly remarked that his falls were more interesting than his climbs. . . .

For, after all, it is the existence of evil, not the recognition of evil, which overcasts life. Just as the existence of a moral law lifts our souls from doubt, so the transgression of a moral law is the acid test by which judgment and justice are made clear to us. A great deal has been said about the atrocious "crime news" published in the American papers, but the atrocity lies in the crime rather than in the news. The little catechism we learned as children told us there were nine ways of being accessory to sin, and one of these is silence. It may be, and sometimes is, an evasion of duty. Professor William James, a man whose ucompromising candor was ill calculated to soften the harsh outlines of reality, wrote to his more famous brother Henry: "I cannot bring myself, after the fashion of so many men, to blink evil out of sight, and gloss it over. It's as real as the good; and if it is denied, good must be denied also. Evil should be accepted and hated and resisted while there is breath in our bodies.[11]

Second, pandering to depraved curiosity about details of crime, and especially of the more loathsome crimes, is an offense against both public morals and public taste. This principle applies to all sensational news, whether it deals with crime or any other shocking events or situations. "Crusades" against vice conditions have sometimes been little more than camouflage for the exploitation of salacity.

We hasten to concede the debatability of matters of taste — or rather, as the old Latin tag had it, the undebatable nature of taste. It may be contended, moreover, with some convincingness, that public taste may sometimes have to be outraged in the cause of honest presentation of realities. But after we have made all proper allowances for such arguments, we must still condemn, on the grounds of both taste and morals, the unnecessary sadism and pruriency in news and pictures which some newspapers sometimes flaunt before their readers.

Was it necessary to print columns of details about Harry K. Thaw's seduction of an actress in 1905? Or about the "Fatty" Arbuckle or Chaplin trials? Or about the indecencies of the Errol Flynn rape case a few years ago? Few episodes in the history of American journalism have been more disgraceful than the "war of the tabs" in New York in 1924–1928, with the Hall-Mills and Snyder-Gray and "Peaches" Browning stories based on the alleged sex offenses of obscure and stupid buffoons. Oswald Garrison Villard once called this "gutter journalism" — which was an insult to a good clean gutter.

But one does not need to go even so far back as the Errol Flynn case to find plenty of examples of the gleeful exploitation of dirty details of sex incidents which have come into the hands of authorities and thus become public matters. Every day not a few but many papers and broadcasts overplay offenses which have little "importance" beyond that which newsmen find in the morbid interest of thrill-seeking readers.

The third principle which emerges is that crime news should be written with far more understanding of its causes — psychological, social, and economic — than is commonly the case. It was near the end of the "war of the tabs" episode just referred to that the wise Marlen Pew wrote an editorial in *Editor & Publisher* which ought to be remembered:

Consider the volume of newspaper space in a year that has been devoted to the so-called "news-facts" in relation to conspicuous instances of sex perversion. Clippings of all that has been printed about the Snyder-Gray and Hickman cases alone would fill a warehouse. No prurient detail in such sex scandal is missed by reporters and the public is fairly gorged with the who-when-where-what-how facts, endlessly told and retold. But the "why" question seems rarely to concern our press; and this is strange, for in answer to "why" lies the wonderful constructive and enlightening story that science may tell bearing on the psychology and chemistry of sex.

For instance, take the Hickman case: how many readers of average newspapers have received from the mass of information laid before them any understanding of the meaning of that instance of moral depravity? To the ordinary reader Hickman represents a criminal monstrosity the like of which the country has never before seen and may never see again. But any experienced police reporter knows exactly what this youth represents in psychopathology and that while his offense is extreme his type is by no means uncommon. If any benefit is to come from the wide-spread and continued publication of the facts in this horrible case it will lie in a dissemination of the scientific facts so that society may the better protect itself from such abnormal human specimens.

Pew might have mentioned a story by Thomas S. Rice in the *Brooklyn Eagle*, in which that great reporter and criminologist wrote about Hickman "for soundly constructive social ends."

The presentation of crime news with such understanding is not easy, but more and more it is being done. In his *Backgrounding the News* (Baltimore, 1939), Sidney Kobre tells how the press in 1924 "played" the case history of Celia Cooney, the "bobbed-haired bandit," which gave her social background; but he also points out that these facts were dug out by a probation officer and not a newspaper reporter. The thesis of Kobre's book is that modern reporters must be better grounded in the social sciences. That certain papers now take this attitude is a gratifying fact. A good example of the new method of handling a crime story was printed in the *St. Louis Post-Dispatch* on January 21, 1951. It dealt with the killer Bill Cook, whose capture had recently been chronicled, and was entitled "Case History of a Badman." It was written by Peter Wyden, a staff correspondent of the paper, and told of the criminal's rootless uncared-for childhood, deserted by his sharecropper father, educated in "reformatories," and so on. The story was interesting, to be sure, but full of meaning.

J. Edgar Hoover's rebuke of the press for alleged romanticizing of gangsterism in 1937, with its suggestion of more scientific attitudes, has undoubtedly had some effect. Increased understanding of modern penology, and especially of parole laws, and some knowledge of abnormal psychology and of sociological problems on the part of writers for the press, have improved crime reporting. As editors and reporters become better educated in these fields, we shall have more constructive handling of our crime news.

Fundamentally, the evil of sensational news is not that it is sensational, but that its significance is too often obscured or distorted. The news of a murder, or a series of murders, may be of great importance from several points of view — that of public administration, that of social causation and responsibility, that of immediate dangers. But if reporter and editor lose sight of such significant aspects of crime, and shovel in details of horror, sex, moronic emotionalism, and low vulgarity, then the appeal is made simply and baldly to morbid curiosity, and the result is clearly immoral.

As to crime news in general, there is no question of printing or not printing. Of course it must be printed. But that arbiter whom Carlyle delighted to call the "able editor" prints it not as titillations for the prurient, nor even as a kind of sadistic exercise in Gothic romance, but as a part of the news-scene without which our knowledge of contemporary society and government would be incomplete and defective.

One of the chief sins of the sensation-monger on both the newspaper and the radio is the effort which he makes to "jazz up" his story, and to make an exciting report out of news that is not really exciting to begin with. To do this, he drags in some of those "elements of interest" upon which some newsmen are wont to rely far too much. To "write it straight" is to be honest; to sensationalize a set of facts is not only a cheating kind of hocus-pocus, but an outrage upon journalism and upon society.

Just how much overplay of highly sensational stories actually goes on in the newspapers, on the radio, and through other news media, it is difficult to say. Since the failure of the *National Police Gazette*, the United States has never had a prominent weekly which has battened on that kind of stuff as does the London *News of the World*, with its phenomenal circulation. But some have said that the chief reason for the *Police Gazette's* failure was that the general newspapers had stolen its thunder. Certainly there is far too much violent and morbid sensation in the American press and radio today. Some modern tabloids retain the traditions of the old "hot" tabloidism. Some eight-column papers, by no means all of them in the Hearst group, are true heirs of the techniques of the old era of yellow journalism. Some columnists and commentators deal chiefly with scandals, and spice their offerings not only with salacious details, but with tricks of style in writing and hysterical voice effects on the air. Even some "respectable" newspapers — too many of them — like to have an occasional fling with the highly sensational story.

The whole question of sensation in the news is difficult and complicated. We have to begin by a realistic recognition of its value as a legitimate response to a demand for what is interesting and even exciting; but we must end by repudiating and condemning at every opportunity all mistreatment of news by "writing in" sensation, all overemphasis on violence and horror and scandal, all pandering to morbid tastes and appetites. It is a part of the continuing "cold war" which all intelligent and high-minded newsmen have to carry on against subversive forces in our journalism.

CHAPTER SEVEN

The Human-Interest Story As News

A distressing confusion in discussions of the human-interest story has been caused by a common failure to define the term. Even Helen MacGill Hughes's suggestive *News and the Human Interest Story* (Chicago, 1940) fails to be as helpful as it should be because the author does not discriminate between news that is interesting to human beings, which is one thing, and news that is interesting because it deals with the life of human beings, which is quite another and more special thing.

Human-interest news is a report which is interesting not because of the importance of the specific event or situation reported, but because it is amusing or pathetic or striking or significant as a bit of the texture of our human life. Little incidents of the street and the home, in words or pictures, in the newspaper, on a radio broadcast, or on the television screen: these furnish the human-interest material that lends variety to the news. A blind man selling pencils on a street corner has a word of philosophical advice for everyone who drops a nickel into his tin cup; a sharecropper tries to raise a loan on a medal he won in the First World War; a girl gets on a bus with her dress on backwards, and, when her friends call her attention to her mistake, draws her arms out of the sleeves, gives a couple of wriggles, and readjusts the belt, to the amusement of spectators (including a reporter); a little three-year-old on a hot afternoon takes off all her clothes to play in a street puddle, a big policeman makes a mock arrest, and a photographer gets a picture that gives a chuckle to thousands of perspiring readers that evening. Of such is the stuff of human-interest news.

It will be perceived immediately that this is a notably "literary" phase of the news. Literature is concerned with the interpretation of phases of universal human life by means of the portrayal of specific exemplars. Ruth, in the Old Testament, exemplifies loyalty; Oedipus represents expiation; Macbeth illustrates the punishment of lawless ambition; Tom Sawyer pictures boyish adventure, and so on. Any good story you read in a magazine brings you some phase of human life and feeling. Brunetière used to refer to *une tranche de vie* — the realistic presentation of a "slice of life." That is precisely what the human-interest story is — a slice of life. Short-story writers often get their ideas from human-interest items in the news.

One finds little of this concept in the early newspapers. There were, to be sure, a few editors who were more perceptive or less conventional than the others — like Thomas Fleet, of the *Boston Rehearsal*, who had a notable liking for the small and sometimes diverting episodes of homely, common life. It was Fleet who published a little paragraph, for example, about a drunken barber at Harvard:

Saturday last a remarkable Accident hapned at *Cambridge*. A Man whose Name is *Edward Farrow*, a journeyman Barber of this town, being on the top of one of the Colleges, and 'tis tho't a little mellow, fell from thence into the Yard; and tho' he lay for dead some Time, yet when he came to himself, it appeared he had only received a slight Hurt in his Back.

There was little of such interest as long as newspapers were published for the upper classes. But when the six-cent papers were pushed aside by sheets which sold for a penny and thus reached the lower social levels, the situation changed. The penny papers, made to suit the pocketbooks of "merchanicks, porters, and dray-men," must also suit their interests and tastes. Stories had to be more direct, more sensational, and more witty. Also they had to rescind the rule that only very important persons were newsworthy.

The penny papers, offspring of the industrial revolution, were also a result of the new growth of industrialized cities. To the reader of old newspaper files it seems as though suddenly, in the middle 1830's, a few young printers woke up one morning and rubbed their eyes and saw all about them crowds of busy artisans with valid interests in what was going on not only in the world at large but in their own changing society, and exclaimed with one voice: "See what we have here! These fellows are human beings! Ergo, they are news-hungry! Let us make newspapers for them and about them!" In fact, James Gordon Bennett, with his strong democratic convictions, had some such comprehension of the situation.

One of the great hits of the first successful penny papers was made by reports of what went on at the early morning police courts. In these courtrooms at four o'clock in the morning were lined up all the vagabonds, wife-beaters, sots, and streetwalkers who had been dragged in by the police during the night. The hearings furnished material which contained a considerable element of sensationalism, but which made its appeal largely because the items were bits of the real life of the streets.

The pattern for these reports had been set by John Wight, an English journalist, who exploited the tragicomedy of early morning hearings in London's Bow Street Court for readers of the *Morning Herald* of that city. A collection of Wight's sketches in book form, called *Mornings at Bow Street*, made a big success in England and was reprinted in America in 1826. George W. Wisner, called by an admirer "the Balzac of the daybreak court," wrote such reports for the first successful penny paper, the *New York Sun*. William Atree did them a little better for another penny sheet, the *New York Transcript*, sometimes using the dialogue form:

Wife. Mr. Judge, Mr. Judge, I'm a poor dead and gone distracted creature that's all cut all to pieces by my crazy husband and killed into the bargain.
Husband. She lies, Judge, she's an ungrateful creature, besides, I never hit her in earnest, but only by way of *coaxing* her.
Wife. Oh, you dreadful villain, was it coaxing you was when you cut my cheek asunder, when you knocked my eye out, and took all my drink away and swallowed it yourself?
Magistrate. Did he knock your eye out?
Wife. He did so, sir, he knocked it clane out wid his dirty fist.
Magistrate. But you appear to have two very bright blue eyes today.
Wife. It's blue they are now, sir, but it's black they were a short time since. . . .

Rowdy and ribald these items often were, and a tawdry sort of humor. But it was the first time in the history of American journalism that the papers had made a practice of printing the domestic misadventures of the lower classes; it was better than a play, and readers were vastly amused.

Occasionally there was a little word-caricature, as in this item about a sailor on shore-leave, which appeared in the *Philadelphia Public Ledger*:

James Holmes, a rough-looking tar, with a pair of James Watson Webb whiskers, was found last night in a court which leads down to Water St., drunk and asleep; he was arrested. He stated that he came home on the U.S. Ship Delaware, took a drop too much, and "lost reckoning and got out of his latitude," as he expressed it. He was permitted to clear out.

So common as to be almost a convention of such reporting was the incidental sermonette against strong drink. The *Public Ledger* man had a new way of presenting the idea when he quoted an "oration on whisky" which had been delivered by one John Corbit, an old offender, in the Mayor's Court. This speech, which bears a resemblance to other bibulous disquisitions, ran as follows:

Whisky is a curious article; it is both sweet and sour, a poison and an antidote. It creates war and is used in making peace, it breaks heads and mends them. Governments encourage its use and punish people for using it. It is paradoxical and contradictory. I cannot understand it.

In spite of this effort, Corbit went to jail, there further to pursue his philosophical reflections.

Facetious court reporting as a regular feature did not last long. Bennett never used it in the *Herald*, and moralists very justly condemned it. It has little standing in the modern newspaper.

But the human interest story as introduced to American journalism by the penny papers was by no means confined to courtroom materials. Human life everywhere came to be used as newspaper material. People on the streets, in their homes, in the shops and factories, in the theaters, at fairs and at sports events — all of them were subject matter for the writers of these little stories.

Among the most notable of series of street sketches published in American papers at the middle of the nineteenth century were Solon Robinson's "Hot Corn" stories in the *New York Tribune*.

They were distinctly reformatory in nature, and designed to tell *Tribune* readers about "the ways of the poor to eke out means of subsistence in this over-burdened, ill-fed, and worse-lodged home of misery" — the New York slums. Robinson's chief characters were the "hot corn girls," who sold roasting ears on the streets — dirty and ill-kempt children whose cry, "Here's your nice hot corn, smoking hot, just from the pot!" was familiar to New Yorkers.

But it was not until Charles A. Dana took over the *New York Sun* in 1868 that American journalists learned how human-interest stories could brighten and enliven a great newspaper. Dana gathered around him editors and reporters who learned to produce excellent human-interest pieces, which were sometimes run on the first page alongside more important news. "Boss" Clarke's young men sought out the color and variety and intimate vitality of the life of a city which had now grown to a million population. One of them wrote a story of hot-weather living conditions in the tenements in July, 1878, with no special attempt to point a social lesson or to be amusing or to be pathetic, but with a natural vividness and liveliness. "Here is a bit of life, Mr. and Mrs. Reader; it will interest you in this hot weather; the *Sun* shines for all." Another wrote a story of a gentleman burglar, which might have suggested (but probably did not) the character of "Raffles" to E. W. Hornung. Another, in 1872, wrote a wonderful story of a discreet Chinese servant for whom a half-daft sailor had conceived a malignant hatred born of fear, and of the assault and trial which followed. Yet another told of how a mob took possession of the ballroom of a hotel in Flushing for a 73-round prize-fight, and a few days later gave us the story of the efforts of "The Mouse" and "Owney Geogeeghan's Rat" to find a place for a fighting match. The unknown writer of these fight stories caught the very mood and color of these early, illegal ring-contests — a mixture of cruelty, gangsterism, and sport.

This was not comic writing. Occasionally there was a flicker of wit, a bit of caricature. Yet the essence of caricature is exaggeration, and there was nothing broad or overdrawn in these sketches. It is clear that "Boss" Clarke instructed his young men not to overwrite, not to gild the lily, never to exaggerate; it is clear that the stories are amusing largely because of the selection of materials. For the most part, they were even severely objective, restrained, and unpretentious. Usually they were not more than a quarter of a column in length, and they almost never reached a full column.

Typical is a little story of a steamboat excursion. It begins:

A small man with a yellow beard and a blue badge on his breast stood yesterday morning at 8 o'clock at the foot of West 24th st. and wiggled his fingers at all who passed. Some comprehended the pantomime and in response turned off to the wharf at 25th st. Others regarded the nimble fingers of the man in a simple amazement and passed on. The man wiggled his fingers because the boat that was to bear the Manhattan Literary Association of Deaf Mutes to Columbia Grove lay at the foot of 25th st. instead of at the foot of 24th as had been announced. In a short time a hundred persons were gathered at the pier.

Space is not available for the remainder of this story, which displays charm and a quiet humor in telling of the chattering of thumbs and fingers on board the boat, and of an after-dinner speech by the Association's president.

The *Sun* rather specialized in stories of the excursions, picnics, and clambakes in which organizations of all kinds in the New York of the seventies indulged. There was one, for example, about the annual excursion of the Fat Men's Association, with a clambake, and a dance on shipboard. The charm of this occasion was somewhat marred, however, by an altercation between two of the oversize members, in the course of which, the deck being a little slippery with spilled beer, some six hundred pounds of avoirdupois went down and an ankle was broken.

These reportorial techniques of the *New York Sun* were, in the course of years, highly influential on the development of American journalism. They brought circulation leadership to the *Sun*, which in some years outstripped even that phenomenal but now forgotten paper of the tenement districts, the old one-cent *Daily News*; and techniques that win circulation are always imitated. The *Sun* became famous as "the newspaperman's newspaper," and many editors held it before their young men as a model. Among others, the *Kansas City Star*, founded in 1880,

made much of the type of amusing story which was so important
in the *Sun*, and to this day the *Star* will occasionally run a human-
interest story alongside a Washington dispatch on its front page,
in true Dana fashion. But the *Star* was by no means the only
follower in this technique; in varying degrees and with greater
or less promptness virtually the entire American press adopted the
clever story of common life as a component part of their news
budget.

In 1916–1917 the *New York Evening World* used to run each day
a page of short pieces sent in by readers describing interesting
things they had observed on the streets. Prizes were paid for
the best of these short articles, and together they made an extremely interesting picture of the life and color of a great city.
Papers in other cities followed the *Evening World's* example for
a time. Later, O. O. McIntyre's "New York Day by Day" became
a popular syndicated column. Ernie Pyle traveled about the
country picking up interesting bits about people and things.
Papers everywhere trained their reporters to watch for usable
human-interest stuff.

And so it goes today. Editors and newscasters like the human-
interest bits in the news grist — the little pieces which reflect
fragments of common life — because they know from their surveys of the interests of readers and listeners that the public likes
them. They bring variety and brightness into the paper and
broadcast. Dana valued them for what he called "sprightliness."
It will have been noted from the examples given that incidental
humor is often an element of such writing. Occasionally pathos
is used effectively. Commonly human-interest stories get an easy
emotional response; they are attractive and readable. They are
"soft" news.

Perhaps it is enough that human-interest stories should be entertaining. We all need diversion, and such writing, if done with
skill and restraint, makes admirable reading. Moreover, a good
case may be made for the essential *importance* of little stories
of common life. They have something of what critics of fiction
sometimes call "universality": they deal with matters in which
we all participate. And if an objector rises to remark, "But the
persons involved are so unimportant and the incidents so trivial!"

we shall be forced to observe pontifically that no human being is unimportant and that homely common life is itself deeply significant.

The human-interest stuff of the news has such values only, however, when these bits of flotsam are chosen for their meaning as representation of the life about us, and then presented with the deftness and restraint of the literary craftsman. Occasionally a talented reporter writes a little masterpiece in this kind — a bit of writing that deserves a better fate than that of tomorrow's wastepaper. Those minor Balzacs and Dickenses and O. Henrys flourish from time to time in the busy city rooms of some of our newspapers, and often go on into the somewhat prouder fields of fiction and drama. It is significant that so large a proportion of American novelists began as journalists.

But one great danger of human-interest stories in the newspapers is in over-writing. Their effect on the average reader, and certainly their appeal to the discriminating critic, may be ruined by blatancy, striving for effect, insincerity. Worst of all are the "sob stories" written to work up popular sympathy for the prisoner in some notorious criminal case. Restraint is a factor in all good writing, but particularly in human-interest feature stories; and when it comes to "color" stories in crime and disaster reporting, restraint is often necessary if such work is to be saved from gross vulgarity.

Measures of what we have called "significant importance" are not easy. Social criticism, patterns for reform, and moral and religious teachings may lift the human-interest story to a very high level of significance. Solon Robinson's "Hot Corn" stories in the *New York Tribune*, and those written in the 1880's for the *World* and the *Morning Journal* by Police Reporter Jacob A. Riis and subsequently worked into his book *How the Other Half Lives*, were social criticism with suggestions of reform. Who shall say that the little stories of a booming metropolitan society written by Amos Cummings and Mr. Dana's other bright young men in the 1870's were not also significant? George Ade's "Stories of the Streets and of the Town" in the old *Chicago Record* were amusing and at the same time meaningful. Contributors to the record of the *comédie humaine* of Chicago were later welcomed and trained by Henry Justin Smith, of the *Daily News* — Ben Hecht, Bob Casey, and others. Finley Peter Dunne's "Mr. Dooley" was a moralist masquerading as a bartender. Best known of all writers of human-interest news in recent times was Ernie Pyle, in his last phase the friend and diarist of the GI in the Second World War.

If an editor or reporter, or both, have a feeling for social values, they will tend to emphasize in their human-interest news such factors as the hardships of the poor, the courage of the under-privileged, the lessons of success or failure in obscure lives. Such stories are frequent in our newspapers; we often clip them out, carry them about in our wallets for a time, show them to our friends, remember them. It is a pleasure for the present writer to mention Lincoln Barnett's "Apple Annie" story in the *New York Herald Tribune* of January 10, 1934, in which the reporter told very simply of the death from poverty and hardship of the apple woman who, a few months before, had been picked off the streets of New York to live in luxury for twenty-four hours, as a pub-licity stunt for Columbia Pictures' "Queen for a Day." He recalls also Stuart Welch's story of the tailor Florio, who took his favorite sewing machine into service with him when he went to Europe in the American Expeditionary Forces so that he could mend his fellow-soldiers' uniforms, and afterward kept it in his little shop, decorated with medals. Welch's story was one of several such pieces which he wrote for the *Tacoma News-Tribune* in 1935–1936. And also part of a series was Paul Fisher's story of "Joe Doakes," in the *Kansas City Star*, June 4, 1939, which told of the character and daily activities in his job of a precinct captain in the Pendergast machine.[12]

Of course, many of these stories are looked upon by the editor as "features" rather than "straight news." Some of them, like the one based on the death of "Apple Annie," are "news features." But whatever the distinctions used in the newspaper office, these pieces have very real values in the newspaper. If they are socially meaningful and written with a certain literary skill, they may reach a high mark in journalistic achievement.

CHAPTER EIGHT

Objective News *versus* Qualified Report

It is inevitable that much of our information about what happens in the world should come to us by a process which may be called *qualified* report.

Rumor, which is the name we have for popular reporting, has little respect for the bald and exact fact. Indeed most persons have little capacity for exact observation, or for careful reporting. In the swift race of rumor, facts undergo qualifications and changes which are often grotesque and almost incredible. It is like the old parlor game of "Gossip," in which a statement is whispered from one person to another around a ring, and the words that return to the first whisperer are ludicrously unlike those he spoke into the ear of his neighbor.

All news came by rumor in ancient times. After specialists began gathering the news for governments and for businessmen, rumor still played a large part in the shaping of the reports; and though the professional letter-writers of the centuries preceding printed newspapers often felt some responsibility for the authentication of their news, they were, in the main, a gullible and uncritical lot.

When the printing press took over, there was a change in all this. Perhaps the change was more apparent than real; but there is no doubt that printed news is more likely to be responsible than written or spoken news, and that it is so regarded by the reader. Indeed naive readers often go too far in accepting whatever appears in "the sanctity of print." There is something definitive about type printed in black ink on white paper. Print carries an implication of care and responsibility. It seems to give a mere rumor something of what Voltaire called "le sacrement de confirmation." The very first news-broadside printed in the American Colonies was entitled *The Present State of New-England Affairs*; and under that heading was the line: "This is Published to Prevent False Reports," as though print were a sure cure for the ills of rumor. And we have already noted that one of the chief reasons which Ben Harris gave for publishing the first American newspaper was "the Curing . . . of that Spirit of Lying which prevails amongst us."

Thus printed news gained acceptance, which gave the printer both power and responsibility. It was natural that as soon as regular newspapers appeared, the editors, who were specialists in gathering and handling reports, should assume authority in dealing with news. Now, power often begets abuse, and many editors came to exercise their control over the news with a reckless disregard for what we have called the "bald and exact fact," exploiting the popular regard for the printed word, which should have been precious to them as the basis of their profession and their prosperity, for devious purposes. Usually they were not themselves free agents, but exercised their power under the domination of Government.

The attitude of these editors may seem cynical to a modern student; but often editors had no high opinion of the capacities of the common people, and they regarded themselves as competent directors of their readers' opinions. If it was expedient to qualify the news, to twist and garble and embellish it, that was their business. Sir Roger L'Estrange, licenser of the press under the Restoration, remarked candidly in the first issue of his *Intelligencer* (August 31, 1663) that a gazette of news, prudently managed, had certain values:

'Tis none of the worst ways of address to the genius and humor of the common people, whose affections are much more capable of being tuned and wrought upon by convenient hints and touches in the shape and air of a pamphlet than by the strongest reasons and best notions imaginable under any other and more sober form whatsoever.

This may be regarded as the classical statement of the technique of the qualified news report: such "convenient hints and touches," together with prudent selection, have always been at the heart of biased or "angled" news reporting.

It must not be thought that there was no candid reporting in the seventeenth and eighteenth centuries. There was a great deal of it, not only in those departments which were not offensive to Government, but also in news which bold editors printed in defiance of authority.

But rarely did any editor print bald and exact fact. Even honest Ben Harris, writing copy for the first American newspaper, peppered his facts with comment; here was no attempt to garble or distort, but reporting without "convenient hints and touches" was virtually unknown. When Harris told of the conduct of the Indian allies of the British in the current war against the French, he could not restrain a mild criticism of the alliance with fighting men who were given to the unpleasant practice of burning their prisoners alive. This got him into trouble and ended the career of his *Publick Occurrences* before it was fairly begun. Nobody doubted his facts, or the propriety of his commenting on the facts as he went along; but Government would not permit criticism of its behavior.

Somewhat later the careful John Campbell qualified his reports in the *Boston News-Letter* according to the demands of the royal governor, acknowledging in each and every issue that his paper was "Published by Authority." Other papers submitted to similar qualification of news by Government; still others defied authority and colored the news as their editors saw fit, sometimes very lightly and harmlessly, and sometimes with deeper dyes. But they all touched it up more or less. To cut the news to pattern, to dress it up with color and frills and proper costume accessories was an editor's trade. Such was journalism in the eighteenth century.

The unadorned, unqualified news fact was seldom found in eighteenth-century papers except as it appeared in lists of ship clearances and prices current and meteorological tables. This universal system of "dressing up" the news often seems to a modern reader quaint but rather pleasant. Here is a typical item from the *New London Gazette* of June 16, 1769:

Last Sunday evening was married here Mr. Daniel Shaw, of Marlborough, to Miss Grace Coit, of this Town, a young lady embellish'd with every Qualification requisite to render married life agreeable.

A story of Boston's 1785 Fourth of July celebration in the *Centinel* began thus:

> Monday last, being the anniversary of the ever-memorable day, on which the illustrious Congress declared the then Colonies of North-America, to be Free, Sovereign and Independent States, all ranks of citizens participated in the celebration of the happy event, and even Nature put on more than usual mildness, expressive of her joy on the occasion — Ere the Eastern ocean was yet bordered with the saffron hue, the feathered choristers sang their early matin, and to usher in the auspicious day, Aurora unbarred the ruddy gates of the morn, with sympathetic smiles. — The roar of artillery . . .

This method was commonly harmless when applied to social events; but when it came to public affairs it is obvious that coloring and patching were sure to be dangerous to honest news. During the Stamp Act controversy, and even more noticeably when the Townshend Acts were in force, the political attitudes of the newspapers strongly affected their presentation of their reports. The abuses of partisan handling of the news were accentuated when American political parties developed in the last decade of the eighteenth century. Outrageous personal abuse of political opponents was woven into news stories. Scurrility, vituperation, vulgar insult, became common in the reporting of political affairs. These were the Dark Ages of American journalism, lasting for some forty years (*c.* 1795–1835). A good party paper in those days never published fair news of the opposition. A Jackson organ would never print a speech by Henry Clay, nor would a Clay organ print a speech by Jackson, except to garble it in an abusive criticism. Apologists for the party-press system often said that a reader could get a fair picture of the situation by reading papers on both sides; but this was not true, since political news was not honestly reported on either side.

It is necessary to review the development of qualified news with some care because we cannot understand the news-handling of the middle of the twentieth century without this historical background. The problem of qualified news is neither old nor new: it is perennial, because it inheres in the nature of reporting by human agencies in the midst of social situations.

Modern attitudes toward the problem began to appear with

the advent of the penny press in the 1830's. The success of the penny papers, with their emphasis on nonpolitical news, resulted in a gradual movement away from partisan control of the press. The next hundred years saw the growing political independence of American papers. Just as the first century of our journalism was marked by a struggle against control by Government, so the century beginning in 1830 was characterized by the slow emergence of the press from party control. Technological advances helped, for fast presses and cheap paper made mass circulations possible, and large and profitable papers tended toward independence from partisan dictation.

The movement gained greatly by the "bolts" of party papers in the presidential campaigns of 1872 and 1884, both motivated in many cases by resentments against corruption in office. The "bolting" papers were contemptuously dubbed "mugwumps" by the faithful party journals; but once these editors learned to jump the fence, they were never again safely corralled by party herdsmen. By 1880, a fourth of the papers in the United States were listed in the directories as independent, neutral, or merely "local." Ten years later, the proportion had reached one-third. By that time nearly all the profitable, big-circulation papers were independent, and Editor Horace White declared: "Business prosperity has increased with all papers in the proportion that they have maintained their independence and their freedom." "Only an independent newspaper is in a position to be honest," cried Charles H. Grasty, then editor of the *Baltimore Sun*, in an address at the University of Virginia.

Today about half of the English-language daily papers of general circulation in the United States label themselves "Independent," and one-fourth call themselves "Independent Republican" or "Independent Democratic," leaving only one-fourth to bear the old party labels. Of course, the tag that a newspaper gives itself for the record in the directories may or may not mean much in a given case; but the shift of party labeling just reviewed indicates unmistakably the movement toward independence which seemed revolutionary in the seventies, but commonplace by 1900.

However, a declaration of independence from partisan control did not necessarily carry with it a renunciation of qualified news.

It did remove one of the strongest reasons for coloring news, and it helped immeasurably the cause of honest and straightforward reporting. And at the same time another journalistic reform was working in the same direction — the separation of editorial comment from the news story.

This reform also had its roots in the penny press. It is true that the first editorial columns appeared in some of the older six-cent papers, where they had developed with the news under the local heading. But when local news, in the penny press, assumed a larger space and greater importance, it was necessary to find another place for editorial comment if it, too, were to be important. It was in Horace Greeley's *Tribune*, which began as a penny paper, that the full-fledged editorial page first developed in America.

This divorce of editorial comment and the news in the make-up of the paper had a salutary effect on reporting. It was not immediately a complete divorce, and it did not by any means prevent entirely the qualifying of the news by hints and touches; but by recognizing the line between news and comment it made "straight" reporting easier, and it simplified the task of the reader.

Political independence and the separation of the news and editorial departments brought about a situation in which the truth and accuracy of the reported fact might be sincerely sought as the goal of the best journalism. In this modern insistence on unbiased and uncolored news, it would be wrong to disregard the part played by the great news services. The Associated Press, United Press, and International News Service serve many clients. They must please editors and publishers of diverse attitudes and communities, and the only way they can please them all is by carefully factual and uncolored news reports. Anyone who has ever attended a meeting of managing editors of papers served by one of the great wire agencies, or read accounts of the proceedings in such meetings, knows how sharply bureau chiefs and managers are brought to task on any suspicion of bias in their reports. Frank J. Starzel, general manager of the Associated Press, must be presumed to have spoken with absolute sincerity when he made the following remarks at the dedication of the *Minneapolis Star* and *Tribune* building in 1949:

We are seeking only to obtain facts and the truth. We have no axe to grind in politics, economics, or personalities. The intense interest of hundreds of American newspapers in obtaining factual, unbiased, uncolored news founded and prospered this organization. . . .

Our correspondents operate on the theory that people everywhere want facts and information, irrespective of whether these fit the reader's or listener's own preconceived points of view. Any competent newsman knows, of course, that the search for truth is never-ending. The best he can do is to present intelligently each day the information he can obtain.

In general, this is the attitude of the American press today. In general, American news ethics are summed up in the simple statement in the "canons of Journalism" of the American Society of Newspaper Editors: "News reports should be free from opinion or bias of any kind."

It may be hard for participants in the great national game of criticizing newspapers and radio to realize that for most American newsmen the ideal of accurate and objective news reports is fundamental and paramount. It is distinctively an American contribution to journalism, and it is prized by most American newsmen as the keystone of journalistic practice. Alan Barth, of the *Washington Post*, writing in the *Guild Reporter* for November 24, 1950, declared: "The tradition of objectivity is one of the principal glories of American journalism." Will Irwin, in one of that admirable series of articles on "The American Newspaper" published in *Collier's* in 1911, wrote: "Truth, fogged by the imperfections of human sight, hidden under the wrappings of lies, stands the final aim of a reporter when he goes out on a news tip" — and he named such great reporters of his generation as Julian Ralph, John P. Dunning, Nicholas Biddle, and Frank Ward O'Malley as devoted to this ideal.

Newspapermen now in important positions throughout the world still remember sitting in a lecture room in a midwestern school of journalism in 1929 and hearing an astringent, hard-hitting address [18] by a thin, tense man named Paul Y. Anderson — the great Washington correspondent of the *St. Louis Post-Dis-*

patch. His address was far removed from sentimental glorification of his craft; it was utterly sincere and desperately practical. But it ended with this paragraph:

How then shall we finally characterize the business of a reporter? Does it offer an ideal worthy to be dignified by a genuine sacrifice? Does it require the best gifts which a man or woman can bring to the service of a profession? The ideal which it offers is the unending search for truth. There is no higher. For the fulfillment of its function, it demands courage, intelligence, devotion, incorruptibility, and the divine curiosity which has been behind every ascending movement of the human race since the first Neanderthal man lifted his head to gaze at the stars. For myself I have no greater ambitions than those to which a reporter does and should aspire. If man is ever free, it will be because he knows the truth, and if he knows the truth it will be because there were honest reporters.

And then, in a mood of grim whimsy which was not uncharacteristic of the man, Paul Anderson concluded:

When the inevitable day arrives, and this gaunt, limp form is cut down and carted away from the gallows to its last melancholy resting place in the potter's field, my only wish is that some old subscriber, touched by a little feeling of gratitude, will stick a clean shingle in the earth to mark the spot, inscribing thereon these simple words: "Forty Years a Reporter — Dead he lies here now, but nobody ever caught him at it while he was alive."

Herbert Brucker, editor of that grand old paper, the *Hartford Courant*, recently wrote, as a kind of climax to his candid and realistic book, *Freedom of Information*, the following sentences:

Without benefit of law or any other compulsion, this exceedingly powerful tradition of objective reporting now keeps the vast majority of American news reports free from bias, and leads editors and publishers to segregate their opinions about news in clearly identifiable editorials, columns, cartoons, and special articles. The tradition that the news must be reported objectively is beyond question the most important development in journalism since the Anglo-Saxon press became free from Authority.

Mr. Brucker makes this striking and entirely proper generalization at the end of a comprehensive summary of the historical development of the concept of news as objective fact.

We could go on quoting outstanding reporters and editors on

this point, but it is now time to take a square look at this thing that we call objective news.

The term is doubtless unfortunate. It means, of course, reports which are written or broadcast without any bias or influence from opinions of the reporter or editor, as opposed to subjective news, which would be controlled and presumably distorted by the ideas and views of the reporter and editor.

The trouble is that complete objectivity, in this sense, would never be possible even for a robot to achieve, for there must have been some mind behind the creation of the robot. News is gathered, written, edited, and distributed by human beings, all of whom have certain ideas, feelings, attitudes, opinions, and prejudices. These men very generally make a conscious effort to handle what they call "facts" with an open mind. As Mr. Starzel recently said, the membership and staff of the Associated Press "have aimed to produce a news report just as objective, just as unbiased as human beings could make it." But complete objectivity is no more than a concept, an unattainable absolute.

What shall we say, then, of an objectivity that is less than complete — practical, working objectivity? Fine-sounding as the term is when it is used as a challenge against the dishonest, fraudulent distortions so common in the older reporting and in that of many countries today, objective reporting falls far short of perfect communication.

Let us see how it works. It begins with the observations of a single reporter. Now, a good reporter has sharp eyes, sensitive hearing, and ready perceptions all 'round; and he has been trained to be an acute observing agent. But he is not a machine, and he is subject to fatigue, shock, and surprise, as is any other person. Also he has certain mental backgrounds, many of them helpful in his work as a reporter, but some of them constituting deep-seated prejudices of which he himself may be unaware. No human being can be totally free of prejudices and prepossessions.

Further, all observation has position in time and space, and this position limits what the reporter sees, hears, and feels.

Observation of a stock exchange at the moment stocks are crashing might be interesting, but not very informative; complete observation of such a phenomenon would include that of the development of financial institutions and the phases of change in many economic and industrial movements over a long period.

The limitations of the observer's position in space are even more obvious. We all remember the old fable of the four blind men who described an elephant. One, who had approached the animal from the rear and seized his tail, said an elephant was shaped much like a snake; the second, who had laid hold on the trunk, said it was much larger than any common snake, and tapered toward one end; the third, who had found a leg, said the beast was more like a column; and the fourth, who had come up against a flank, said they were all wrong, and an elephant was like a wall. While news reporters are far from blind, they are at best limited in the scope of their observation by their positions only a little less strikingly than the blind men of the fable. Frederic Hudson, managing editor of the *New York Herald* under Bennett, apologized for the omission of many details in his premier history of American journalism by pointing out that both newspaper reporters and historians are severely handicapped by their restricted viewpoints.

> In all great battles [he wrote], there are thousands of men on the field of operations, formed into companies, regiments, brigades, divisions, and corps, with private soldiers, captains, colonels, brigadier generals, major generals, and marshals. . . . Space, on the pages of history, has never permitted a detailed description of Waterloo or Gettysburg. Waterloo, where all Europe was engaged, was described in one-third of a column of the *London Morning Chronicle* in 1815! Sedan, where 300,000 men were engaged, an empire overthrown, and 120,-000 prisoners taken, occupied only five columns of the *New York Tribune* and *New York Herald* in a comprehensive and graphic account.[14]

In short, any account of any event or situation must be biased not only by the observer's peculiar abilities and attitudes, but by his physical point of view. His report must be partial, and even meager. George Santayana wrote, in one of his essays:

> The most exhaustive account which human science can ever give of anything does not cover all that is true about it. All the external relations and affinities of anything are truths relevant to it; but they radiate in space and time to infinity, or at least to the unknown limits of the world.[15]

The appalling multiplicity of detail thus suggested as necessary to complete reporting of anything forces us (1) to admit that a complete objective news report is, in practice, unthinkable; and (2) to consider what the good reporter actually does in face of such a plethora of relevant detail.

The general-semanticists have a word for it. That word is "abstraction." What we all do in our daily lives and language is to abstract some details from the available total and make them do as a basis on which we can get along. In this process we commonly do a good deal of generalizing, placing great emphasis on likenesses between things and people. We try to reduce the incomprehensible multiplicity of the universe to a comprehensible simplicity. In doing so, we often do violence to the qualities of individuals, as when we talk about "Japs," or Wall Street, or "the brass," or Jews, or "the cloth" as though the individuals included in these class designations were all about alike. To avoid these speech dangers, say the semanticists, we must do more and more "indexing"; that is, after accepting the categories, we must indicate the differences. For actually, the clergy, or the Japanese, or the army officers, or the Jews are far more unlike than like within the groups indicated.

These language difficulties (which are based on thinking difficulties) are forced upon us by the bewildering complexity of the universe in which we must live and carry on our daily tasks and try to think and to understand our problems. The first commandment which the semanticist gives us, in order to lead us out of this wilderness, is that we must realize what we are doing when we speak and write: the *consciousness of abstracting* must be with us all the time. We have got to realize that we are not saying it all, that we do not know it all, that no language and no press service and no newspaper or broadcast can even approach a complete statement about any thing, event, or situation. If we are aware that we are constantly "abstracting," we shall be more careful, more tolerant, and more adequate in our reports; and we shall give more attention to our "indexing."

Let us note one other technique of semantics before we examine the applications of these theories which working newspapermen have been making in recent years. Alfred Korzybski, whose book, *Science and Sanity*, set the pattern for general semantics, pointed out that there were two categories of abstractions on the verbal level: first, descriptive words, which are functional and apply to what we are acquainted with; and second, inferential words, which involve higher generalizations and judgments. Although the distinction between these categories is not always easy, it is extremely important.[16]

This is precisely the distinction which American newsmen have been trying systematically to make since about 1930.

It was not until the turbulent 1920's that leaders in American mass communication began to realize that we were all living in a new and vastly more complex world than that of the early 1890's. They were doubtless tardy in their realization. The expansion of our horizons and responsibilities had begun about the turn of the century, when McKinley's "expansionism," a far narrower thing than that of the 1920's, was a political issue. The reader of old newspaper and magazine files is impressed with the increase of attention to international questions from the late nineties onward. The United States had suddenly become a World Power after the war with Spain. But that was not all. The tremendous expansion of industry and finance, the growth of urban population, the revolution in transportation and communication, the conflicts of labor and capital and of social and racial groups, the developments in science and education and culture — all these phases of change in a vast and dynamic society — together with the impact of international problems, had given American newsmen something to report transcending in intricacy, turmoil, and confusion anything that had ever before challenged them or any other body of reporters.

The bald and exact fact was no longer enough to make the new world understandable. The "descriptive words" of Korzybski's first category, telling the story in terms of things readers were all acquainted with, were inadequate because the phenomena were too strange and complicated and the panorama too large.

When Kent Cooper became general manager of the Associated Press in 1925, he lauded "the journalist who deals in facts diligently developed and intelligently presented" — a phrase which seems now to have caught a glimmer of the new reporting which was to come. The United Press was already adding color and elucidation to its bald facts; and soon Silas Bent, watchful critic of the newspapers, was complaining that the A.P. had yielded to "United Pressure" in dressing up its own reports. But what nearly all newsmen were actually doing was a modest job of explaining the bald facts. The Associated Press Managing Editors Association began in 1933 its drive for more explanatory writing in the A.P. report, which was climaxed a decade later by Cooper's memorandum to his staff calling upon it for "the direct, factual, and wholly objective news reporting that digs below the surface and tells the true story."

Note that Cooper stuck to the word "objective" in this statement. It is still an honorable word, although, as has been pointed out, not quite a happy choice to describe what good newsmen really do. What Cooper meant in this famous memorandum was that his reporters should stick to facts, but go beyond *overt* news. Walter Lippmann, in his *Public Opinion,* declared that "before a series of events become news, they have usually to make themselves noticeable in some more or less overt act." That most news stories will always start from overt acts is incontrovertible, but to many of his readers Lippmann seemed too much an apologist for the reporter who was satisfied with the obvious. Cooper and his successor Starzel, as well as Karl Bickel and Hugh Baillie of the United Press, and Seymour Berkson and Barry Faris of the International News Service, all believe today in the obligation of the good reporter to "dig below the surface" of the overt act or the "handout" for deeper significances.

Thus in the decade of the Great Depression and during World War II there developed the emphasis on what has come to be called "interpretive reporting." Professor MacDougall revised his book *Reporting for Beginners* and retitled it *Interpretative Reporting.* Interpretation in the news story had come to stay. A writer in the *Nieman Reports* for April, 1950, is a good spokesman for the prevailing point of view.

Let us make clear that this isn't a condemnation of objectivity as such. But if the newspaper is to do the job it should do in a democracy, where things are eventually decided by the people, the reader is entitled to his objectivity served up in a form that he can understand. Not everybody is an expert on the ECA. Some readers can't tell a clearing agency from an international monetary fund without a scorecard. And it's up to the interpretive reporter to provide the scorecard, in the form of explanatory material, definitions, and background. The writer should come down from the clouds of "international financial and monetary problems" and tell his readers, frankly and informally, "This means that . . ."

Throughout this development there have been critics who have considered it dangerous, and who have deplored writing which seemed to them to go so far beyond the bald and exact fact that it became editorial comment. Have we turned back toward the qualified report of our early press? Are we retracing our course to the "hints and touches" technique of the Machiavellian news directors of the seventeenth and eighteenth centuries? Are we on the way to such a mixing of "straight" news and editorial comment as will confuse the trusting reader?

To such questions there seems to be only one answer. Interpretive reporting gives more opportunity for careless or dishonest bias than "straight" reporting of overt events; but *all* reporting has to be watched and double-checked for carelessness and dishonesty, and interpretation seems to be necessary in our era. It is a matter of increased precautions. Erwin D. Canham, straight-thinking editor of the *Christian Science Monitor*, ran a series of page-one discussions of this matter in his paper in April and May, 1951, which arrive at this conclusion:

Rightly carried out, this [interpretive] function need entail no more editorializing than is involved, for example, when an editor decides to print one story and not another. But interpretation requires integrity and knowledge and understanding and balance and detachment. . . . This is a problem newspapers can solve in the long run by steadfast news objectivity and honest interpretation. But it sometimes seems to be an uphill road.

The type of news story we have been discussing up to this point is the regular run-of-the-mill report, usually without by-line, emanating from a news service or written by a local reporter. But it must be remembered that there are many types of news report which are current in the United States in the mid- twentieth century. It will be helpful, in connection with our thinking on this matter, to review a few of those which make a specialty of interpretation.

There is the weekly news-magazine style of report, which abounds in opinion, conclusions, and running criticism. Prepared by shrewdly intelligent, trained, wise, careful, and conscientious reporters and editors, with a passion for fairness, such articles might be almost ideal from the point of view of significance and interpretation; but all this, alas, seems a kind of unattainable counsel of perfection. These magazines differ among themselves, of course; but too often, in any one of them, reports are marred by false emphasis, "smartness," or sheer carelessness. Yet sometimes they have reached high levels; and, on the whole, the weekly news-magazine report has achieved a wide acceptance in American news dissemination.

The weekly summaries of news which appear in the Sunday or Saturday issues of many daily papers are difficult to characterize. Some of them are distorted by opinion, most of them try to be fair, many are marred by poor and haphazard selection.

The self-styled "confidential" reports, which are not confidential at all, are the oddities of the news scene. They try to produce the illusion of omniscience on a limited capital of wisdom, and of special revelations on a limited supply of real information. They deal much in prophecy, without climbing far out on many shaky limbs. They pretend to follow the ancient tradition of the written newsletter, even to using typewriter faces for their printing types; but some of them have built up considerable circulations at high subscription prices. They are at pains to give the impression that they can print news which papers and magazines of general circulation cannot touch, but they are subject to the same principles of reliability and responsibility that limit, or should limit, any news medium.

Then there are the news departments of general magazines, such as the *Atlantic Monthly*'s always stimulating "Report on the World Today," which are usually more in the nature of informative editorials and are often wise and thought-provoking.

Radio news has almost as much variety as newspaper news. The chief difference is that radio generally has as yet no regular editorial page which separates opinion from "straight" news. It has its commentators, to be sure; but they are the columnists of the air, giving the news along with free play of opinion. Much as one may like certain dogmatic commenators whose opinions agree with one's own, candor forces one to the conclusion that a broadcast which ostensibly presents the news of the day, but mixes it with a given set of prejudices and prepossessions, is a disservice to fair and honest reporting. Paul White, of CBS, was right in his contention of 1943 that these men should be "analysts" rather than "commentators."

Newspaper columnists appear in such variety that we cannot generalize about them. Even the late Harold Ickes, who spelled the word "calumnists," granted that there were "good and bad, decent and discreditable" writers among those who wrote syndicated letters on public affairs. The commonest criticism of them as a class has been based on the assumption of infallibility characteristic of many of them. One of them, the gladiatorial Westbrook Pegler, once wrote:

Of all the fantastic fog-shapes that have risen off the swamp of confusion since the big war, the most futile and, at the same time, the most pretentious, is the deep-thinking, hair-trigger columnist or commentator who knows all the answers just offhand and can settle great affairs with absolute finality three days, or even six days, a week.

But we are concerned here chiefly with the practice of these writers in mixing comment with news. Most public-affairs columnists are recognized as editorial writers; as such, several of them have gained respected and influential places in our modern journalism. An editorial writer commonly takes a "peg" of news for the starting point of his article, and so it is with some of the columnists. And just as an editorial writer sometimes devotes his whole article to information, so some columnists deal almost entirely with news. But the point is that if either editorial writer or columnist does not make it clear just where his fair and unbiased news leaves off and his comment and opinion begin, he commits a major sin against honest journalism. Like the news commentator on the air, the columnist dealing largely with news always has to watch his step if he is to avoid distortion and fraudulent "angling." As for the gossip columnist, he is in another category; he, or she, seldom knows what ethics is, or are.

There is another type of article combining news and opinion which deserves notice here; it is what we have called in an earlier chapter the "editorial feature." Though often written by a staff correspondent, and sometimes syndicated, it is neither a by-lined news story, a column, nor an editorial. It is an interpretive article, nearly always signed, by a newsman, publicist, or scholar, usually printed on the regular or auxiliary editorial page. The sin of slanting the news to suit a thesis always threatens in such writing, and more especially when politicians and leaders of movements are given space to expound their ideas. The reason that this type of article, in the hands of some of our ablest journalists and in our best newspapers, ranks among the finest offerings of modern American journalism is not merely that these men are good analysts and sound thinkers, but also because they have profound respect for news facts.

By-lined news stories also require special consideration. There is a general feeling that a by-line gives the writer license to voice opinion in somewhat the same way the columnist does. Thus political news, controversial stories (as in a "crusade"), reports in the fields of science or economics, correspondence from Washington or the state capital, are commonly by-lined. Some of the worst distortion in American news reporting appears under the by-lines of special Washington correspondents. It cannot be said too strongly that no by-line in any paper ever gives any reporter a right to deal fast and loose with news as news. The A.S.N.E., in its Canons of Journalism, excepts from its rule of unbiased news "so-called special articles unmistakably devoted to advocacy or characterized by a signature authorizing the writer's own conclusions and interpretation." That is all right, so far as clear "advocacy" in a signed article is concerned; but it is fundamentally and clearly wrong for editorial arguments to masquerade as news reports on news pages, whether signed or not. If the article purports to be a news story, it should be as "objective" and undistorted as possible; and comment and "advocacy" should be shown frankly for what they are. Interpretive reporting, if allowed to become a cloak for propaganda, would take us back to the bad old days of unrestricted "qualified report."

And now, having discussed some of the dangers into which

interpretation and comment lead the unwary newsman, we must consider the inadequacy (and worse) of certain kinds of reports when comment and interpretation are withheld. One of the oldest, and in mid-twentieth century still one of the most troublesome editorial problems in our journalism is how to handle misleading statements and ill-founded charges uttered by men of apparent standing and importance. The bald and exact fact is that the statement was made, by a prominent man, in a public place. The reporter knows the statement is false. A denial will be made, by another prominent man; but it will not have the force of the original statement. Here is involved not only the question of interpretive comment by the reporter, in case he can make a succinct, authenticated denial (based perhaps on the record); but also an editorial question as to how to handle the story in space, display, and position.

Secretary of State Acheson made a remarkable address to the American Society of Newspaper Editors at its 1950 meeting, followed by an off-the-record talk which he prefaced by a remark to the effect that, while he had been put on the spot by his critics in the preceding months he recognized that these criticisms had also put the members of his audience on the spot. His observation showed an understanding of the fact that reporters and editors cannot always be sure of the fair and honest way of handling such matters as the McCarthy charges against the State Department. Alan Barth, whose laudation of "the tradition of objectivity" we quoted earlier in this chapter, wrote further in the same issue of the *Guild Reporter*:

But indiscriminate objectivity too frequently makes the press a tool for those best versed in the uses of publicity. Stories such as the McCarthy charges were hard to handle because straight reporting of what the senator said merely gave currency to gossip, innuendo, and, in many instances, outright falsehood. It is not enough in a situation of this kind to balance accusation with denial. The denial always seems self-serving and never quite eradicates the imprint of the accusation.

Secretary Acheson was right in saying that such matters gave the editors many headaches, and he was right in implying that most editors are tremendously concerned with the problem of just what "play" to give such news reports. Irving Dilliard, chief editorial writer for the *St. Louis Post-Dispatch*, tells how Oliver K. Bovard, the great managing editor of that paper for the thirty years ending in 1938, once called his attention to a short news story which had been printed below the fold on page one of the latest edition of the *P-D*, saying:

Here is a lie. I know it is a lie, but I must print it because it is spoken by a prominent public official. The public official's name and position make the lie news. Were the source some unknown person, I could and would gladly throw it in the wastebasket. I have done what I can to show that I know that the statement is untrue by putting it under a small headline and printing only enough of it to make an entry in the record of the day's news. Printing these lies, even in this way, is one of the hardest things I have to do.[17]

Did Bovard have the right answer? Obviously, thoughtful journalist and conscientious citizen that he was, he did not look with any satisfaction on that little story below the fold. He did not like to print lies in his paper, no matter whose lies they were.

Mr. John Q. Reader would have a simple solution to the Bovard problem. He would say without hesitation: "Throw 'em out! D'you think I want to be fed lies?" But the answer really is not so simple and easy as that.

In the first place, the journalist, however skilled, is not an automatic lie-detector. To separate truth from falsehood often takes superhuman wisdom. " 'What is truth?' said jesting Pilate, and did not pause for an answer" — because he thought there could be none. "No," says the news editor. "There may be some truth in the Senator's statement, though I suspect it's mostly hokum. But it's objective news. Didn't a duly elected Senator of the United States utter it on a public platform? And besides, another Senator or somebody will come along day after tomorrow and deny it, and that will be objective news again, and I can use it."

"All right, all right!" replies John Q. Reader testily. "I'll let you off on statements and charges that are close to the line, and you don't have time to look 'em up, and maybe you don't have brains enough to tell if they're true or not anyway. But I stick to it that the things you know are lies, you ought not to print."

"Now look here, John," the editor argues. "I don't print Senator

Whoosis' blow-off yesterday, which even I know was a lie; and the paper down the street does print it, and so you say I'm trying to cover up, and suppress the news, and all that. And maybe the people have a right to know about the lies, too, if their public servants make them."

"But that's just the point!" interrupts John Q. Reader. "Half the time we don't know they're lies, because you don't put the lie tag on 'em. Now, listen: I'll settle for this. Whenever you print a lie, hang a tag on it. I don't mean sprinkle in the word *lie* in parentheses, the way they used to sprinkle the word *applause* into a stump speech, but sticking in a modest correction where the Senator's facts have gone haywire, or pointing out that this here's the opposite of what he said before."

Such are the chief arguments in the debate over a question which becomes more important year by year. The greater complexity of the modern political and governmental pattern, the growing emphasis on Congressional and extra-judicial investigation, and what Elmer Davis describes as "the new doctrine of Congressional jurisprudence called 'perpetual jeopardy'" have served to sharpen the problem. Of course, there are some papers that have no qualms whatever about not only printing but prominently displaying misleading statements, if they are exciting — and politically acceptable. This John Q. Reader is learning to resent — just as John Q. Hearer resented the Fulton Lewis exploitation of the Jordan charges regarding the alleged gift of atomic information and materials to Russia — and just as John Q. Viewer is going to resent demagogues and liars on the screen unless accompanied by competent and fair comment.

For the interests of truth are not always best served today by the bald and exact fact — by what is commonly miscalled objective reporting. About the time these lines were being written, Mr. Elmer Davis, the distinguished radio commentator, was speaking at the Minnesota School of Journalism on this question of the mixture of interpretation and news — a subject on which he should be an expert. It was a fine, pungent, and occasionally acrid address, from which we borrow a paragraph for insertion here. In the phrases that follow, fans will hear the cadences of Elmer Davis' voice:

This kind of dead-pan reporting — So-and-So said it, and if he's lying in his teeth it isn't my business to say so — may salve the conscience of the reporter (or of the editor, who has the ultimate responsibility) as to his loyalty to some obscure ideal of objectivity. But what about his loyalty to the reader? The reader lays down his nickel, or whatever, for the paper, in the belief that he is going to find out what is going on in the world; and it does not seem to me that the newspaper is giving him his nickel's worth if it only gives him what somebody says is going on in the world, with no hint as to whether what that somebody says is right or wrong. . . .

I believe the present tendency is toward more interpretation. But just how it can effectively be done — not in the columns or the radio commentary or on the editorial page, but *on the front page* — that is something that must still be worked out. . .[18]

Yes, it must still be worked out, as so many things must. But it is heartening to know that there is so much concern over the matter of labeling lies on the part of both newspaper and radio men. The interpolation of interpretive comment in brackets and italics, the "playing down" of spurious and phony attacks in the editing process, the pooling of reportorial information as suggested by Davis: such techniques may be useful in "working it out."

And in all fairness, we must end this chapter on the bald and exact fact *versus* interpretation by pointing out that despite all the difficulties of dividing truth from falsehood, despite censorships and propagandists, despite pressures from within and without publishing and broadcasting organizations, day in and day out, American reporters and editors generally do an honest and tremendously painstaking job. To be sure, we criticize them on the one hand for allowing interpretation and comment to run away with the news and produce an "angled" report; and then we criticize them on the other hand for *not* commenting on what they believe to be definitely misleading statements and tagging them as lies. If we seem to attack them on both flanks, it is because they are vulnerable not merely to criticism but to error on both flanks. Good newspapermen know this, and do their best to protect both sides. It is a big battle and a long one. Clarence K. Streit wrote in 1932: "Always we journalists have had to fight for accuracy against heavy odds. Our human proneness to err has been only one of the obstacles against us." [19] But the good fight goes on. Anyone who has intimately observed the work of American newsmen over a long period of time knows that when Streit and Anderson and Davis and Barth speak of devotion to truth and enmity to error, they are not using romantic terms, but are describing a grimly realistic attitude characteristic of the great majority of American reporters and editors.

CHAPTER NINE

Local News

Dame Gossip had charge of local news until the 1830's. During the first century and a half of the history of the American newspaper, little news of the home communities reached the dignity of print. Of course, the early papers were small and often crowded, but that was not the chief reason for slighting the local news. There were two other reasons which eighteenth-century editors held to be conclusive.

The first of the two was that everybody knew about the local happenings anyway. Why waste precious paper and ink on news that could be circulated by means as cheap as talk? "There were too many spectators there to make it now a piece of news," said the *New England Courant* about a popular demonstration of interest in an eclipse of the sun in Boston in 1723.

The second reason was that local news was not, as a rule, considered to be very important. To be sure, the doings of the Governor and the local great, all bad storms and shipwrecks, most public ceremonies, and the deaths and marriages of eminent persons were worthy of note in the home paper. Such events as had more than merely local interest, or had to be printed "for the record," were important enough for the editor to write up himself and place under a heading composed simply of the name of the home town. But the common life of the community was not considered print-worthy.

Once more in our inquiry for the origins of modern news prac-

tices we turn to the penny papers of the 1830's. The journalism of
that yeasty decade furnished the springs of modern news techniques. The chief innovator of those years, James Gordon Bennett,
is called by his leading biographer "The Man Who Made News,"
and he doubtless did have more to do with molding news to its
modern forms than any other man because, more than other
journalists of his times, he understood the new society created
by the industrial revolution. Bennett saw the growing power of
the laboring groups in a tremendously expanding industrial center. He noted that New York now had a quarter-million population and was losing most of the characteristics of an informal
rural society. He realized that "mechanicks, shop-keepers, porters,
and draymen" were now accumulated in sizable groups, and he
knew they were beginning to have a strong consciousness of their
own importance.

These groups wanted news. They wanted it cheap, and Bennett
and his fellow-editors of the little papers supplied it at a penny
a day. They wanted it interesting and readable; and the penny-
paper reporters gave them spice, human-interest, crime. They
wanted not only news of the great and near-great, but also stories
about themselves and what was going on around them in the
burgeoning city they were making; and Bennett and his fellows
gave them local news.

The neglect of local news had been tolerated by an earlier,
more homogeneous society in which such matters circulated easily
by word of mouth; but now neighborhood attitudes were disappearing under pressures of urban living, and the family in the
next "flat" were no longer "neighbors" in the old sense. Conse-
quently, if people wanted news of what was happening about
them (and they always do), they had to have new means of information. This was exactly what the penny papers offered. Wrote
Bennett in the *Herald*: "We shall give a correct picture of the
world [he meant the world of New York] — in Wall Street, in the
Exchange — in the Post Office — at the Theatres — in the Opera —
in short, wherever human nature or real life best displays its
freaks and vagaries." Bennett also introduced society news into
his paper, for gaps were developing not only between families

on the same social level, but even more notably between the rich and the poor.

Thus the penny papers supplied the growing need for local news, not only in New York but in the swiftly growing urban centers all over the country. The methods of Bennett and his fellows were continued and improved upon. Throughout the latter half of the nineteenth century, city news continued to develop, local reporters increased in number, the prestige of the "city desk" in the newspaper organization grew apace, and local news crowded other departments to an extent which alarmed some astute observers. Whitelaw Reid, thoughtful editor of the *New York Tribune*, observed in 1875 that the average newspaper of that city gave more space to the clambakes which New Yorkers on holiday held on Long Island than to the meetings of the American Academy for the Advancement of Science.[20] That reminds one of the famous remark of Fred G. Bonfils, of the *Denver Post*: "A dog-fight on Champa Street is better than a war abroad." The Bonfils epigram is quoted by Stanley Walker, an experienced metropolitan editor, in connection with his own statement of 1934: "The space devoted to local news in most New York papers has increased fifty per cent in the last fifteen years."[21] A measurement of five New York papers for a week in September, 1951, shows 58 per cent of their news space devoted to local life and institutions. Even in the great New York newsroom of the Associated Press, where news from everywhere is processed, the largest group of newsmen is the one serving the New York city desk.

The pattern thus set in New York with regard to "city news" was followed without much differentiation in all the great eastern centers. The *Boston Globe* under General Charles H. Taylor distinguished itself by taking to heart the ancient truism about local news which has been current among editors and reporters time out of mind, "Names make news," and actually printing the names of more persons in its day-to-day issues than any other newspaper has ever been known to publish.

In other regions there has sometimes been even more emphasis on local news. In the Midwest, the Rocky Mountain area, and the South certain great papers have won almost unassailable leadership in their various home cities and states largely by untiring local news coverage. Any mention of specific papers is likely to be invidious; but outstanding are the *Chicago Tribune*, whose news not only of Chicago but of a large surrounding region has given it a remarkable circulation and placed it in an impregnable position; the *Kansas City Times* and *Star*, which are the home-town papers not only for their own city but for large parts of Kansas and Missouri; the *Denver Post*, which maintains its traditional paternalistic attitude toward the whole of what it calls the "Rocky Mountain Empire"; the *Oregonian*, with its morning home delivery in many Oregon towns, and the *Oregon Journal*, with its state edition; the *Des Moines Register* and *Tribune*, which cover all Iowa in both news and circulation; and the *Atlanta Journal* and *Constitution*, which boast of covering Georgia "like the dew." It is probably a mistake to attempt any list which does not run to scores or hundreds, for virtually all the great papers which have built large circulations and established themselves as recognized local institutions have done so largely by an emphasis on local news. And they did this before the days of the *Continuing Studies*, which show a reader-interest ratio of about two to one in favor of local over other kinds of news.

Now, it is important to an understanding of the news in America to know something about the mechanics by which it is handled; and since it was the emphasis on distinctively local news that upset the balance in the old, small, tightly organized editorial staff and brought into existence a new kind of newspaper organization, it will be helpful at this point to see just what the rising flood of news did to the group on the job. Let us first note how an early staff was organized.

When Alexander Hamilton promoted the establishment of the *New York Evening Post* in 1801, two men were enough to start it off — Editor William Coleman and Printer Samuel Burnham. Of course, Coleman had assistance from many gentlemen who were willing to write pieces for the paper without remuneration, and Burnham had apprentices in his department. Editor Coleman was a very busy man, for he had to take care of the paper's business affairs as well as do the editorial work every day. He had not a single reporter, and therefore he printed only such local news as drifted in or as he himself thought it necessary to write. He did badly on the business side, but soon made his printer a full partner and the paper's business manager, which saved the venture from failure. After a while Coleman brought his son in as an editorial helper; but it was not until the paper was twenty-five years old, and an established success, that he hired young William Cullen Bryant as assistant editor. And this splurge in staff-expansion was really caused by an accident which had incapacitated the editor-in-chief for a few weeks. Allan Nevins tells all about it in *The Evening Post: A Century of Journalism*.

This small staff made the editor a marked man. Readers knew the editor's name as well as that of his paper, and the *Evening Post* was likely to be referred to as "Coleman's gazette." This was what came to be called "personal journalism." Before Hamilton's death in 1804 the *Post* was often called "Hamilton's gazette," for everyone knew who the chief promoter and adviser was.

But when local news was expanded in the thirties and forties, it was necessary to have more help. Newspapers could no longer rely on whatever drifted in. A "reporter" was necessary, and soon more than one. By midcentury nearly every daily paper the country over had its local reporter, commonly called the "local," who had a column or two to fill each day with the news of the community. Some of these "locals" were talented individualists and were allowed great latitude as to what they wrote. Such a man was Charley Browne, "local" of the *Cleveland Plain Dealer*, who, one day when community news was scarce, filled his column with an ill-spelled letter from an itinerant showman whom he named "Artemus Ward," and then, encouraged by the chuckles of readers, followed with similar letters, until a famous comic character emerged. Such a man, too, was Sam Clemens, who adopted the pen name "Mark Twain" while he was a "local" on the *Virginia City Enterprise* out in Nevada Territory.

But local news was taken a little more seriously in the great cities of the East, where it had become so important by midcentury that considerable staffs of reporters became necessary; and the position of "managing editor" was set up on some papers in order to place an experienced man in charge of the flow of news — local, national, and foreign. Later dailies came to need also a "city editor" for supervision of local news and a "telegraph editor" for news that came by wire, as well as a sports editor, a society edtior, a financial editor, a Sunday editor, and so on.

Note what this did to the old editor-in-chief. He was still in his "sanctum" writing editorials, but he knew very well that the newsmen were taking over the paper. In 1851 Horace Greeley was a visitor in London, and while there he consented to answer a series of questions put to him by a Parliamentary Committee which was considering the removal of stamp taxes on English newspapers. In the course of his answers, he declared that in the United States "more weight is laid upon intelligence [news] than on editorials; the paper which brings the quickest news is the one looked to." Here was America's greatest editorial writer pointing out, as early as 1851, the victory of the newsmen and, by implication, the decline of personal journalism in the United States. It was inevitable that the emphasis on news as the chief function of the American newspaper should destroy the prestige of the editor-in-chief.

So the Greeley type of editor was shouldered aside by the newsmen, and the old era of personal journalism was dead or dying. But it is a mistake to say that contemporary journalism has no personalities. The names of certain columnists and of a good many by-lined correspondents (especially in Washington and abroad) are well known, and their characteristics and attitudes are recognized. Moreover, it would be easy to make a list of a score or more of editor-publishers all of whom are well known in their own regions, and many throughout the nation. (See Chapter 18.) But a survey of the best-known American journalists would show that most of them have won their fame and achieved their present positions chiefly through their work, not in editorial writing and opinion commentary, but on the "news side." And even our columnists, as has been pointed out already, are often more reporters than commentators.

Thus far we have been discussing chiefly the local news in the metropolitan papers, but it is in the small-city dailies and the community weeklies that such news has its greatest emphasis. Some large-city papers, such as those singled out for mention above, make a special effort to come close to their readers; but

in the smaller communities this close and sympathetic relationship is easy, natural, and usual. On the lists of the community
papers are the "old subscribers" who talk of "our paper" and
consider it as necessary a part of their homes as the kitchen sink.
And why not? It chronicles births, weddings, and deaths in each
family, and has done so for years. It tells about the sicknesses,
the social events, the honors and successes, as well as the mis-
fortunes, of the childhood, youth, adulthood, and age of every
person in the town and the outlying countryside. Trivia? Rubbish?
Not if human life is important, and the individual personality
precious.

This essentially democratic nature of local news is not always
realized. In such a record we have repeated recognition of the
importance of human life and experience on all levels.

Moreover, when it brings together a multitude of persons in
the record of the life of a community, the newspaper performs a
valuable service to democratic solidarity. One of the most important things a newspaper ever does is to promote the social
integration of its community, and this it does by news and comment on local matters. Ralph D. Casey, speaking at the dedication of the *Daily News* building at Faribault, Minnesota, in 1950,
described the process:

In an earlier society, the members of the average community "dwelt,
worked, worshiped, and played with approximately the same group of
people in the same place." In face-to-face communication, the members of this older and simpler society could reach understanding and
agreement without the intervention of any mediating device like the
newspaper. This is not possible today. Even in a relatively homogeneous community like Faribault and its trade area, the common body of
knowledge to hold the community intact is obtained through the columns of your newspaper . . .

The communication process exemplified in the press maintains the
necessary agreement on how a community is going to live and what
are to be its goals for living. . . .

The press helps a community arrive at a consensus. If you have social cohesion in this city, and I think you do, it is a consensus arrived
at by the people of Faribault who read in the *Daily News* the stories
of public affairs, of the many good and sometimes sorry deeds of your
area, of the actions and behavior of your individual residents and organized associations. You are then prepared to debate, argue, and ar-

rive at conclusions on the basis of these tidings; in short, consensus
finally has been arrived at.

The press is a substitute for the town meeting of Colonial days, and
the coffee-house and tavern where news could be exchanged. The con-
tact which today's press provides is . . . vital, significant, and necessary.

Radio stations are nowadays devoting more and more time to
local news. Some of them began to cultivate the local field early
in the history of broadcasting, as may be seen by Mitchell Charnley's *News by Radio*; KMPC, at Beverly Hills (Los Angeles),
used ten reporters for local news as early as 1930. After the
Second World War, partly in response to the prodding of the
Federal Communications Commission, and partly because there
were no longer any colorful war stories to rely upon, stations
began to turn more and more to the interesting field of events in
their own communities for their newscasts. Small stations are
often hampered by inadequate staffs, and are wont to rely too
much on the ready-to-read stuff of the news services; but the
increase of local news on the air is still one of the most striking
trends in radio. And, of course, special events on the television
screen are necessarily local for the audience where the program
originates.

And so local events and conditions, and the activities of local
persons and institutions furnish a large part of the news. The
great metropolitan papers, and even more markedly the small-city
dailies, the suburban papers, and the community weeklies, as well
as the radio and television, all respond to the demand of their
readers for extended treatment of local affairs.

After all, local interests come first; we were all local readers
to begin with. The child's first interests are in its own fingers and
toes; later it explores the home scene, then it gets acquainted
with neighborhood and school. Many persons never have any real
interests outside their own community environment. St. Paul's,
the Arc de Triomphe, the beautiful "blue" Danube, the burnoosed
and bearded Mohammedan and the Chinese with queue, Fuji-
yama, Taj Mahal — these all have the unreal quality of the movie
dream-world. Even a visit to California or New Orleans or the
Maine Coast leaves our isolationist with the feeling that, after all,

the only realities, for him, are at home. The shipment of locals abroad in two world wars was merely a temporary displacement; Ernie Pyle, true historian of that excursion, told of Gordon Uttech of Merrill, Wisconsin, or Ed Bland of Waurika, Oklahoma, whose father was railroad agent there.

Of course, loyalty to family and home is a fundamental virtue. We cannot find fault with it and ought never to sneer at it. And it is a proper interest-basis for the local report which newspaper and radio furnish.

But civilization is, by definition, advancement in *social* culture, progress in adaptation to society; and such advancement and progress cannot stop at local boundaries. Pitifully inadequate is any civilization that does not include world society. In this country, the increased mobility of the population and the great regimented hegiras of recent wars have doubtless served to increase general awareness of world society, and news in all its phases has helped with stories of the visits of foreign statesmen and monarchs, new appropriations and taxes, and such changes in control of farm, labor, and industry as bring world and national affairs home to us. But the process is very slow. It is not a matter of abandoning home loyalty, but of adding to that virtue a genuine interest in regions outside of the local community and a sympathetic appreciation of life in other countries of the world. The civilized reader is interested not only in local news, but in a far wider area of domestic and international reports.

Thus there is always the danger of excess in the play of local news. Whitelaw Reid's complaint about disproportionate space given to clambakes is as valid today as when it was uttered, though other fads have replaced the parties for which Long Island beaches were famous. There is always danger of isolationism, of ingrown interests, of disgraceful ignorance of the world at large. But in general it must be admitted that the local report which furnishes a broad base for the total news structure is sound both in practical journalism and in its service to society on the community level.

CHAPTER TEN

Domestic News and the News Services

Geographically, there are four classes of news — local, state, domestic, and foreign. State news, however, is scarcely to be distinguished from local news; many papers consider both state and city as the local field. To be sure, "string" correspondents do most of the work on state coverage, assisted by staff men occasionally sent out from the home office; and small-city papers depend chiefly on the state wire report issued by a news agency. Nevertheless, so far as news problems are concerned, state and local news are one. But there is another class of news which has attained large proportions; this is governmental news, which includes not only the Washington report, but news originating in state capitals and city halls. Thus there are, for our discussion, still four classes — local, domestic, governmental, and foreign.

Domestic news consists of reports from American cities and towns outside the local field in which the newspaper is published. Let us see how this type of news developed and what it amounts to in modern press and radio.

In early American newspapers, non-local news came chiefly from clipping other papers, from stories brought in by post riders and sea captains and chance visitors from a distance, and from casual correspondence. This clipping was not news-piracy in any degree; it was the recognized system by which newspapers got their news from other towns and Colonies. All the editors exchanged papers with each other; and William Parks, of the *Virginia Gazette*, expected to get his news of Connecticut from Thomas Green's *Connecticut Courant* or the New London or Hartford *Gazette*, while Green and other New England editors looked to Parks for the news of Virginia. Some editors, indeed, felt the obligation to print the important news from their own bailiwicks as much for the use of papers at a distance as for the perusal of their own subscribers. This was the earliest technique of coöperative news-gathering in America, and it supplied most of the domestic news in the Colonial newspapers.

This system actually continued throughout the first third of the nineteenth century. Even the news of the Mexican War was handled in that way: other newspapers relied on those of New Orleans to gather the news, though they then competed with each other in the speed with which they brought it north for use in their own papers. Such competition, largely by means of horse expresses, had a tendency to break down the old system; and the development of the telegraph network in the fifties and sixties changed entirely the communication situation. Now it was necessary for enterprising papers to have their own part-time correspondents, usually newsmen working on other publications, in all news centers in the country. This was too expensive for the individual papers, and more and more of them were forced to turn for help to the New York Associated Press, a news-gathering agency organized by a group of strong New York city papers.

After the midcentury, nearly all important domestic news, including most Civil War stories, came into newspaper offices by "magnetic telegraph." The three great machines which, in the first half of the nineteenth century, transformed the newspaper business from a musty, back-street undertaking into a big and prosperous industry were the Fourdrinier paper-making machine, the Hoe power-press, and the Morse telegraph. Of these, the one most directly connected with the news itself was the telegraph. For about three-quarters of a century, telegraph desks in newspaper offices were equipped with Morse receiving sets, and the important non-local news came directly off the wire. Not until recent times has the Morse key been displaced by the teletype. By this new device, a tape is punched by the operation of a typewriter keyboard, and this is fed into a telegraphic sending machine which controls a typewriter at the receiving end and causes it to write out the copy automatically. The Associated Press adopted the teletype for its New York service in 1914, and the United Press followed the next year. Gradually these machines came to supplant Morse-code telegraphy on all the press circuits, doubling and later tripling the speed and therefore the capacity of the systems. By 1935 the old Morse men, so long a fixture in newsrooms, had virtually disappeared.

The early history of the news associations was tied up with that of the telegraph companies. It is a complicated story; but probably the success of the Associated Press was due largely to the ability of its managers to maintain an affiliation with the Western Union Telegraph Company, which was the concern that came out on top in the cat-and-dog fight among the early wire companies. At any rate, any news syndicate had to be a wire service chiefly; and it took both syndicate organization and wire availability to achieve adequate coverage.

Since domestic news in our papers and on our radio broadcasts is gathered and transmitted almost wholly by the news associations, this is the appropriate place to describe briefly each of those three great national services. It is true that they handle also governmental and foreign news, which will be discussed in ensuing chapters, and also (for papers at bureau points) some local news, but they first come prominently into the picture in connection with the domestic "budget." Needless to say, these services are tremendously important in a survey of the news in the United States.

The Associated Press, like all early news services, was a coöperative organization. Organized in New York in 1848 by the *Sun, Herald, Tribune, Express, Courier and Enquirer*, and *Journal of Commerce* (the *Times* was taken in when it was founded three years later), it had for its purpose the pooling of the resources of these papers for gathering domestic and foreign news. Though the member papers retained ownership, they soon began selling their report to others in Boston, Philadelphia, Baltimore, and other cities in the East, the South, and the rapidly growing West. Whenever they sold their service of pooled news, they contracted to receive from the new subscriber the important items of his own local news report. The A.P., under a series of aggressive "superintendents," did not stop with pooled news; it established its own correspondents in all important centers of domestic news, and also built up a strong foreign service.

Space does not permit us here to follow the competitive struggles of the New York Associated Press. Its strong financial position, based largely on its fees from subscribers, and its rich flow of news, based partly on subscribers' contributions and partly on its own correspondence, together with bold and skillful management of its relations with Western Union, kept the New York Associated Press far ahead of would-be competitors. The great revolution in its affairs took place in 1893, when various events forced a reorganization under Illinois laws on the basis of membership and participation in management by all subscribers. Chief changes in more recent years have been a second reorganization (in 1900) under New York laws, and certain amendments in rules required by the federal anti-monopoly laws. Following a Supreme Court decision in 1945, existing provisions for "blackballing" a new applicant for membership by a competitor were removed. At the midcentury the A.P. has over 1700 member papers, including some weeklies, semi-weeklies, etc., as well as about a thousand radio stations which came in as associate members. It is undeniably a leader in efforts to improve the gathering and writing of news and to maintain a high quality of reporting and editing.

"The United Press Associations" is the full name of the modern U.P. It has no relationship to the old United Press, which perished in 1897. It was formed as a consolidation of three news services, one of which was a coöperative, by E. W. Scripps, chiefly in order to gather news for the Scripps-McRae (later Scripps-Howard) group of papers. But almost immediately the U.P., under Roy Howard's aggressive management, went after clients outside the Scripps "chain" and succeeded in enrolling several hundred for its full or abbreviated service within a few years; eventually it had a thousand or more daily clients in the United States. It began selling its service to radio newsrooms in 1929, and many stations today use the U.P. wire. It was early in the South American field, and has many foreign clients. It sometimes leads the field in good writing, and always takes special pride in its foreign correspondents and coverage.

W. R. Hearst in 1909 supplanted earlier news services designed for the use of his large group of papers by setting up the International News Service for morning papers and the National Press Association for the "evenings." Both sold their services to papers outside the Hearst "chain." They were merged in 1911, but six years later a similar separation of morning and evening services was put into effect, I.N.S. handling the budget for the "evenings" and Universal Service for the "mornings." A second merger was effected in 1928, and since then International News Service furnishes the news "round the clock." It is said to have in the neighborhood of a thousand clients, some in foreign countries. It has had some brilliant, outstanding writers, especially in the foreign field.

Only a score or so of daily papers of general circulation in the United States do not use one or more of these great national news services; with them may be grouped perhaps fifty which use a "pony" service by telephone and mail. These are papers published in towns of a few thousand population which find it advantageous to confine themselves almost wholly to local news and to allow the larger papers which are circulated in their territory to furnish the national and foreign reports. But nearly five hundred papers use two or more of the three services, and no less than 183 use all three.[22] Of course, a paper which receives more than one of the reports deals with a tremendous amount of duplication; but editors benefit by a wide freedom of choice. Some stories will be better written than others dealing with the same events; one service's state or regional coverage may be better, another's Washington news is more satisfactory, while a third's by-liners abroad may be more pleasing. At any rate, such opportunity for picking and choosing permits the editor to produce a less stereotyped and more individual newspaper.

The A.P., U.P., and I.N.S. are not the only services which furnish news to the newspapers and radio stations, however. The *Editor & Publisher Year Book* for 1951 lists 115 "news services." These are all, in one way or another, more limited in scope than the three great general agencies. Some are restricted in geographical spread, like the Westchester County Newspaper Service in New York. Some are limited or specialized in subject matter, such as Science Service, Religious News Service, Educational Newsfeatures, Universal Trade Press Syndicate, Daily Sports News Service, and so on. Then there are the Associated Negro Press, Chicago, and the National Negro Press Association, Washington. Some great agencies are general in scope but specialize in the feature side of news and articles of comment, as the North American Newspaper Alliance (NANA) and Newspaper Enterprise Association (NEA). Several great dailies syndicate the work of their own special correspondents, so that we have the Chicago Daily News Foreign Service (now including more than foreign news and handled through the Des Moines Register and Tribune Syndicate), the Chicago Tribune Press Service and the Chicago Tribune-New York News Syndicate, the New York Times Syndicate, and the New York Herald Tribune News Service. Some of these syndicated services have special leased wires direct to the offices of their newspaper clients.

Nor do these 115 news services exhaust the list of the organized agencies which supply news to the daily and weekly newspapers, the weekly news-magazines and class periodicals, the trade press (business papers) in various fields, and the radio and television stations and networks.

Pictures, for example, are often quite as much news as the word-reports; and we have no less than 77 news-picture syndicates located in various cities in the United States, more than half of them in New York. Prominent among them are Wide World Photos, organized by the *New York Times* in 1919 and later taken over by the Associated Press; Acme Newspictures, set up as a United Press and Newspaper Enterprise Association subsidiary in 1924, the U.P. later selling out its interest to N.E.A.; and International News Photos, a Hearst unit, organized as International Film Service in 1910 and now associated with King Features. Such services supply pictures by wire and mail, picture pages, photographs by special assignment, and so on. There are also many photographic services which sell pictures to special and occasional clients.

Most of the early radio newscasts were based on domestic news. Apparently the first news on the air waves was that of 8MK (later WWJ), the *Detroit News* station, when it broadcast reports of Michigan elections in 1920. The Detroit newscasts were quickly followed in Pittsburgh by those of KDKA. The early news programs were nearly all those of special events. "We take you now to Boyle's Thirty Acres in Jersey City, where World Champion Jack Dempsey is facing Georges Carpentier, the

French challenger," and so on, with a ringside blow-by-blow account. KDKA broadcast big-league baseball from Forbes Field in 1921.

Radio was hampered in its use of the national news services by newspaper opposition for several years. Many daily newspaper publishers were afraid that the new medium would make their printed news reports "stale and unprofitable." Their alarm was groundless, for, as events proved, hearing the news is never enough for most people; they must also see it in the full printed reports. But for a time, newspaper pressure prevented the great news services from furnishing their reports to radio. To fill the gap, several news-gathering agencies were set up for the newscasters, most important of which was Transradio Press Service. But by 1935 the U.P. and I.N.S. were accepting radio clients, and the A.P. finally set up in 1940 an organization, first called Press Association (P.A.) and then A. P. Radio, to serve radio newsrooms. This was just in time for World War II, during which nearly all the reports brought us tidings of the war or of national defense activities. Today radio news balances fairly well its local, domestic, Washington, and foreign reports.

Certain specialized kinds of domestic news require brief attention here — reports in the fields of science, labor, agriculture, and religion.

Prior to the third decade of the twentieth century, the greatest anomaly in our news system lay in the fact that, in the midst of a dominantly scientific age, science itself was very badly reported. Reform came from several directions. An important factor was the recruitment of a group (very small at first) of men educated in the natural sciences and in writing, and their assignment to the science field. Another development was the change in attitude toward the press of some of the great scientific societies, notably the American Association for the Advancement of Science, which set up a press section to coöperate with working reporters to the end that its great meetings might be properly presented to the general public. Many scientists still maintain that science cannot be at once accurately and popularly reported; but many others, realizing how important to scientific movements a general understanding of them by the public may be, have en-

couraged science reporting. The A.A.A.S.–George Westinghouse
Science Writing Awards are important prizes. Still another factor in the improvement of work in this news field was the founding in 1921, by E. W. Scripps and Dr. William E. Ritter, of
Science Service, a syndicate edited on a high level first by Edwin
E. Slosson and later by Watson Davis. As a result of these in-
fluences and others, this field of news is now far better cultivated
than formerly. The romantic pseudo-science story of the Sunday
supplements has not entirely disappeared, nor has the idea that
the scientific meeting or address must yield something funny or
sensational; but most newsmen now take their science seriously.
Less than 10 per cent of our dailies have designated "science
editors," and less than a score of these give a major part of
their time to science writing; but a large proportion of them
print good science stories pretty regularly. The National Association of Science Writers is a flourishing organization.

E. W. Scripps was a pioneer not only in the development of
science news but also in labor reporting. He thought of labor as
representing "the ninety-five per cent," and his papers supported
the unions when most of the press was against them. Pulitzer and
the young Hearst leaned in that direction also; but it was not
until the years of the First World War, with its many wage dis-
putes and strikes, that the newspapers generally accepted labor
as "big news." The employment of specialists for such reporting dates from this time. Came the great depression a little
more than a decade later, with its National Industrial Recovery
Act and its Section 7-a, guaranteeing the right of collective bar-
gaining; and now labor matters required the full-time work of
many reporters on the various papers and in the wire agency
bureaus. The enactment of the Wagner Act in 1935 and the Taft-
Hartley Law in 1947 and the growth of the Congress of Industrial
Organizations added to the complexity of the labor picture and
to the difficulty of the job that must be performed by press and
radio. There is no doubt that the positions of labor, especially
in strike situations, are still inadequately and unfairly presented
in many papers; but the situation is greatly improved over what
it was a generation ago. Louis Stark, labor specialist for the *New
York Times*, wrote in 1942:

Imperfect as the handling of labor news may still be in some cases, nevertheless the quantity of such news which is published has vastly increased. On the whole, one may say that the quality also has enormously improved.

Today, many metropolitan papers dispatch their labor reporters to all parts of the country to cover labor conventions, strikes, and other events of labor management significance. Labor news has come into its own as a feature of American newspaper coverage.[23]

Similarly, agricultural news has shown a great increase in the last few decades. Such factors as the "dust bowl," sharecropping, farm legislation, and reclamation projects have been important in the news; and most dailies and weeklies in the agricultural regions tend to give increasing space and emphasis to such matters. About one-fourth of our American daily newspapers have "farm editors," though comparatively few of those so designated give full time to agricultural news.

An even larger proportion of the daily papers name "church editors," but often the staff member given that dignified appellation is merely the reporter who covers the churches and two or three other beats as well. Whether religious news is better handled today than it was fifty or a hundred years ago may be doubted. Some papers do excellent work in that field, however, and sometimes the by-line of a religious newsman will come to be highly regarded. The Religious Newswriters' Association is a national organization.

CHAPTER ELEVEN

News of Government

News of government begins on the local level, continues at the State capitals, and reaches a spectacular climax at Washington.

The activities of local government may not be showy, but they are extremely important to the people. Most American newspapers cover the work of city Councils, and that of city and county officials, boards, and bureaus, with a fair degree of thoroughness. Many radio stations have come to report on at least the top news of local government. Courts usually receive better coverage than offices, because the news found there is more dramatic.

In fact, a large part of the local news grist comes from city government, if we include, as we must, courts, police, fire department, public schools, utilities, planning and zoning, parks and playgrounds, health commission, etc. All these activities are, of course, covered by local reporters on regular "runs," or "beats." A reporter becomes well acquainted with the officials on his "run" and with their office forces; he cultivates their friendship, and they "protect" him on important news-breaks by giving him immediate information.

But there is an obvious and ever-present danger in such friendships. If the official protects the reporter, the reporter may end by protecting the official. Every good reporter knows that his friendship for a news source must never extend so far as disregard of official dereliction or incompetence. But competent observers point out that a notable fault of the reporting of local government, especially in a one-newspaper town, is the tendency to go along with the administration in power. It is only when a paper, well managed and able to earn its own way, and therefore unafraid, tells what it knows and all it knows about what is going on in city government that it is an honest servant of the people.

The line between muckraking and candid reporting is, in actual practice, often hard to draw. But thousands of papers — dailies and weeklies — have found, through many years of active experience, that they do not have to be constant crusaders, with chips on their shoulders and holier-than-thou attitudes, in order to report honestly the blunders and incompetence as well as the successes and efficiency of local government. The candid and honest paper, although inevitably it will often give offense to officials and sometimes make enemies, is pretty sure in the long run to win the respect of both government and people.

Coverage of State government presents greater technical problems. Except for the papers located in the capital, such news must be gathered and reported by special correspondents and the wire services. Papers in the larger cities of a State will have their own correspondents, and sometimes bureaus with staffs of three or four men; while the wire services will supplement the work of the "specials" for the larger papers and furnish the sole report for the smaller ones. Sometimes weeklies have their own correspondence from the capital, usually sent by mail.

It is not an easy task to report intelligently and intelligibly what goes on at any one of our State capitals. It is a job for a shrewd and knowledgeable man, and it is full of pitfalls. Its three greatest difficulties are fairly obvious.

First is the problem of centering upon significant matters. The Statehouse and the State office buildings are busy places, and every official and bureau wants publicity — of the right kind. All these things, it is easy to argue, should be of state-wide interest. They all have their importance; and it takes intelligence, industry, and experience to fit a correspondent to work effectively in the complicated pattern of State governmental activity. It is always easy — too easy — to peg the story on some clash of personalities or opinions, because a fight is always good copy. It is easier to write that kind of story, which is more or less on the surface, than to dig down into something which may be less spectacular and dramatic but is really far more significantly important.

The second great difficulty is that of keeping free of entanglements. Here is not merely the danger of bias for or against the administration in power, but the ever-present peril of being "used" by propagandists. The Statehouse is full of lobbyists, especially during the sessions of the Legislature; and lobbyists are a friendly lot, with liberal expense accounts for entertainment. Many of the causes and projects for which they are working are fine and admirable. Most officials, members of the Legislature, and lobbyists are good fellows. The reporter thinks he too must be a good fellow in order to keep close to his news sources and enlist their help. Yet there is much to be said for the general principle that a reporter in such a situation should be soundly hated and deeply feared. If this positive statement is too strong, it may at least be asserted that the reporter who always tries to be a "good fellow" is sure to betray his readers by uncritical friendliness to special, and sometimes sinister, interests.

But perhaps the commonest fault of the more experienced and seasoned Statehouse reporter is political partisanship. The history of the development of journalistic independence from party bonds has been traced in a former chapter, but there is still plenty of partisan bias; and more of it is to be seen in the newspaper reporting from some of our State capitals than anywhere else in the journalistic scene. In many cases, the whole threat to good State government reporting is comprehended in that which is posed by dogmatic partisanship. That is, the lobbyists are sometimes important only as partisans, and the significant question is submerged under partisan propaganda.

Generalized evaluations in this field are hazardous, as they are in respect to other phases of journalism. Certainly there are many excellent newsmen doing consistently fine jobs in State capitals. It is probably a disadvantage to reporting of State governments that work in the capital of the home State is so often regarded as training for a berth in a Washington bureau; but it is fortunate that not a few good reporters like to work in Albany, or Springfield, or Sacramento better than in the mad mazes of the national capital.

Washington is the world's greatest news center. There are larger national capitals, of course; but nowhere is there a comparable operation of reporting the activities of a government. This is no more than we must expect of our combined news agencies, for a great democracy cannot function without adequate reporting of government.

There are about 1400 men and women doing this job at Washington. More than half of them work for newspapers; in fact, if you include news photographers, about three-fifths serve the daily press. Another fifth serve radio and television; and the last fifth, including writers and photographers, work for magazines and periodicals. This army of news-gatherers, news-writers, news-processors, news-broadcasters, and news-photographers is organized in a rather complex pattern. Every man and woman works for some news-distributing agency — a newspaper, a magazine, a radio station, or a syndicate serving a group of such outlets.

Large metropolitan papers have their own special Washington correspondents, and many are represented by individual bureaus staffed by two or three up to a dozen reporters and editors. Some have even more: the *New York Times* has a large Washington bureau and holds twenty-seven Gallery seats, the *Herald Tribune* sixteen, the *Wall Street Journal* fourteen, the *Baltimore Sun* twelve, the *Chicago Tribune* twelve, and so on.[24] Such well-staffed bureaus provide a wide general coverage of Washington's multifarious activities; they include specialists in various kinds of news, "leg-men" and rewrite-men, feature writers, and columnists who are virtually editorial writers.

But many daily papers throughout the country have a single correspondent each at the national capital. Even commoner is the device by which a number of papers combine to hire the services of one man, who is then said to have a "string" of papers. Some of these "strings" have been built up to a score or more of clients, so that they require the services of a small bureau rather than a single reporter. Each of these papers wants a special representative mainly to serve its own local economic and political interests. It feels that the reports of the national news services need to be supplemented by stories from a man or small bureau familiar with the special interests of its own readers and whatever particularly affects the people of its own region. Besides, it likes to have its own report, written with the individual distinction of the "special correspondent."

Another type of bureau is that of the newspaper group, or "chain." The Scripps-Howard Newspaper Alliance has fifteen Gallery seats, the Hearst Newspapers eight, the Gannett News Service five, and so on.

The weekly news magazines have large Washington staffs, and many more general periodicals have representatives.

There are about a hundred and fifty men and women accredited to the Radio Press Gallery, occupied by representatives of the national networks, some individual stations, some groups or "strings," and the radio services of the national news associations. The National Broadcasting Company has twenty-four men on duty; the other great networks somewhat fewer.

But the largest Washington news bureaus are those of the great national press services. The Associated Press has about ninety Press Gallery seats, the United Press sixty, and the International News Service thirty-five; but the actual staffs of these bureaus are much larger, including, as they do, editors, wire-filers, rewrite men, teletype operators, etc. — all the personnel of big wire-service bureaus. If we add about two-thirds to the number of Gallery seats assigned to each, we shall get the approximate total staff sizes of the three services — a hundred and fifty, one hundred, and sixty.

These bureaus perform one of the most important, exacting, and responsible operations in the whole range of American news-gathering. It is a highly detailed and carefully organized job. To use the expression common among Washington newsmen, these national service staffers must "watch every rathole." Theirs is the most meticulous coverage of government known anywhere in the world. Moreover, serving a great variety of papers, they must be on their guard against bias and unfairness, or they will hear from their members and clients. They will hear from them anyway, hard as they may try to keep an even keel; they are continually aware of the critical watchfulness of hundreds of editors.

Fifty years ago, reporting Washington was a fairly simple problem, centering chiefly on the proceedings of Congress. There were no regular news conferences at the White House. Less than two hundred newsmen were needed to report the total activities of our national government. When the First World War came upon us, there was an increase in the Washington press corps, which was maintained throughout the twenties. But at the time of the financial collapse of 1929, bureaus were about one-third the present size, and life was comparatively calm on the Washington news front. What then happened is well summarized by Thomas L. Stokes, veteran Washington correspondent and well-known columnist:

Washington really became the news capital of the nation during the great depression that began to manifest itself publicly in the 1929 stock-market crash and continued well into the 1930s. The advent of the Roosevelt New Deal, with all the measures it took — first, for salvage and recovery and, second, for reform on a wide front — turned the attention literally of almost every citizen constantly upon Washington; for every citizen had a very direct and personal interest sooner or later in what was done during this amazing and breath-taking span.

It meant food, shelter, jobs, safety of bank deposits and investments, safety for homes and farms, higher wages, social security for unemployment and old age, and the like — all very personal matters.

News about these things originated from Washington. Every development was of keen and often anxious interest to millions all over the country. Nearly every household had a stake in what was being done in Washington. This meant more and more people in Washington to gather the news and more to handle it and get it out over the wires, over the radio, in pictures.[25]

And then we entered the Second World War, with America as the arsenal of the Allies as well as a chief power in the liberation of Europe and the repulse of Japan; but it was not until the postwar years, when this country became the leader of the world's finance, production, and politics, that Washington suddenly found itself, as Mr. Stokes pointed out, not merely the greatest American news center, but the news capital of the world.

Today coverage of our national capital is a terrific challenge to conscientious reporters. The size, variety, and complexity of the Washington maze is appalling. The background information and training in economics and finance, in politics and diplomacy, in the natural sciences, history, sociology, agriculture, industry, and virtually all fields of human knowledge, necessary for the proper reporting of Washington affairs seem beyond practical attainment. Of course, they *are* beyond attainment by any one man, and the best work in Washington is done by specialists who devote their energies to specific facets of the total scene. It is amazing, however, what a wide range of activities a really intelligent, industrious, and conscientious reporter can cover reliably and adequately.

The Capitol is still the center of the Washington news system. Covering sessions of Congress is hard work, often requiring long hours. The mornings are filled with committee meetings which are often far more important than the sessions of the House and Senate. Public hearings sometimes afford the most important open forums for the discussion of vital controversial questions to be found anywhere. The great American leaders, not only in government but in industry and business, in the labor movement, in agriculture, in education, and in scores of other fields, appear in such hearings; and there are sometimes dramatic clashes of opinions and personalities. Nor are the so-called executive sessions of committees neglected by reporters. We have come a long way from the days of 1787, when the newspapers respected the secrecy of the deliberations of the Constitutional Convention; nowadays reporters group about the closed door of a committee meeting, ready to buttonhole members as they leave an executive session and to find out what has just happened. No reporters and by no means all legislators have much respect for star-chamber methods in government.

During the meetings of House and Senate in the afternoons, the press Galleries are filled more or less completely, according to the importance of the sessions. Radio men have their own Galleries. Senators and Congressmen are often to be found chiefly in the lobbies rather than on the floor, and reporters often find it more profitable to seek out and interview them in the House lobby, or the President's Room off the Senate lobby, than to sit in the Gallery listening to perfunctory proceedings on the floor. The newsmen will go where the news is, and very often the really important information develops outside the legislative chambers.

Second in importance as a news source is the White House. Of course, it is at times the top news spot, especially when Congress is not in session. It was Theodore Roosevelt who first had a room set aside for the White House correspondents. One day he noticed some reporters standing outside the mansion in the rain, waiting to interview visitors who had just called upon the President; forthwith he had a small anteroom assigned for their use. When new Executive Offices were added to the White House, a sizable room equipped with telephone booths for direct lines to bureau offices, and with desks, etc., was provided. There and thereabout the White House correspondents spend their days.

Their central news source is the President. He is their man. His conferences, his visitors, his utterances are their business. When he leaves town, the regular White House correspondents travel with him.

In the White House group is a representative of each national news service and radio network. Every metropolitan newspaper with a well-staffed bureau has a man there. Then, besides the regulars who watch the place from morning to night, many other correspondents drop in from time to time, often coming because some visitor to the President's office has a special interest for the newspapers which they serve. Always there are some photographers about.

Every morning the President's press secretary holds a news conference, which is commonly attended not only by those regularly stationed at the White House but by many others. Presidential press relations were formerly handled by the chief executive's private secretary; but with the growth of Washington reporting in the thirties, Franklin Roosevelt decided to put a special assistant in charge of correspondents. Such men as Stephen T. Early and Charles G. Ross have lent prestige to this position. At the press secretary's morning conference, names of that day's visitors, usually with some data about them and the purposes of their calls, are given out, together with other information about the President's program and activities. The secretary has later informal conferences to keep correspondents in touch with what has been going on in the President's office. Some of this is mere routine, but sometimes highly important news comes from the secretary's office.

But the most important statements of presidential opinion and administration policy are made at the weekly news conferences of the President himself. Though President McKinley sometimes gave out news to correspondents in groups, it was Taft who inaugurated the custom of regular weekly conferences. Wilson at first established semiweekly press meetings, but in 1915 he canceled them altogether. Harding, a newspaperman himself, revived them, often talking more freely than his friends thought wise. Coolidge, though he had a reputation for terseness and laconism, talked a good deal at his conferences; but he did not allow himself to be quoted directly. Harding and Coolidge held fairly regular semiweekly meetings; Hoover's were less frequent from the first, and dwindled until, in the last few months of his administration, there were none. Franklin Roosevelt resumed the two-a-week schedule; and, except for his periods of absence from the White House, he kept to this program rigorously through the tumultous years of his administrations. Truman, when he succeeded his dead chief, adopted the policy of weekly meetings with press and radio correspondents.

The Presidential news conference is a distinctively American institution. In it the Chief Executive talks to the people. Here is a clear recognition of the people's right to inquire into what government is doing and the reasons behind its actions. It is a recognition that prepared handouts are not enough, that the press (representing, in this instance, the people) have a right to cross-examine the responsible head of their government. With all its faults, its shortcomings, and its occasional break-downs, the Presidential news conference is one of the greatest object lessons in the working of the democratic principle in government that has ever been devised.

Men and women representing newspapers, radio, and magazines sit in folding chairs in Room 437, Old State Department Building. The President stands behind a desk. Questions and answers come thick and fast. The President has to be shrewd and careful. He has to withhold information the release of which might injure the national security. He has not only to state matters truly and accurately, but he has to guard against misunderstanding. He has also to guard against stating things so that they can easily be garbled or distorted, and yet the correspondent can defend himself with: "Well, this is what you said." Throughout the conference, it is evident that the correspondents are asking questions and listening to answers with minds intent on the question, "Is this a story? Will this make headlines? " Newsmen must have news. Then the senior wire service man says, "Thank you, Mr. President," and they all break for the telephones. It is a stampede, and there have been occasions when someone was hurt. [26]

The Departments of State, Defense, Agriculture, the Treasury — indeed, all of the major departments and many of the hundreds of minor bureaus and agencies and boards — must be covered daily by the Washington newsmen. Now that government has come to exert — for good or ill, and regardless of what party may be in power — such a powerful and direct effect upon the daily lives of all people, daily information about the plans and activities of many of these agencies is demanded by all readers and listeners. All of this may be news of acute, immediate, vital interest to everybody, and it must be gathered and processed with intelligent care.

Some experienced Washington correspondents consider the State Department a more important news source than the White House. It has much the same kind of coverage, with men from the staffs of the big news services and the bureaus of metropolitan papers regularly stationed there. The same practices of interviewing callers as they leave are followed; and Mr. Secretary of State holds regular news conferences not unlike those of Mr. President, often attended by as many as a hundred newsmen. The Secretary has a "special assistant for press relations" who holds daily conferences.

These latter years, during which the United States has attained a leadership in international matters, have seen the rise of a specialized type of Washington reporter known as the foreign-affairs, or "diplomatic," correspondent. He has unusual backgrounds of study and experience in international affairs, speaks two or three languages, possesses a measure of shrewdness in evaluation and analysis of information received, and can write an understandable news story. This diplomatic correspondent spends much of his time at the State Department, with its multitude of bureaus and geographical "desks"; but he must also cover the foreign embassies and legations. Nor can he neglect the White House, or the Senate and its committees on foreign relations. He is a specialist not only because the work to which he confines himself is of premier importance, but also because it has peculiar difficulties which he has learned to understand and at least partially to overcome. Diplomatists are rarely straightforward or candid; that is putting it mildly. Reticence and deception are their characteristics, and the tricks of Machiavelli are their stock in trade. Dealing with such news sources, the diplomatic correspondent must be astute and wise. Moreover, his department of the news is delicate and dangerous. Peace and amity between nations may be injured or destroyed by press reports; and it is the duty of the press to redouble its care in dealing with international relations in order that its reports shall be both accurate and fair.

Some of Washington's diplomatic reporters often visit Lake Success, which, in a manner of speaking, is on their beat. New York bureaus of the wire services, newspaper staffs, and feature services cover the deliberations of the United Nations Assembly and Security Council, and representatives of many American and foreign papers and services have seats in the press gallery. About fifty newsmen have such places, though half that number do most of the work, and 770 correspondents — including a large number from abroad — are accredited to the U.N. Booths, lighting, and facilities are provided for motion picture companies, for radio, and for television. The broadcasts of Assembly meetings have been a leading feature of television news since 1950.

By this time the patient reader will be willing to agree that the field of government news reporting is both extensive and complex. But a large force of reporters is engaged in the task, and we have to inquire whether the many men and women working in this vital center of our American news system are doing an adequate job. What are their chief difficulties, and how do they meet their problems? While the basic principles of newsgathering are the same everywhere, and good reporting is good reporting in any news center and any situation, nevertheless there are always special issues characteristic of a given news field.

Washington, for example, is the native home and natural habitat of the "handout." A "handout" is a prepared statement furnished to the press, commonly on mimeographed or multigraphed sheets, to be published on or after a specified release date. This staple fare of the Washington news banquet is officially known as a "news release," but reporters generally refer to it by the name originally used for a sandwich or other donation passed out to a tramp at the back door. The name is appropriate enough: a "handout" is freely given, and more often than not it has good nutritive news value.

There are about twice as many government press agents in Washington as there are newsmen employed by the various newspapers, magazines, radio stations, and wire services.[27] Of course, these press agents, who include secretaries, clerks, etc., perform many duties in the general field of information and publication besides working up press releases; but the preparation of these "handouts" is no small part of their work. Every executive department, bureau, board, committee or commission, legation, association, or organization of any kind in Washington has its press assistant or information specialist; and nearly every group issues press releases more or less frequently.

"Handouts" are valuable aids in news-gathering. Washington newsmen, indeed, could not get along without them. They provide needed information which reporters could not otherwise acquire without great expenditure of time and effort. The men who prepare them are specialists in their own fields of government activity; moreover, they know they have to avoid inaccuracies and misleading statements if they are to keep the confidence of the newsmen. The National Press Club in Washington provides a capacious rack in its clubrooms which is daily filled with press releases from all over the area, so the reporter does not even have to visit all the bureaus and commissions.

At the 1951 meeting of the American Society of Newspaper Editors, the opinions of several anonymous Washington correspondents on the subject of "handouts" were quoted. One said:

It often seems we are weighted down by handouts, but when it comes to complicated stories such as those on price ceilings, they are completely necessary to make the story mean something. All in all, we're glad to have them. We're much better off with them than without them.

Another newsman made a frank confession:

The long standing charge that information offices kill initiative of reporters I believe holds true. As to whether they are good or a menace, I know that I use their services scores of times daily. I know that I rely on them too much. But I don't know how I would get along without them.

Obviously the great danger in this flood of prepared statements is too much reliance upon them. This is not so much a matter of trusting them too much, as failing to go beyond them. There are doubtless some Washington correspondents who manage to get along on "handouts" and "blacksheets" and the gossip of fellow reporters; but their careers at the capital do not often last long. The good newsmen have to do a lot of digging, and the excellence of their work depends largely upon the perseverance, intelligence, and courage with which they pursue such investigations. Paul Y. Anderson's stories to the *St. Louis Post-Dispatch* in 1928 on the Teapot Dome scandal brought him a Pulitzer Prize and are still examples of the best investigative reporting in Washington.

"Handouts" are usually issued after actions are taken and the matter is all packaged and wrapped up, but the people must have the news before it reaches that stage. "A good reporter must ring a lot of doorbells to dig out the truth at a time when decisions affecting the course of world history are being formulated behind closed doors," says the 1950 APME report on Washington. James B. Reston observed in an address at the University of Minnesota School of Journalism in 1949:

> Good, enterprising reporting of ideas on basic issues can in many cases be as important as the reporting of action. The decisive point in many great events comes long before the event happens. It comes in what the diplomats call the "exploratory stage," when influential officials and legislators are making up their minds what they are going to do. The Marshall Plan was a great story in Washington before General Marshall ever heard about it. Few papers, however, paid any attention to it because it was "just an idea." In fact, the *idea* behind it was all laid out in a speech made by Dean Acheson weeks before General Marshall announced the plan at Harvard; and the only paper in the world, to my knowledge, that carried the text of that speech was the *Times* of London.

This presupposes a measure of friendly coöperation on the part of informed news sources. And it must be recognized that in general, and by and large, Washington government agencies try to help the correspondents in their work. "Do your job just like you were working for a newspaper," said Steve Early to the departmental press assistants when President Roosevelt put him in charge of them in 1933. Delbert Clark, of the *New York Times*, in his *Washington Dateline*, stated the general situation truly and fairly:

The history of the Washington assignment is the history of the free press in America. In no other country does the press have so great advantages; nowhere else are the members of the press permitted and encouraged to hobnob daily with the great. Freedom of the press, literally construed, is the freedom to publish anything at all, subject only to the laws of libel; in Washington it has come to have a much broader construction, a construction which presumes that government will not only permit publication of news, but will also make it freely available, with sundry aids and conveniences to lighten the task of the reporter.

But Clark goes on in his informative book to relate many an anecdote about uncoöperative news sources in high places, departmental and bureau press agents who have tried to conceal important news and release only routine stories, and officials who have denied reports which were embarrassing though true. Suppression of news by secrecy at the source will have to be discussed in a later chapter of the present volume, but it must be said here that the greatest obstacle to adequate reporting of the Washington scene is now and probably always will be the unwillingness of highly placed officials always to be frank and fair, and never to hold back legitimate news.

Heads of the government, on the other hand, do not find press relations anybody's pink tea. Some are temperamentally unfitted for the give-and-take, the needling and sparring, and sometimes the downright abuse involved in dealing with newspapers and newsmen. Many Presidents, beginning with George Washington, could not "take it." In modern times, Presidents have usually (Hoover was an exception) started off with a kind of "honeymoon" with the press, only to find themselves treated unfairly somewhere along the line, to lose their tempers, and to settle down, for periods, at least, of armed truce. Wilson and Hoover ended by discontinuing their press conferences entirely. Harding talked too much and too often without knowledge, and had finally to resort to answering only questions written out and submitted in advance; Truman's remarks were occasionally ill-considered.

The President, especially in his news conferences, suffers from the sharp competition among Washington newsmen. So many correspondents, representing so many rival news agencies, produce a highly competitive situation in which significantly important news is often sacrificed for whatever can be depended on to make headlines — the "hot news" that most editors want. The men who crowd the President's office at a conference are not primarily sensation hunters; but not one of them would refuse startling or exciting news, and always there are lines of questioning thrown out in the hope of landing a big story which the President does not really intend to release. When the President is tired, or loses his temper, or does not fully realize the import of a question, or is careless about conditioning or hedging his own statements, he may be seriously misrepresented.

An example of bad news handling occurred on November 30, 1950, when President Truman, having issued a "handout" regarding the war in Korea, submitted to a barrage of questions about the prospect for the use of the atomic bomb in that unfortunate country. How much of the fault was the President's in not explaining in words of one syllable that his insistence that the A-bomb was an ever-present threat did not mean it was being considered at the moment for immediate use in Korea, and how much of it can be laid upon the eagerness of the White House correspondents for a sensational story is still debated; but the distressing fact is that a carefully prepared release received comparatively little attention, and the President's oral statement (which he apparently considered a fairly obvious matter) that the atomic bomb was a continuous threat was given a great "play." [28] The repercussions were international. It was, on the whole, as some newsmen involved realized in looking back on it, bad reporting, for it did not give clearly and fully the idea that was in the mind of the President. It is, of course, the proper business of reporters to dig behind "handouts," but it is grave distortion when eagerness for headlines gives to words uttered in the give-and-take of shrewd questioning an emphasis beyond their proper meaning.

This search for whatever is immediately startling and shocking at the expense of what is duller but more significant is characteristic of certain types of journalism — as has been amply pointed out in the foregoing pages. But such practice in Washington reporting is especially dismaying. Whereas the news from our capital is profoundly important, and reporting it is a serious business, the unusually sharp competition among newsmen there tends to encourage sensationalism. Delbert Clark refers to "the dog-eat-dog competition which characterizes the Washington correspondents at work." The late J. Frederick Essary, of the *Baltimore Sun*, once dean of capital correspondents, observed in his book *Covering Washington*, "Ours is the most competitive field of active journalism in the country, if not in the world." Now, competition among reporters may be highly valuable when it is directed at digging for facts and ideas, but it is far too easy for it to degenerate into rivalry in sensationalism. In Washington, especially, it is important for reporters to keep their balance and to respect their calling, instead of sinking to the level of what Neil H. Swanson, executive editor of the Baltimore Sunpapers, recently called them — "a tribe of head-hunters."

Such idealism, however, is not likely to amount to much unless the editor at home also respects his calling. Too many editors keep their correspondents under continuous pressure for more and more "good stories," more and more striking and exciting copy, at the expense of significant reporting. Tom Stokes closes the article on capital coverage from which we have already quoted with a notable sentence: "There's nothing wrong with Washington news coverage that the newspapers themselves cannot cure."

What Stokes was really talking about when he said that, however, was the evil of newspaper pressure for political bias. Such pressure and such bias he believes to be the chief abuse of Washington reporting. But it is difficult to measure and difficult to generalize upon the total amount of bias in reporting the activities of the federal government. There is perverse and outrageous partisan distortion on the part of some papers, but a persistent effort to be fair by more of them. The great wire services may slip from time to time, as any system operated by human beings will; but hour by hour and day by day, those services do a pretty good job of fair and "objective" reporting.

If a serious, thoughtful newspaper reader were asked to say what the chief fault of Washington correspondence is, he would probably — after some serious, thoughtful hemming and hawing —

pronounce the verdict that it is the same thing that is the chief fault of American news reporting in general, namely, too much insistence on elements which appeal to the naive and casual reader, and too little emphasis on vitally important developments of ideas, plans, and patterns. Quarrels and attacks, "clashes" and "flaying," and surface excitement in general tend to displace significant news. Whether this is the fault of the reporter, or of the editor, or of the publisher, or of the readers, or of all of them, it is a great fault. And it is a fault which is more noticeable at Washington, because Washington is the high-lighted news capital of the world.

CHAPTER TWELVE

Foreign News

Do American readers and listeners receive adequate news from abroad? What is adequacy in this field of reporting? By what criteria can we set a quota for foreign news?

The facts are, of course, that the proportions of local, domestic, governmental, and foreign news have never been set and that editors do not select news for publication by such a pattern of proportions; but that they are ruled instead by the test of relative importance, and that the application of this test causes great variability from day to day and paper to paper in the proportion of the different classes of news which is published.

Here we again confront, as we have in respect to other problems of news content, the double standard. The editors want to give us most of what is most important. But most important by what standard of importance? Shall the news be evaluated by the conventional newsroom tests of unusualness, combat, sex, and so on; or shall it be considered important in proportion to its probable or possible effect on the world, and therefore on local readers? In regard to some pieces of news, such as that of a violent uprising in a European tinderbox, there is no question; by *all* tests it is important. But for most news the double standard of importance does exist, and it affects the use of foreign reports profoundly. Newspapers which have a strong feeling for what we have called "significant importance" in the matter they print will use more international news than those which are governed chiefly by the old rule-of-thumb reader-interest tests of money and sex, unusualness, and violence.

The significant importance of foreign news to the American people has increased tremendously in this generation. As has been pointed out, two of the chief factors in this higher importance are probable consequence and proximity; and the chief reason that probable consequence has risen so high in foreign news is that the status of proximity has changed so greatly. In other words, Europe, South America, Asia, and even Africa are today so close to all readers in communication, commerce, and political influence, that much of what happens abroad has immediate effects on our own people.

These incontestable and well-known facts lead many to the opinion that the average American newspaper prints too small a proportion of foreign news. Many feel that we could spare a lot of the more frivolous and even vapid content of our papers if we could gain thereby a larger volume of thoughtful reports on important events abroad. They feel that there exists here a professional editorial lag of newspaper performance behind the actual need of American readers in the modern world.

Some papers give only three or four out of a hundred non-advertising columns in an issue to foreign matters. Scores of metropolitan daily newspapers and hundreds of small-city dailies assign to news and comment dealing with foreign and international affairs (including such matter in pictures, news-features, Washington letters, editorials, columns, etc.) less than a tenth of their total news-and-comment space. The better papers increase this proportion to an eighth or even to a fifth. Outstanding in their attention to international matters are the *New York Times*, the *Baltimore Sun*, the *Christian Science Monitor*, the *St. Louis Post-Dispatch*, the *New York Herald Tribune*, the *Chicago Daily News*, and the *San Francisco Chronicle*.

The objection to our inadequate foreign news is not a matter of specialized interests on the part of a class of readers sometimes

called the "intelligentsia." The better educated group are doubtless more conscious of the editorial lag referred to; but the average reader has latent and underdeveloped interests in a world
with which two great wars have given him a certain familiarity,
so that it is unbelievable that good reporting and good editing
should not bring home to his own living room his natural interest
in overseas news and international problems.

Nor is it a question of the criticism of visitors from abroad, who
invariably find fault with our papers for paying too little attention
to news from their own countries. Our papers may be guilty of
some such neglect, but it is not the lack of an impossibly thorough
news coverage of all the countries of the world to which the
reasonable critic objects. It is, rather, the lack of an entirely possible minimum presentation of the significantly important news
from abroad.

Anything that gets into any newspaper, broadcast, or periodical
is admitted in the face of competition. The reader of earlier chapters of this volume may have been impressed with the importance
of local, state, domestic, and government news. The editor under-
stands these values, and also the great importance of feature material and advertising; and the critic, too, should be aware of these
pressures for space and position. But when all factors are considered realistically, the conviction remains that, in this new world
of the mid-twentieth century, the American people are being inadequately informed of what is happening to us abroad.

The news situation is certainly far better in this respect than
it used to be. A half-century ago only the more picturesque and
historically impressive events abroad got into our newspapers.
Measurement of ten leading metropolitan newspapers for the first
week in 1910 shows them devoting only 3.1 per cent of their non-
advertising space to news and features with foreign datelines.
Ten years later, just after the close of World War I, the proportion had increased to 8.8 per cent; but by 1930 it had fallen to
4.8 per cent. In January 1940, with the Soviet war against Finland
in full swing, the proportion of foreign news was up to 7.9 per
cent; and measurements a decade later place it at 8.2 per cent.
These statistics are of value only in their indication of trends;
the quotas themselves have comparatively little significance.[29]

Perhaps we can learn something about the adequacy of our service of foreign news by inquiring into the means and techniques of gathering such information for American readers and listeners.[30]

Most important in this task, because of the large number of papers, magazines, and radio and television newsrooms served, are the national news agencies — the coöperative Associated Press, the Scripps-Howard United Press, and Hearst's International News Service. Probably more than half of the full-time American correspondents abroad work for these associations. It is upon their tireless, 'round-the-world services that American readers, hearers, and viewers chiefly depend for their foreign news.

Reuters Limited, whose American agency is devoted wholly to foreign news, distributes about twenty thousand words daily to its American newspaper and radio clients. This is a report collected in London from a large corps of correspondents. Reuters is allied with the A.P., exchanging its United Kingdom domestic report for A.P.'s similar report from the United States; but each retains the right to market its extensive report in the other's territory as foreign news. Thus Reuters serves a dozen or more important eastern papers over its leased wires, and a somewhat greater number west and southwest of Chicago over the wires of the Chicago Tribune Press Service.

Some feature syndicates also furnish notable foreign materials. The Newspaper Enterprise Association has good foreign coverage on pictures, as well as in news and features. N.E.A.-Acme bureaus are located in London, Paris, Berlin, Frankfurt, Rome, Milan, and Tokyo; and the organization also uses roving correspondents and "stringers" abroad. The North American Newspaper Alliance, more than half of whose service relates to foreign news and features, recently secured American rights to the Kemsley Foreign News Service, an agency which maintains over a hundred foreign correspondents to serve a group of English papers. The Overseas News Agency has several correspondents abroad, as well as a good many "stringers"; it is primarily a feature service. All foreign news bureaus have their photographers; and several motion picture outfits are constantly making newsreels overseas for American audiences.

Half a dozen American newspapers add to the foreign service they receive from the great news associations and the syndicates by maintaining small bureaus of their own at leading news centers abroad. Outstanding in this kind of representation is the *New York Times*, whose overseas bureaus and staff outnumber those of any other paper. The *Christian Science Monitor*, notable for its world-view, has an excellent foreign news and feature service of its own. Three Chicago papers have full-time correspondents abroad — the *Tribune*, the *Daily News*, and the *Sun-Times*. The *New York Herald Tribune* is another paper with foreign representatives; and a number of papers (notably the *Baltimore Sun*, the *San Francisco Chronicle*, and the *St. Louis Post-Dispatch*) occasionally send their own news, feature, and editorial writers overseas for firsthand observations. Most of the papers that maintain foreign bureaus syndicate their reports to others which like to supplement their news-agency stories by special articles less generally distributed.

The great broadcasting companies keep some Americans abroad in active news centers, bringing them in directly on network newscasts. *Time* and *Life* have full-time American correspondents regularly stationed overseas, as have *Newsweek* and *United States News & World Report*; these weekly news magazines, like the great dailies named above, use press agencies as well as their own men. McGraw-Hill's World News, established in 1945, maintains bureaus in eight foreign news centers for a service which it supplies to thirty or more magazines.

From these various agencies American newspapers, magazines, and radio receive perhaps two hundred thousand words on an average day — much of it overlapping, but still a tremendous torrent of news, comment, and features on the foreign scene. New York A.P. foreign desk gets considerably more than 25,000 words on an average day, and the San Francisco foreign desk of that service almost half as much.

It is evident that this is lavish abundance. It is certainly far more than is poured into any other country by foreign correspondents for the instruction of a nation's readers on the subject of world affairs. If this flow of news and comment represented full world coverage, and if all editors used it liberally on the printed page and on the air waves, and if readers and hearers and viewers made full use of it, then the American people would indeed be better informed about international matters than any other people in the world. But we have seen that the average American newspaper uses a very small proportion of its space for news from abroad, and a similar disinterest in the foreign scene becomes increasingly evident in radio broadcasts. Moreover, our coverage of news in many parts of the world leaves much to be desired.

We have referred repeatedly to "American reporters" and "full-time men" abroad. This is because the overseas news bureaus serving American papers often employ nationals of the countries in which they are located, either on full-time or part-time basis, as well as a number of non-American "retainers" who assist with the technical details of their offices. Besides these, there are probably close to a thousand "stringers" scattered over the world, who are paid at space rates by the various foreign bureaus for whatever usable material they send in. There is much difference of opinion about the value of the foreign national as a correspondent for American press services. It has often been pointed out that the national lives in constant fear of punishment for anything he may write which is unfavorable to his own government or people. Says one critic:

I will admit to some exceptions, but in the main I contend that news intended for the U.S. press, magazines, and radio should stem from Americans, unfettered by natural native biases and government pressures. I do not believe, for example, that a Hungarian or an Argentine national can provide factual coverage out of Budapest or Buenos Aires. Such a correspondent works under fear of reprisal and imprisonment; the worst that can happen to an American is expulsion.[31]

Those words were written just before William N. Oatis, American A.P. correspondent in Czechoslovakia, was jailed and tried on trumped-up spy charges. American correspondents, too, sometimes work in danger of personal reprisals other than expulsion; but the fact remains that nationals are even more vulnerable. Furthermore, it is often claimed that these foreign reporters are ill trained and have too little respect for objective news facts to be allowed to write for the American press.

On the other hand, it is obvious that, when well selected, these men contribute much by their intimate understanding of the life, customs, and attitudes of their own people. Their bias in favor of local attitudes is sometimes cited against them; yet this may serve to counteract misunderstanding and prejudice on the part of the American correspondent himself. But probably the strongest argument in favor of the employment of nationals by foreign news bureaus is a very practical one: the agencies simply could not afford financially to replace them with Americans. Foreign nationals always have been used for this work in the past, and the practice will undoubtedly continue. We can only hope that they will be used wisely, under correct principles of selection, training, and editing.

That the American press is too meagerly represented in most foreign fields is beyond question. Budgets for foreign news are severely limited; barring increased demand for the commodity on the part of editors (ultimately, of course, on the part of the public) they will continue to be limited in peacetime. During the last two years of World War II, we had approximately five hundred full-time American correspondents stationed in the belligerent countries (constantly changing but maintaining about that number), and probably less than a hundred in neutral countries; today we have about three hundred abroad all told.[32] It is not enough, as was demonstrated when war broke out in Korea in June, 1950; even though men were rushed to the front, by the "firehouse coverage" technique, they were not properly backgrounded reporters. But what can you expect? Pity the poor chief of foreign correspondents, who can only guess which volcano of international antipathies will erupt next, and who must jealously count his men and his dollars under the careful eyes of the auditor and the director of the budget. High international telegraph and cable rates are always a threat, though the situation at midcentury is a fairly favorable one.

Also there is another reason why our news systems are underrepresented abroad. That reason is the effectiveness of the Iron Curtain which surrounds the Soviet Union and her satellites. Why station scores of correspondents in those great regions where every precaution is taken, with great rigor and tireless patience, to prevent any leakage of news beyond that which is contained in propagandic handouts? A few representatives of the American press are kept in Russia, to pick up whatever is permitted (and more, in case anything should jar loose); but most of our more significant news from that country has to come from reading between the lines of Russian publications, from contacts in Washington and at Lake Success, and from trickles of information which seep in through other countries. William L. Ryan, of A.P.'s foreign desk, learned to read Russian in order to acquire such information. "You get the feel of *Pravda* quickly," he says, "and soon find yourself able to read between the lines for what they are driving at. You find they are bad at keeping secrets. There may be no word or phrase you can put your finger on to say 'This is it,' but the overall tone gives you a clear impression." Of course, the wire services, which are very alert in the use of these techniques, pick up a considerable amount of information from the forbidden areas from points just outside the Iron Curtain. In 1951 the Foreign News Service was set up to gather precisely this kind of information "along the rim of the Red orbit," process it in a New York office, and syndicate it to the American press. That is also the way Paul W. Ward, of the *Baltimore Sun*, got the material for a remarkable 1951 series of articles entitled "What the Iron Curtain Hides."

It must be kept in mind that much of our information about foreign affairs and events and situations abroad comes from Washington. A considerable proportion of the news from the national capital deals with such matters. "United Nations, N. Y." has also become a familiar dateline, and foreign problems may be the subject matter in dispatches from New York, Chicago, San Francisco, or any other news center in the United States.

But it is upon our correspondents overseas that we must rely chiefly for our knowledge of what is happening in foreign lands and that understanding of the politics and economics, the thinking and traditional cultures of other peoples, which are so necessary to us in our present position of world leadership.

The foreign correspondent faces an extremely difficult job. Although he is usually an adept in journalistic practices and in the special techniques of his own news service, it takes him some months to learn the ways of a foreign capital; and a bureau chief abroad commonly figures that a new man will scarcely pull his own weight before he has had a year's seasoning. Foreign assignments are usually looked upon at home as "plums" with which to reward bright young Jack Horners ambitious to see the world, and there is even a tendency to look upon these posts as sinecures. A famous American managing editor cabled his Paris bureau chief back in N.R.A. days when government regulations had shortened the working week of editors and reporters: "New York staff going on forty-hour week. Paris staff will continue to work thirty hours a week." But the foreign bureaus generally consider themselves both understaffed and underpaid, doubtless with much reason.

There are both disadvantages and attractions to the life of a foreign correspondent. He is an expatriate; and if he is a family man he must rear and educate his children far from American society and schools. He runs greater hazards than newsmen at home, especially in times of wars, insurrections, and plagues. On the other hand, many men find a desirable freshness of experience in a few years' tour of duty abroad, and some like living in a foreign capital so much that they make a lifetime career of it.

The foreign correspondent always has to keep in mind the American angle. He may wish to write long pieces on the internal economy of Spain, but he has to ask himself, "What do our editors want? What will our people read?" He is not running the bureau for himself, or for Spanish readers. Also he has to keep in mind the time-map of the world, especially in view of the varying deadlines of morning and evening papers between New York and San Francisco. When it is 11:00 P.M. in New York, it is already 1:00 P.M. the next day in Tokyo. This is often confusing, especially to American copy-desk men. When the Emperor Yoshihito died in 1926, one American paper, whose head-writer must have undergone agonies of composition, carried the headline: JAP EMPEROR DEAD TOMORROW. But troublesome as the time-map for varying editions is, the foreign correspondent has to work with it and soon masters it.

And despite its difficulties and hardships, the field of overseas reporting is a powerful magnet for many newsmen. Whether the motivation is the spirit of adventure, an ambition for "by-lines," a curiosity about other lands, or merely an itching foot, many a young reporter would give his eyeteeth for a foreign assignment. It is, however, a task for which comparatively few are fitted. Mastery of languages, understanding sympathy with other ways of life and appreciation of another civilization than the one to which a man has been born and bred, the ability to live comfortably and work hard in an alien environment — these things are not easy for most men to achieve. Anyone who has observed the work of American correspondents in any foreign news center knows that there are always some who, though they would never admit it, are actually suffering from a kind of sublimated homesickness for the sidewalks of New York, or the carbon dioxide of "Boul' Mich," and can never do their best work outside of "the States." But difficult though the task is, many have performed it admirably, and the roll of great American foreign correspondents of the past and present is a long one.

CHAPTER THIRTEEN

No. 50, Rockefeller Plaza

The fabled gathering-place of the winds on Mount Olympus has its modern counterpart on the fourth floor of No. 50, Rockefeller Plaza, New York, where the news of the world swirls in, passes through a system of channels, and flows out in the A.P.'s wire reports to newspapers.

This is the world's largest newsroom, covering about three-fourths of an acre of space, with hundreds of teletypes, a regiment of trained newsmen, a multitude of busy typewriters. There is no confusion, no litter on the floor, no running or shouting or waving of arms. Fast movement of the news is of the essence from one end to the other of this great room, and in every corner of it. "Move" is the key word: they move news of full national interest on the A-wire, they move other stories on the regional wires. Everything moves, but there is no appearance of rush or frenzied haste. If there is anything that could be called the prevailing mood of the Associated Press newsroom at Rockefeller Plaza, it is an intelligent routine in which quick decisions based on "know-how" direct the constant flow of news on the wires.

The A-wire is an extraordinary performance. It goes on and on, clickety-click, day and night, in its three cycles each twenty-four hours, without pause for holidays or anything else, clickety-click, carrying news from Oshkosh and Missoula and Hongkong and Iran and London, with scheduled budgets from Washington, with occasional high-priority "95's," with rare four-bell bulletins, and with routine announcements to editors, clickety-click, going on forever. There is something symbolic about this A-wire. Like the Vestal fire of ancient Rome, it is continually replenished; it never ceases to radiate the light of information.

The basic reason for the three cycles of the A.P. service lies in the fact that members issue both morning and evening papers, and editions are going to press around the clock. Moreover, when the Early Cycle closes at eight in the morning, five-o'clock editions of A.M.'s on the Pacific Coast are just going into press. The Day Cycle of the New York Associated Press runs from eight o'clock in the morning to six in the evening. The Night Cycle then takes over, but some of its men have already come on five hours earlier to acquaint themselves with the news picture by reading over the report which has just gone out over the Day Cycle, to watch developments of the late afternoon, and to map the upcoming report. Putting aside this overlap, the Night Cycle runs from six P.M. to two in the morning. The Early Cycle, which serves especially the western morning papers but which is also the nightwatch for the whole system, covers the hours from two to eight in the morning. Not all the wires are busy throughout the twenty-four hours; the D-wire, for example, which carries financial news, is on from ten in the morning until six in the evening.

The A-wire is the great trunk line of the New York A.P. bureau. It serves all the one hundred and one regional bureaus which are located at news-gathering and news-distributing points throughout the country and those member papers which receive the service directly in their newsrooms, as well as news-magazines and foreign news agencies. It goes to the eastern half of the United States — to all important newspapers located in the vast area bounded by a line from Maine to Florida to Louisiana to Kansas City to Minneapolis and through the eastern states adjacent to Canada, all their teletypes copying the same news simultaneously. At Kansas City, the "Great Divide" of the A.P.'s domestic service, the trunk line is broken, and the bureau at that point controls the western circuits; from midnight to ten in the morning, however, the A-wire is cut through Kansas City (that is, mechanically repeated) to the Pacific Coast, forming a full national circuit that flows into hundreds of newspaper offices in all states of the Union.

This A-wire carries all the most important and interesting news. A story worth the A-wire, nominally, should be of as much interest to Miami, Florida, as it is to Portland, Oregon. Its editor keeps feeding it with selected stories which have to come to the A.P. from its staffers and "string" correspondents all over the world. Most of the domestic bureaus can send direct on the A-wire. They break into the moving copy with a bulletin, the sending operator simply giving a bulletin signal, marking the moving copy "more" and then coming in with a short "take" of the bulletined story. High priority stories that can be "wrapped up" in two hundred words or less also have bulletin right of way. The general run of stories or new "leads" usually are scheduled to New York and taken in when, in the editor's judgment, the story offered is more important or interesting than any in the large pile of copy before him at the time. Washington, especially when Congress is in session, commonly contributes the largest file.

The A-wire is the great supplier of top news to all A.P. papers. Those which do not receive it directly obtain a condensed file of it from the nearest bureau on state or regional "single circuit" wires.

The B-wire is a supplementary trunk line connecting the New York office with all the A.P. bureaus throughout the country. It carries important stories of regional interest, together with many messages and schedules having to do with the service. These messages may be queries or requests for additional coverage wanted by some member paper. It runs only to Kansas City, which, as has been noted, has its own western and southwestern trunk lines. For the South, there is the G-wire, which performs the same function for its region that the B-wire performs for northern quarters of the United States and the West to Kansas City. And then, for New England, there is the E-wire; for New Jersey, the C-wire; and for New York State, the S-wire.

These latter wires, carrying state services, are served from the New York office; but other state wires run out of the various regional bureaus. On each of the state and limited regional circuits, on which all members are served by one of the bureaus, is carried a version of the A-wire report, cut and edited for the region, together with the state and regional news which has come into the bureau from member papers and "stringers." These "single circuits" also carry service messages and queries.

What is called the "New York Bureau" includes the A.P. "local" desk, which serves New York papers with local news of their own city. Most large cities at one time had city news bureaus which papers combined to support in order to save duplication of effort in covering the more routine types of news. New York's old "city bureau" is now the A.P. "local" desk, which has a considerable force of reporters and editors covering the New York scene. Some of these are "leg men" who are rarely or never seen at 50 Rockefeller Plaza but receive their assignments and make their reports by telephone. Also included under the "New York Bureau" are rewrite men who select news which comes to the "local" desk and prepare it for the regular A.P. wires.

The Associated Press maintains foreign desks at both the San Francisco and New York offices, the latter chiefly devoted, of course, to European news. About 85 per cent of the news of the New York foreign desk comes by way of London, whence it is transmitted directly by teletype. This teletype connection makes London the clearing house; even with the relay required, there is usually faster transmission from European points via London than from cableheads on the Continent.

There are also the export news staffs which prepare American news for La Prensa Associada, the South American distribution agency, and for the cable to London, where it is fed to the European clients of the A.P. A similar organization in San Francisco sends news by wireless to the Orient, Hawaii, Australia, the Philippines, Tokyo, Singapore, and so on.

Several special services are supplied by the New York office of the Associated Press to which members may subscribe. The D-wire handles financial news, from 10 A.M. to 6 P.M., with a separate service of tabulated stocks and bonds. The SP-wire carries sports news from 2 P.M. to 6 A.M., with a separate racing wire giving horse-race results and charts.

A staff of some fifty men and women at Rockefeller Plaza serve A.P. Radio. They edit the A-wire in a style suitable for news announcements to go over the air, and distribute their service to the radio stations which are associate members of the A.P. This operation, like the A-wire itself, goes 'round the clock.

A.P. Wirephoto is another special service for which members may subscribe. This consists of photographs sent by wire for production as halftone engravings by the subscribing papers. The pictures are received at the New York bureau just as the news is obtained, from photographers serving bureaus and member papers all over the country, and illustrate, for the most part, "spot news" stories which are sent out over the various wires. Weather maps are part of Wirephoto, and "A.P. Telemats" is a mail service of the most important of the pictures sent by wire.

Wide World Photos was formerly located in the general newsroom on the fourth floor; but floor space there, once deemed more than sufficient, is now inadequate, and WWP has been moved farther up in the building. It is a "mat service" — that is, it furnishes, by mail, matrices from which newspapers can cast the halftone engravings from which pictures are printed. It shares quarters with A.P. Newsfeatures, which supplies, also chiefly by mail, a full line of features — comics, columns, fashions, cartoons, crossword puzzles, juveniles, book and theater reviews, weekly summaries, etc. All of this material (much of it closely related to the news) is sold to both members and nonmembers.

But we mention these auxiliary services, interesting and important though they are, only because Wide World Photos was formerly located on the fourth floor. It is the great newsroom which engages our attention.

Air-conditioned, well-lighted, high-ceilinged, the unusual area of the room impresses the observer less because of the variety of activity on every side. Men in shirt sleeves bending over typewriters, other men at desks reading copy with pencil in hand, others scanning newspapers, still others busy at the teletypes, conferences in groups of two or three. Teletypes along one wall, files of the old reports, a library of reference works. A girl distributing copies of the new issue of *A.P. Log*, the weekly house periodical published for the thousands of A.P. employees around the globe. An occasional quiet vendor of candy and peanuts, which furnish a kind of stimulant to men working at high speed. There is here an extraordinary feeling that "everything is under control." There is no shouting or aimless dashing about. These men know what they are doing, and they are doing it intelligently and without bluster or show.

Let us look at certain kinds of news in process in the Associated Press system.

Stephen X. Jones, aged 90, dies in Americus, Georgia. He was once prominent in the city's affairs and his death is worth three-quarters of a column in the *Times-Recorder*, the local daily. But the deceased was once a candidate for governer of Georgia, and the *Times-Recorder*, which is an A.P. member, asks the Atlanta bureau of the A.P. how much they want on the death of S. X. Jones, once prominent in state politics. The Bureau editor calls for four hundred words, which he puts on the Georgia state wire. But he notes in the story the statement that Jones was a delegate to the Democratic national convention of 1912 and made a picturesque speech seconding the nomination of Champ Clark, and so he queries New York on the G-wire to see if they can use something on S. X. Jones' "houn' dog" speech of 1912, pegged by the orator's death. "Send 200 words Jones, A," comes the reply. The schedule for the story moves on the G-wire; it is handed to the editor of the A-wire, who gives Atlanta a "go-ahead"; the next morning the little piece about the "houn' dog" speech is in papers all over the country.

Or Mrs. Susannah Rowson Smith is elected president of the Iowa State Federation of Women's Clubs. Of course, the Des Moines Bureau picks this up and gets it on the Iowa state wire; but the bureau also offers it on the B-wire. In New York, it is noted that Mrs. Smith belongs to the Rowson family of Amsterdam, New York; and so the story is placed on the S-wire for upstate papers, chiefly as a service for the *Recorder*, of that city.

But let us take a more important and an actual piece of news. A few minutes after midnight on April 10, 1951, in the city of Washington, White House telephone operators began calling newsmen with the announcement that there would be a news conference in the office of Joseph Short, the President's press secretary, at one o'clock. The calls went out to the wire services, the radio chains, the bureaus maintained by individual papers, and the news-photography syndicates. Newsmen raced to the White House from all over the city, from offices and homes, probably from poker-games and parties, on foot, in taxis and cars. Not since the anxious times of World War II had there been a similar after-midnight news conference at the White House. As the men gathered in the wide lobby, speculation was what is sometimes called "rife." Perhaps the favorite theory was that General MacArthur's resignation from his Far East command was to be announced. Few believed that the general was to be removed; a "high authority" had recently said that the President had decided against such a course.

Promptly at one o'clock, the doors of Mr. Short's office were opened; at these doors were posted White House guards to prevent anyone from emerging before the conference was over and thus getting a time advantage on the announcement. As soon as all had crowded in, mimeographed sheets were distributed giving the President's statement about the ouster of MacArthur, the official orders to both MacArthur and Ridgway, and some background documents compiled by the secretary and his staff relating to MacArthur's attitude toward United Nations policy in the Far East. Mr. Short, standing behind his desk, remarked that the President felt that General MacArthur was not sympathetic with our foreign policy. A reporter immediately asked, "Do you mean that he has disobeyed orders?" "The statement," replied Short, "speaks for itself." "Why is the statement issued at this hour?" asked another. "It is three P.M. in Tokyo," observed Short. Then the doors were opened, and there was a grand rush for the telephones in the press-room and for taxis and cars.

The first intimation of the one o'clock conference came to the New York Associated Press office from Wirephoto's "squawk-box," which has direct connection with the Washington bureau;

it brought the information that photographers were being sum-
moned to the meeting. Announcement of the impending news
conference then went out over the A-wire as a warning to editors
that some top news could be expected shortly after one. When the
big news came, at 1:07, there was no "flash"; "flashes" have been
discouraged by the A.P. as time-wasters, in view of the fact that
the first ten words of the "lead" give the news anyway. But the
four bells of a top-news bulletin were heard in newspaper and
bureau offices over the whole length of the A-wire, and then the
teletype began to tap out the story:

BULLETIN

WASHINGTON, APRIL 11 — (AP) — PRESIDENT TRUMAN EARLY TO-
DAY FORCED GENERAL DOUGLAS MACARTHUR FROM ALL HIS COM-
MANDS.

At the same time, the story was put on the cables to London and
South America, on the C-wire to New Jersey, and on the S-wire
to up-state New York. In San Francisco it was relayed by wireless to Hawaii, Australia, Hongkong, Tokyo, and so on. All the
bureau chiefs over the country were putting it on their morning
reports for state and regional wires.

But this was only the beginning of a story which ran for days
and weeks. Washington newsmen, as soon as they filed their
initial stories, got senators and representatives out of bed and
obtained from them quick reactions to the news. Foreign correspondents, especially in Tokyo and London, had good stories
about the repercussions abroad. From individuals, official and private, from associations, from editors, came a flood of views and
actions, all picked up by reporters and gathered in by the great
news-gathering net of the Associated Press.

Such is the newsroom at 50 Rockefeller Plaza, and such are the
devices and techniques of its news-gathering system. The New
York bureau of the Associated Press is a large and important news
center, but it is only one of many notable offices where the news
is gathered and processed for American newspapers, radio stations, news-magazines, etc. The New York bureaus of the United
Press and International News Service are quite as interesting.

Apologies are due those great wire services for our failure here to describe their operations in detail; one service might do as well as another for our exposition, but only one is required to give the curious reader some insight into the complex mysteries of the operation of an international wire news service.

The difference between the privately owned U.P. and I.N.S. and the mutual A.P. in respect to the coöperation of members or clients in the news-gathering for the whole system is not as great as it may seem to be at first glance. The clients of the U.P. and I.N.S. certainly are not, as a rule, uncoöperative. Those agencies employ paid, part-time "stringers" in hundreds of small cities and towns where they do not have regular correspondents. But the A.P. also employs a great many "stringers," not only in places where it has no members but even in the offices of a large number of member papers. Paying for work which is supposed to be the duty of members in a coöperative system is frowned upon in some quarters, but the use of "stringers" who are on the staffs of member papers seems to others a necessary and efficient part of the system.

The International News Service, the United Press and the Associated Press have devised, and now maintain, an international and domestic news process which continues day and night, without interruption for Sundays or holidays, three hundred and sixty-five days of each year. As someone has said, "They never put the world to bed." Their service is about as constant, and almost as reliable in its even performance, as the precession of the equinoxes. This threefold system of news by wire, the intricate techniques of which are unknown to the reader of the daily newspaper and the listener to radio broadcasts, furnishes the framework of a large part of the news in America.

CHAPTER FOURTEEN

The "Daily Tribune" Goes to Press

American journalism was born in very humble surroundings. Our first newspapers were by-products of our first printing offices, and these were often located in the homes of the printers; or, if they were in the business district, they were on side streets or alleys. Basements were popular for printing offices because of the weight of presses, and newspapers continued to have an affinity with cellars throughout most of the nineteenth century. By the middle of that century, however, a few papers (notably the *New York Herald*) had good buildings of their own, and shortly after the end of the Civil War fine new homes were erected by the *Philadelphia Public Ledger*, the *New York Sun*, the *Chicago Tribune*, and several other big papers. From that time on, metropolitan newspapers occasionally built and proudly dedicated to journalism large buildings on the main streets and squares of our leading cities. But it was not until recent years that great newspaper buildings, modern, roomy, well lighted and well equipped, became common in cities throughout the land.

With better buildings came cleaner and more orderly newsrooms. Wastepaper on the floor, dark stairways, grimy copyboys, noise and confusion were once common in newspaper offices. Now they are not only uncommon; they are almost unknown, except in motion pictures.

Likewise, drunkenness and immorality were once all too common among newspaper reporters. The cult of Bohemianism, originated by Henri Murger and friends in Paris in the mid-nineteenth century, exerted a considerable influence upon groups of artists and writers in France, and later in England. In New York, Pfaff's Cellar was a gathering place for the Bohemians of the 1860's. The spectacular successes achieved by some members served to glamorize the standards of loose personal behavior which became a tradition of the cult. Some of the journalists were always attracted to the Bohemian groups, in Paris, in London, in New York; and among these were not a few who knew little of art or literature, but were drawn in by the fascination of clever talk, loafing, bawdry, and drunkenness. Augustus Maverick, writing of the New York Bohemians in 1870, said that "the race has almost disappeared"; but if that was true, many newspaper reporters were still bravely carrying on the tradition of dissipation which they had received from such groups. As late as 1890 President Charles W. Eliot, in a moment of exasperation, called reporters "drunkards, deadbeats, and bummers." This produced loud denials from the newspapers, and there is no doubt that by this date there was a general reaction among newspapermen against the drunken reporter.[33]

But if eastern papers were taking a stand against this neo-Bohemianism by 1890, a "cultural lag" had brought it to flower in Chicago at that time. The roistering, prank-loving, tough Chicago reporters of the turn of the century have been so fully celebrated in fiction, drama, and reminiscence that they need no further exploitation in these pages. These are the men whom Hecht and MacArthur put on the stage in their crackling, lusty melodrama, *The Front Page*.[34]

Today one rarely sees a drunk in any newsroom. In an era in which alcoholism is a difficult problem on all social levels, it is no more prevalent among newspapermen than in — say — the brokerage business. Working with the news requires a high degree of attention and judgment, and drinking on the job usually ends by drinking without a job. Drop in at the newsroom of any good daily paper, and you will find a group of hard-working men with no nonsense about them, busy at their various tasks without thought of the romance or glamour of the "game." Sometimes their working conditions are not what they should be; quarters may be crowded, and lighting and ventilation not the best. On other papers, facilities are admirable, with everything needful for fast, efficient work. But whatever the surroundings, these men are not playboys, sots, or stage-heroes. In his column in the *Des Moines Tribune*, Gordon Gammack recently wrote:

Those of you who have visited our newsroom (and you're always welcome) have seen that it is as orderly and quiet as most offices.

Editors don't shout at reporters — and certainly reporters don't shout at editors or, with threats of quitting, tell them how to run their business.

Newspaper men are pretty normal people. Most of them have families, and they go to their homes quietly when they are through work. They mow their lawns, shovel snow from their sidewalks, and play with their children.

Rare indeed is the modern newspaper man who drinks on the job — and he knows that he risks dismissal if he does. He may pass along his hunches to a detective or a prosecutor, but he doesn't make it a habit to play cops and robbers. He is more likely to uncover wrongdoing by painstakingly probing records, official and otherwise. . . .

The modern newspaper man is a trained professional. He has studied and prepared for his work just as lawyers, doctors, accountants, engineers, and architects have. Usually he's pretty crazy about his work. A good story makes his heart beat faster. But, by and large, he's an average guy.

And yet motion picture producers continue to give us newsrooms based upon some of the most disgraceful aspects of the past history of the press, serving them up as representations of modern journalism. A Hollywood actor well known for his rôles as a newspaper reporter told the writer recently that he knew that reporters do not keep their hats on in private homes, "tank up" while on the job, or act generally like rowdies from Skid Row; but that the movies have to give their public what it wants, and what it wants in these rôles is the romantic tough. This sounds a little like the alibi which some editors make in defending the publication of over-sensationalized stories; apparently such editors are getting back some of their own medicine in these screen travesties of the newspaperman.

All this is by way of introduction to a description of how the news is handled in the office of a typical metropolitan afternoon newspaper, which we shall call the *Daily Tribune*.[35]

Central in a large and airy room is the copydesk. In the Old Building, the various departments all had their own rooms or cubbyholes; the Sunday staff, sports, society, pix — each had its own domain within four walls. But here in the New Building everybody is out on the big newsroom floor except the managing editor and the publisher; and their offices, though often used for conferences with visitors, are easily available. Even the editorial writers and columnists have their stalls on the big main floor, where they are studying or pounding away on typewriters. This "universal" newsroom has the advantage of easy access to all departments, rapid movement of news and news-copy, and quick conferences of heads of departments. It emphasizes the unity of the entire staff, all the members of which are centering their efforts on one objective — getting out a good paper on time. It makes for sound, democratic personal relationships; there are no "trained seals" or favorites.

Along one side of the big room are the doors to the newspaper library (including the "morgue" where clippings and "cuts" and pictures are filed), the darkrooms of the photographic department, and locker-rooms. On the other side are the teletypes bringing in the services of the wire agencies — trunk, regional, and special wires from the I.N.S., U.P., A.P., New York Times, Chicago Daily News, N.A.N.A., etc.

And there are plenty of wastebaskets, and plenty of filing "hooks" for unwanted copy; nobody throws anything on the floor. Nor is there any shouting; the reporters' desks are near enough to that of the city editor so that he does not have to raise his voice to call one of his men over, and the news editor can call department heads together without fuss.

The *Daily Tribune* is an evening paper, and its chief home edition goes to press at two o'clock. The city editor is at his desk at seven in the morning, studying his book of "futures" and clippings from rival papers, and outlining his campaign for the day. Most of his reporters do not show up before eight; what is the use of starting on the news rounds before the city is awake? There are fifteen reporters — eighteen if you count three "leg-men" who work in distant parts of the city, telephone their reports in, and are rarely seen at the office. Indeed, there is one "leg-man" whom the city editor has never seen, though he has talked with him nearly every day for the past year. Of the fifteen who report at the office, eight are on regular "beats" — police, courthouse, federal building, hospitals, fire department, labor, Chamber of Commerce, business, and so on. The remainder are assignment men,

though of course any or all of them may be given special assignments when needed, and some may be shifted to "rewrite." The
city editor talks over news possibilities with each of his reporters
every morning, whether the man is going out on a regular beat
or a special job. The city desk is the center of the whole news
picture of a great metropolis. The city editor's mind is full of
background information, of probabilities and possibilities, of personalities and relationships, of news stories that may "shape up"
today or tomorrow, or next year. It is his business to know, to
guess, to inquire, to dig into situations; and he uses his staff to
find out the facts.

But let us see just how a news event is covered and the story
processed. Ever since the date of the convention of the state bar
association was decided upon, and the man on the Chamber of
Commerce run got it from the hotel bureau, there has been a
note of the meeting in the city editor's future book under a date
which has now arrived; the bar association meets today, and Bill
Jones will have to cover it. Not an especially promising job, on
the face of it; but Judge Spencer is on the program, and there
has been talk about the judge for the governorship. The city editor
talks this situation over with Jones before he goes out on the
assignment, and they agree that the Spencer candidacy might
crystallize today in a hotel lobby, with all the judge's friends
around him. "Hope they talk him into it," says Jones, on his way
out. "Right!" says the city editor. What they both hope for is a
story.

This time they get it. Jones is back by eleven. "Spencer's going
to run!" he tells his editor. "Has he issued a statement?" "No, but
I've got an authorized quote from Judge Bonsal on it." "Good! Got
enough for two pages?" He means two typed pages of copy paper,
triple-spaced. As soon as the copy is brought to his desk, the city
editor goes over it carefully, calls Jones over for a consultation
about Bonsal's relationship to Spencer, makes a few changes, and
then places it in a box for the copydesk, whence a copyboy soon
whisks it to the man "in the slot."

The copydesk is a semicircular table, with space on the outer
"rim" for six or eight copyeditors. The chief copyreader sits on
the inside of the semicircle ("in the slot"), and parcels out the

copy to the men "on the rim." It is the business of the copyreaders (in England they call them very appropriately "sub-editors") to read with meticulous care all copy before it goes down to the composing machines; to question anything that may seem to be incorrect, libelous, or in bad taste; to correct spelling, grammar, punctuation, and bad writing; to see that the "style" of the paper as to usages in writing is maintained; and to write heads of the size and kind prescribed by the copy chief for each story.

Jones's story, which has been given the key word "Spencer," having passed the city desk, comes to the copy chief. If this were a busy day, or the story were a little more important, the copy chief would speak briefly with the news editor about the way the Spencer piece is to be handled; but there is no special problem now, and he marks the copy with a symbol indicating the type of headline to be written and hands it to one of the men on the rim. After the copy has been edited and the head written, it goes by pneumatic tube from the copydesk down two floors to the composing room. There the copycutter hands it to one of the linotype operators to be set into type. The Spencer story, with its headlines, makes six or seven inches of type matter; and in fifteen or twenty minutes the operator delivers the story, in slugs still warm from the machine, to the make-up bank, together with the original copy. The bank man "pulls" a proof, which he sends, with copy, by pneumatic tube to the proofroom, which is located on the floor above. There it is read "by copy," the errors, if any, are marked, and the proof is returned downstairs. In the composing room again, lines in which errors occur are reset; and if there are very many, a revised proof is taken, sent up to the proofroom, and O.K.'d. The story slugged "Spencer" is now in the bank awaiting make-up into the page forms.

Meantime the home edition is taking form up in the newsroom. The key man is the news editor. He has his desk close to one corner of the copydesk, and at his other side he has the desk of the picture editor. He has been keeping close watch of stories which have come to the copydesk and conferring frequently with the city, telegraph, and state editors. He is the big boss in the matter of space, position, and display of news, and it is of course his business to plan the make-up of page one and the other news pages. The advertisements have already been in place in the waiting forms on the make-up tables downstairs for hours, and the sports, society, editorial, and stock-market pages are made up separately by their appropriate departments. The news editor works with "dummy" sheets for his pages, ruled in eight-column forms, on which the space preëmpted by advertising has been marked off. He has an earlier mail edition as a starting-point from which to design the new make-up of the two o'clock home edition.

A little before noon, the city, state, telegraph, and picture editors and the copy chief gather around the desk of the news editor and run rapidly through the early mail edition, marking each story with a symbol indicating whether it is to be discarded, used in the home edition, or the later state edition, or all editions, and so on. This is for the guidance of the news editor in planning make-up. In this conference, the news editor is informed of new stories that have come in; the city editor says it is a dull day, and from the list he has been keeping he names half a dozen new stories, including the one about the Spencer candidacy.

The news editor now settles down to design his front page. He keeps the A-bomb explosion story which appeared in the early mail edition for his top line. Also he keeps Princess Elizabeth's visit to Washington, with accompanying "art." He makes room for the Spencer story by transferring an out-state death to an inside page. The picture editor has dug up a photograph of Judge Spencer from the "morgue," but this is discarded in favor of a good shot of the atom-bomb explosion which has just come in by wirephoto.

By one o'clock the page "dummies" go down to the composing room for the make-up. Here the scene is very different from that in the newsroom. The odor of machine oil and hot metal, the orderly hurry to meet a deadline, the many workmen all intent on their own specialized jobs: these factors represent the climax of the handling of the news on a great newspaper. A long double row of linotypes fills one corner of the room; then come the banks of galleys filled with slugs ready for the forms, the proof-table with its chutes to the room above, and in the center the rows of make-up tables. Several of the page forms have their own make-up printers bending over them and moving type from galley to form; and watching all of them is the make-up superintendent, with an eye for any difficulties caused by mistakes in calculation of space or failure to supply the cuts or type required. About half past one the news editor comes down to watch over his precious page one, and make any adjustments that are necessary. One after the other, the forms are locked up, planed down, and wheeled away to the stereotyping room.

In the hot stereotype department, semicylindrical metal plates are cast from the forms. These are locked on the great presses which extend through the pressroom, row on high-piled row. Men stand here and there along the press units, tightening the plates, adjusting paper tension, setting ink-flow — but all with a kind of expectancy, as though awaiting a signal. . . . The chief pressman steps back, raises his hand, presses a button. A hum, a growl, a steady roar, increasing its tempo. And now throughout the whole building is heard the muted thunder of the great presses in the basement — a sound which epitomizes for every newspaperman the whole drama of the news. It is two o'clock, and the home edition is out.

Trucks are drawn up at the great doors of the circulation room downstairs waiting to take heavy bundles of papers to points all over the city where the carriers will pick them up. Copies fresh from the press are soon laid on the desks of all the editors in the newsroom. The city editor picks his up. There, above the fold in the second column on page one, is Jones's story:

SPENCER WILL RUN
FOR GOVERNORSHIP
SAY HIS FRIENDS

In conclusion, it should be pointed out that many important details have been omitted in this brief story of what went on in one morning at the *Daily Tribune* office. The techniques employed by Jones in getting the Spencer story, the process of the telegraph desk in choosing stories from the abundance offered by the wire services, the work of such departments as sports and society, the problems of the news editor in weighing the values of competing stories and pictures: these things are only suggested.

Also we have chosen a dull day, when no great news breaks interfered with routine handling of the news. For drama in the news and composing rooms, give us the big nearby disaster with national angles, breaking at ten o'clock, with important follow-ups on top of the deadline which necessitate breaking up forms already plated. Henry Justin Smith, late managing editor of the *Chicago Daily News*, once wrote an unexcelled story of the impact of such news on a great newspaper organization in his book *Deadlines.*

And also it must be understood that no two newsrooms are quite alike in their organization. For example, the copy chief sometimes doubles as telegraph editor, even on large papers; or the managing editor may serve also as news editor. Sports, society, and so on may move their copy across a so-called "universal" copy-desk; on the other hand, state news and even city news and telegraph may have separate copydesks. The news editor may have all copy put in his box so he can glance at it before it goes to the copydesk and thus keep his finger on everything. And so on.

But here, in brief, is the *Daily Tribune's* operation, presented in the hope that it may give to the uninitiated some idea of how news is handled, day in and day out, by a great newspaper.

CHAPTER FIFTEEN

WZZZ Airs the News

It is hard to conceive of a "typical" radio newsroom. There is so much disparity in buildings, equipment, organization, and policy that significant generalizations are almost out of the question. It is helpful to classify stations by power, but many 250-watt stations are more intelligently news-conscious than some 10,000-watt operations. There are small stations which give eight or ten newscasts daily; and there are big stations which have no full-time news director, have only one teletype, set off in a corner or closet somewhere, and furnish perhaps two or three network commentators and a couple of "rip-and-read" broadcasts from the wire report each day as their total news offering. It may be said, however, that (a) nearly all stations have one or more wire services furnishing domestic and foreign news by teletype, and (b) most of them have network affiliations which provide at least a minimum of newscasts, either of general news, sports, or the talks of commentators — or all three.

In short, news permeates rather thoroughly the entire American radio system; and, as was pointed out in Chapter II, it is currently showing a consistent rise in charts of the preferences of hearers. There is a strong trend toward acceptance of the doctrine which is succinctly stated in the preamble to the "Standards of Practice" code of the National Association of Radio News Directors: "The broadcasting of factual, objective, and timely news is the finest public service radio or television stations can perform."

The newsroom of a great network station such as the Washington NBC office is very impressive. Most of the big stations are modern in furnishings, beautifully lighted, air-conditioned, and carefully sound-proofed. The newsroom of a network station is large, with ample space for desks of some fifteen editors, reporters, and commentators. A large triple-plate window on one side looks into the broadcasting room, on the other side of which, visible through another window, is the mysterious control room, with its dials and switches, its warning lights, its director with his imperious time-signals. In the newsroom itself is the ordered haste so typical of news-handling wherever it is in process, the click of typewriters, low-toned conferences, intent and purposeful work toward deadlines. Along one wall is a row of teletypes; occasionally someone "clears" them, tearing off the new copy from the long rolls, separating the stories, and delivering them to the various desks. A commentator rises from his desk in the corner to consult a map on the wall, a book from one of the reference shelves, or a new dispatch fresh from the teletype. An announcer, script in hand, hurries out to the broadcasting room; he will be on the air in two minutes.

But perhaps a visit to the news department of a 50,000-watt station will be most instructive, and we shall choose one which belongs to a station unusually conscious of its responsibility for the airing of local as well as national and foreign news. WZZZ [36] gets its news from five main sources: three daily commentators from the network with which the station is affiliated, the national and regional wire services, its own staff of local reporters, its "stringers" located at many points of the territory it serves, and its special farm department. The contributions of each of these sources of the news service of WZZZ must be discussed briefly.

Our station is fully committed to the aim and ideal of factual, "objective," and timely news, and it has little use for news commentators who do more "commentating" than factual news reporting and who tend to angle the news to the bias of their own opinions. It does, however, use two network news programs daily — one an early morning commentator, and the other an early evening show bringing in direct reports from all over the world. Besides these, there are a couple of five-minute roundups from the network late at night.

WZZZ is well supplied with wire services. Its choice of the various wires offered has been governed largely by its competition; it prefers services which rival stations and local newspapers do not rely upon too heavily. Currently it is using the Chicago trunk wire and the state wire of the International News Service, the radio and trunk wires of the United Press, and the radio and state wires of the Associated Press. Of course, WZZZ monitors the newscasts of other stations, especially those of competitors; and the city police, state patrol, and fire department wireless reports, instructions, and alarms are picked up in the newsroom.

But the heart of WZZZ's news department is its own staff of ten members. One of these men is a state political reporter who telephones his reports to the office to be written by other members of the staff and comes into the newsroom only occasionally. Another staffer is a young woman who takes the telephone calls of "stringers" and others with news tips, and doubles as the director's secretary. The remaining eight men are divided half to "day-side" and half to "night-side," the dividing line being at 3:00 P.M. All of these eight men are at once reporters, editors and writers, and broadcasters. They have regular beats — police, federal building, hospitals, etc. — which they cover mainly by telephone, though they all go out into the city for firsthand inquiries from time to time. These men also edit the wire copy; indeed, they do more than edit it, they rewrite all they propose to use, whether it comes from a regular press wire or a radio service. WZZZ believes that a smoothly running newscast can be put together only when teletype copy is rewritten in station style, with local angles emphasized, and just the right condensation applied to make it fit properly into the ten- or fifteen-minute broadcast.

And then each man reads his own copy on his own newscast. This by no means is general practice on all stations, but it has the advantage of allowing the man at the microphone to read a script with which he is familiar. It permits him to develop an individuality in which the writing and delivery are harmonized and fitted together. Thus Smith's foreign news spot at 8:00 P.M. comes to have a special value for hearers, to be anticipated, and it is hoped, to be liked, because it is Smith's and his habitual listeners know what to expect. Each of the eight men in the newsroom has one or two shows on the day's program which he strives to give precisely this drawing power of familiar individuality. Of course, it often happens that several men contribute something to Smith's show, especially if things are happening fast just before a deadline; in such case, although he has not written every item of his own script, he tries to familiarize himself with it all before he faces the microphone. Indeed, all four men on the "dayside" are likely to contribute to the big newscast at 12:30, and the same is true for the "night-side" staff in respect to the big show at ten o'clock.

Another source of news for WZZZ is its corps of sixty-five "stringers" scattered over its broadcasting area. Most of them, though not all, are newspapermen, many located in small cities and towns. They know what WZZZ wants, and they telephone or telegraph their reports in at all hours of the day and night. The sports editor, who is a "night-side" man, is proud also of his active list of 350 high school boys and girls who telephone in basketball scores and send other short items by mail without pay.

Finally, the station's farm department includes a considerable amount of news, beyond weather and markets, in its broadcasts. It uses whatever it wants from the newsroom, and often pays for its borrowings with information about crops, storms, and so on, which are usable on regular newscasts.

Special events broadcasts are occasionally a part of WZZZ's program. The sports editor is a good play-by-play reporter of baseball, football, basketball, and boxing; and the station features leading games of the local university and the annual high school basketball tournament. Important public events and ceremonies of general interest are followed in detail, though long tape or phone recordings are not generally looked upon as affording a proper utilization of news time on the air. Indeed, phone recordings (by "beeper") are regarded as of such poor quality in general that WZZZ uses them only on rare occasions when their news value is very high. Tape recordings are more frequently used, especially when a prominent public figure can be induced to give a brief résumé of a newsworthy speech for WZZZ. An excerpt from the network recording of General MacArthur's speech before Congress was used in the station's regular newscast following that event, and a similar excerpt of Prime Minister Churchill's voice was used in connection with the British elections of 1951. Of course, such special events as the great national nominating conventions are handled through the networks.

During emergencies caused by storms and floods, WZZZ listeners know that the station will devote much time on its programs to special announcements of postponed meetings, closed schools, highway blocks, and traffic detours. This is news of immediate public concern; it is an important service to many persons and is of interest to all.

The WZZZ newsroom is a fine, big place with fluorescent lighting and handsome furnishings. In the center are work-tables arranged somewhat in the form of a newspaper copydesk, with the staff at typewriters around the "rim." The teletype machines are ranged along one wall, and shelves filled with reference books, files of local and New York and Chicago newspapers, and leading magazines are placed along another. Maps are on the walls, and a big "world globe" stands on a pedestal. A large bulletin board near the door has schedules and notices posted on it. Adjoining the newsroom is a small director's office and a telephone and secretarial room.

There is a good deal of traffic in the newsroom. An office boy comes in to bring late editions of newspapers. A farm depart-

ment man comes to look over teletype copy or to talk with the
staff man who has the next show coming up. A girl brings in
copies of a new issue of the station's latest house bulletin and
places them on the desks. An editor walks over to consult the
busily clicking teletype and hunts through the long sheets, some
of them drooping to the floor, which have emerged from the
machines. Another staff man is called to the telephone. The director, sitting at his typewriter at the head of the copydesk arrangement, inquires of the man on the courthouse beat whether
he has checked on the Simmons trial for the next newscast; he
has, but there is nothing new. Everything moves smoothly; these
are all knowledgeable men, doing a job they know how to do,
working toward a set of deadlines with careful attention to both
details and the general shape of the finished shows.

Station WZZZ uses close to one-sixth of its time for news, if we
include not only the newsroom's shows but also those farm department programs which are largely news, and the time of the network commentators. But this figure does not include the broadcasts of games, occasional special events coverage, or political
speeches on time arranged-for outside the news department. It is
not always easy to tell what should be classified as "news" on
a radio program; but WZZZ's twelve shows originating in the
newsroom and occupying two hours and twenty minutes each
day represent a large time allowance to such material, as radio
programing goes today.

It will be interesting to follow one story through the process of
reporting, writing, and broadcasting. The story chosen relates to
an actual event of the "soft news" kind — a good story, but of no
very deep significance except to the unfortunate protagonist. Our
narrative of the processing of this story is accurate except for the
names and a slight shift in time.

The facts were as follows. Smithville is a town of five thousand
population some two hundred miles from the city in which WZZZ
is located. A farmer living thirteen miles from Smithville decided
on the morning of May 14, 1951, to drive over to his trading center
nearby and pay some bills which he had allowed to accumulate
during spring work; and with that purpose in mind, he went down
cellar and dug into an old jar in which he kept his cash reserves.

He took out thirteen hundred-dollar bills and put them into a wallet which he placed in the inside pocket of his jacket. Just before leaving, he noted that his son was having some trouble repairing a hog-lot fence and went out to show him how to do it. As the morning was warm, he hung his jacket on the feeding-lot fence. As soon as the job was done, he returned, ready to climb into his car; but as he looked for his jacket he found that the steers in the feeding-lot had pulled it off the fence and down on the ground. Hurriedly examining the garment, he saw that they had eaten the lining, together with the wallet and its contents. He called his son, and they both looked over all the twenty-five steers in the lot, but neither could tell, for the life of him, which one had $1300 in currency inside him. At length they called a veterinarian, who said the only way to retrieve the money was to slaughter all twenty-five animals and examine their stomachs before the bills had disintegrated. So the farmer called the slaughterhouse in Smithville and asked it to slaughter the steers. But the slaughterhouse was already almost up to its quota and said that the government would not allow it to slaughter that many animals; it could take two or three. The farmer said, "Dum the gov'ment!" and hung up.

The slaughterhouse people told the story, with chuckles, to everybody who came near that day, and it was common talk in Smithville that afternoon and evening. WZZZ's "stringer," who works on the local weekly, phoned it in about seven o'clock; the staff telephone girl took it, and handed her notes over to the assistant news director, who is "night-side" boss and who also has the big fifteen-minute newscast at ten o'clock. He had plenty of time to prepare the story for his show.

Let us go with him into the broadcast room at 9:52. He holds in his hand a small sheaf of copy, some of the pages of which were handed to him in the newsroom just as he was leaving. In the large, brightly lighted studio, its floor carpeted and its walls heavily soundproofed, the newscaster settles himself in a chair opposite the announcer, who faces the control room window. There is a microphone on the table between the two men, who now seem lonely and isolated in the big studio. The newsman glances at his copy, reads the few sheets with which he is not familiar, rearranges them, lays them down on the table before him. There is now that half-minute of pre-broadcast expectancy in which the man about to go on the air settles into the radio mood. The announcer watches the man in the control room, who, with arm upraised and forefinger pointing upward, is looking through his window at the men in the studio. Exactly at 10:00:00, the man at the controls throws a switch with his left hand at the same time that he brings his right arm down to point his finger directly at the announcer. "You're *it*," he seems to say. Over the studio door a sign in red lights comes on: ON THE AIR. "This is WZZZ — " begins the voice of the announcer.

As soon as the announcer has finished his brief "commercial," the newscaster begins reading his script. He reads rapidly and smoothly, never emphasizing prepositions, never balking at strange names (he has looked the unfamiliar ones up in pronunciation guides before he came on), never mangling a phrase out of its true meaning. He reads naturally, without striving for any voice pattern; he has in mind his audience of men and women like himself, with whom he is sharing his interest in the news. He has been on the air nearly five minutes, when a newsroom colleague enters silently and places two slips of paper on the table in front of him and as silently retires; the slips contain two bits of news which have just come in and which the newscaster may wish to incorporate in the show.

Midway of the fifteen-minute broadcast, the announcer holds up a finger, and the newsman stops at the end of the item he is reading to allow the insertion of another "commercial." There is now time to glance over the slips which have just been handed him, and he inserts them in position among the sheets remaining in the little pile of unread copy on the table. A few sheets he lays to one side; he probably will not have time for them, but they are an emergency reserve. As soon as the announcer has finished, the newscaster resumes his story of the evening's events. The foreign and national news was in the first half of the broadcast; he is now on local happenings — an accident, a mayor's proclamation, the death of a well-known citizen. Then comes the weather roundup for WZZZ's entire area. He is saving the story of the steer's $1300 meal for the end, as a boy saves the

plums in his pudding until the last. The announcer is watching
the signals from the control room, and relays them to the newscaster. Three fingers are held up, and just as the sign changes
to two fingers, the broadcast, without change of pace, glides into the Smithville story, telling it more briefly and succinctly than
we have related it above. At the same time, the WZZZ sports
editor and another man quietly enter the studio and seat themselves at another table before another microphone. The sports
editor has a show coming up at 10:15, and the man with him is
a baseball coach whom he will interview as a part of his sports-
cast. Now the present broadcast is swinging into its final seconds,
the announcer is slowly bringing one extended finger down; and
as it points squarely at the newsman, he comes to the last words
of his script: "— and still nobody knows which steer ate the un-
lucky thirteen hundred-dollar bills." Full stop, end of script, end
of show. The announcer comes in with his final "commercial."

The story of the steer's meal was a "beat" — no other news
service, radio station, or newspaper carried it. Next day WZZZ
offered the story to its network affiliate, which used it on a national hookup. Two days later a check with the Smithville correspondent brought the information that the farmer had given up
the quest for his $1300 and had asked his creditors to carry him
until his fall crops were in. Whoever ate the steaks from that
voracious steer's carcass would never know what rich meat he
was tasting.

CHAPTER SIXTEEN

The Form of News

If we look at news in the proper sense, and regard it in-
clusively, it is evident at once that it has no single form and fits
into no established pattern. It is Protean, and we recognize it as
news not by the shape of it but by its purpose.

Thus rumor is as formless as the wind, to which it was often
compared by the ancients: it may be cast in the style of the

staccato sentences and paragraphs of a gossip columnist, in the excited utterance of a predicter-reporter issuing from a radio receiving-set, in a whispered phrase heard on the street, or merely in a meaningful wink. And yet rumor is news — often bad and untrustworthy news, to be sure, but always a report of an alleged event or situation.

We are conditioned to forget that news circulates in haphazard and aimless eddies, on the street, in clubs, in a country store or on subway trains, by our familiarity with its somewhat less ephemeral presentation in newspapers and on the radio. And since it is only in those media, and in news-magazines, newsreels, and news-pictures, that current reports have recognizable shapes and patterns, any discussion of the form of news, to be practical, must include such topics as the structure of the news story, the pattern of the newscast, and fashions in news pictures. Those topics, and problems suggested by them, form the subject of the present chapter.

The form of news presentation in American newspapers has undergone many changes since the days of old Ben Harris' *Publick Occurrences.* Harris wrote clearly and succinctly, as good newsmen have since the beginning of journalism, but there was little pointing up of the more important items in his paper, or in any of the eighteenth-century "gazettes." Everything was crowded in together, and there were virtually no headlines, leads, or identification of unusually important stories. The opening sentences of a news report were usually casual and introductory, as they might be in an essay. When headlines came in, during the Mexican War and the ensuing Gold Rush, the structure of the story became less random and more strictly chronological. By the time of the Civil War, and for more than a decade thereafter, it was the rule to observe the strict order of events in each news story.

Thus the *Chicago Tribune*'s story of the assassination of Lincoln began:

Washington, April 14, 1865. — The President and Mrs. Lincoln were at Ford's Theater listening to the performance of the "American

Cousin," occupying a box in the second tier. At the close of the third act, a person entered the box occupied by the President, and shot Mr. Lincoln in the head . . .

When Grant was nominated for a second term as President in 1872, the *New York Times'* story of the event began:

Philadelphia, June 6. — This, the last day of the Republican jubilee, dawned as bright as the prospects of the great party of freedom, and remained throughout one of those days of brilliant early Summer. As on the previous day, the streets were crowded at an early hour with surging crowds . . .

There is a full column of fine print before the reporter gets so far as the opening of the convention. The entire front page of the *Times* is filled with eye-straining print (more than half of it in solid nonpareil type) about the convention, but it is not until the middle of the first column of the run-over on the fifth page that the reporter breaks the news that Grant was nominated. And as late as 1892, in the issue of the *New York Tribune* for September 8, a story of the twenty-one-round championship fight between James J. Corbett and John L. Sullivan ran to a little over twenty-five hundred words before the reporter told his anxious readers that there was a new champion. All this is not as bad as it sounds, however, since the multiple-deck headlines which surmounted the story themselves formed a kind of "lead."

The technique of the "lead" — that is, of the opening statement giving the gist of the most important facts of the story and leading into the more chronologically arranged main report — was developed in the 1880's. E. L. Shuman, who wrote the first American textbook in journalism in 1894, pointed out that "the style followed almost universally in large American newspaper offices at present" was to put the "marrow of the whole story" in the first paragraph. Just who formulated the "Rule of the Five W's" is uncertain; perhaps it was Shuman, who included it in his fuller treatise of 1903. This famous rule requires that five questions dealing with the subject matter of the story, all of them beginning with the letter W, should be answered in the first paragraph of the story: the questions are "What?" "Who?" "Where?" "When?" and "Why?" To which some have added the query "How?"

In the standard news structure, the skeletonized statement of the lead is followed by a paragraph or two giving attendant details, and then the story reverts to the lead and expands it with all the details necessary to give full understanding of the event or situation. In writing a long story, the reporter always keeps in mind the fact that exigencies of make-up may require throwing away the last paragraph or two, especially in a late edition; thus the least important material must come last.

This may seem a tortuous and unnatural structure, but the reasons for it are clear. Most newspaper readers want it that way. They want to be able to glance at a headline; and if it seems to indicate subject matter of interest, to skim the cream off the story by reading a summary; and if interest still holds, to read most or all of the story. The time is long gone when anyone can be expected to read the paper thoroughly from end to end; in this era of impatient readers and forty-page papers, skimming is not only common but the almost universal rule. The structure of the modern news story is suited to the skimmer. Of course, it encourages skimming, and thus defeats the purpose of the longer story.

Indeed, having indulged the reader in his skimming habit (and helped teach it to him), the newspaper is now faced with the necessity of making its stories shorter and shorter. Lending powerful impetus to this trend is the current world-shortage of print paper. The *New York Times* story of the Grant nomination, in the issue for June 7, 1872, ran to about eighteen thousand words under one heading; today even the *Times* rarely prints a story of one-tenth that length, and in most papers even the more important stories are not allowed to run much over a thousand words. In some papers, brevity has become such a fetish that one wonders if they may not wind up with the logical result of the theory behind the rule of the five W's — a paper containing only headlines and leads, accompanied by advertising, pictures, and features.

The contemporary pursuit of brevity, with its inevitable consequence of fragmentation, in all fields of communication is alarming. The reason for it, of course, lies in the feeling that the audience is incapable of continuous attention, or is too busy,

too divided in interests, too impatient and jittery, to be held
very long by any offering. One wonders if the diagnosis of the
trouble is not mistaken — if perhaps the difficulty is not less a
matter of quantity than of quality. Thus, while movie producers
think they must change the backgrounds of a picture every fifty
seconds in order to hold the audience, perhaps if a background
were compelling or satisfying enough it would not bore the
audience if retained ten times that long. And though the magazine publisher thinks he must offer his public shorter and shorter
pieces, until he gets his articles down to digests and his digests
down to quintessences in single paragraphs or sentences, perhaps
if he could only show his readers how vitally his themes touch
their deepest interests they would follow willingly and at length.
Also, though the newspaper editor, having reduced his two-
column story to "a couple of stickfuls" of type, boils it down
further to six lines and a "head," perhaps the long piece, selected
for real significance and written attractively, might be superior
in holding interest. Even the radio newscaster, ever conscious of
the minute-hand of his studio clock, might perhaps make his
show more effective by elaborating the big story and forgetting
the unimportant items.

The daily newspaper has a great advantage over the radio in
its opportunity for fuller treatment of important matters — an
advantage it should be loath to throw away. And if the newspaper asks its readers to await the issue of the weekly magazine
for adequate treatment of affairs, it is selling its birthright for
a mess of bulletins.

Much of the effort put into providing brevity for "the busy
man" is misplaced. Primarily, it is not brevity the man of affairs
wants, but significance. Of course, he does not want prolixity
or babbling, but he will take a lot of time for anything that
seems really important to him. When people say they do not
have time to read, they mean they do not have time to read
what is offered them.

Certainly much may be said for condensation and lean, succinct news writing. Paper shortages in England and many other
countries have forced the development of a crispness and terseness in newspaper writing which not only economizes in the

use of paper and printers' labor but saves readers' time as well. It is a familiar saying of editors and teachers of young reporters that the inspired author of the first chapter of Genesis described the creation of the world in seven hundred words — less than a column in any full-size newspaper. And yet it is hard to believe that the earnest reader (and should we not postulate the earnest reader?) ought not to be supplied with fairly full reports of the more important happenings in the world.

Newspaper writing has doubtless been much affected throughout the 1930's and 1940's by both the radio and the newsmagazines.

Radio style, together with a reaction against a too rigid application of the "Rule of the Five W's," has brought a trend toward leads which are easier to read and more attractive. We have always had some "feature leads," of essay or narrative type, along with the "summary leads." The tendency today is to increase the number of leads which are striking, or which make a definitely interesting statement ("punch" lines, questions, descriptive sentences), even if the "Where?" "Why?" and "How?" have to be postponed until the second, or even the third, paragraph. Of course, radio itself makes some use of the summary lead; but in general, its presentation is more informal.

What is known as "*Time* style" has had some effect on newspaper writing, too. The eccentricities of *Time*'s earlier years have exerted less influence than a kind of *style coupé* which lends itself to terseness and condensation, plus the occasional use of rather bold and vivid adjectives.

In recent years the newspapers have become highly conscious of the need for reforming news writing in order to make it more readable. The complicated problems of economics, science, and government which have become such an important part of the news are likely to make heavy reading unless great care is taken to achieve simplicity and lucidity. The United Press has long had a reputation for fresh presentation, and many of the star correspondents of the I.N.S. have displayed outstanding originality and real literary ability. The Associated Press, too, has had many top-notch writers, and ever since about 1925 it has given special attention to vigorous and lively writing. Then early in 1948, spearheaded by its Managing Editors Association, the A.P. began a readability campaign which has attracted wide attention. Dr. Rudolph Flesch, a specialist in the business of writing so that reading will be easy, was employed as a consultant.

Now, formulas for predicting reading difficulty were nothing new. They had been developed in education departments of universities and in teachers' colleges along with "basic English" word-lists, and spelling lists adapted to various levels. In 1935 the Gray-Leary formula for evaluating difficulties in reading prose was based on the number of "hard" words, pronouns, prepositional phrases, different words, and long sentences in a piece of writing. The Lorge formula, which came along four years later, was a little simpler, being founded on the proportion of "hard" words and prepositional phrases, and average sentence length.

Dr. Flesch's original formula of 1943 proposed a simple "three-pronged yardstick" for testing the readability of prose by measuring the length of sentences, counting the number of affixes, and calculating the number of "personal references." All the investigators in the field had agreed that long sentences are a bar to easy reading, and Dr. Flesch said the seventeen-word length was a good standard for the average reader. The affixes were counted because they make long and complex words. Mark Twain had a different slant on this problem. Late in his life, when he was receiving seven cents a word for everything he wrote, he remarked:

An average English word is four letters and a half long. By hard, honest labor, I've dug all the large words out of my vocabulary and shaved it down until the average is three and a half letters. . . . I never write *metropolis* for seven cents, because I can get the same price for *city*. I never write *policeman*, because I can get the same money for *cop*.

But to go on with the Flesch formula, the first two "prongs" — sentence length and affixes — had to do with ease of reading, but the third related to attractiveness of content. "Personal references" included names of, and references to, persons: proper names, like *President Truman* or *Dr. Flesch*; relationship names, such as *son, aunt, parent, sweetheart*; generic names, such as *woman, baby, miss, folks, fellow.* Included also in this category were personal pronouns.[37]

Such were the leading formulas for measuring (or, more accurately, for predicting) reading difficulty proposed before Dr. Flesch was retained as consultant by the Associated Press. In 1948 the early Flesch formula was revised somewhat. To quote the report made to the A.P. Managing Editors Association:

> The formula [now] estimates "reading ease" and "human interest."
>
> "Reading ease" is measured by the average length of words and sentences — the shorter, the easier to read. My studies have shown that an average word length of 1.5 syllables and an average sentence length of 19 words is a good standard for newspaper material.
>
> "Human interest" is measured by the percentage of "personal words" and "personal sentences." These include names, pronouns, and certain other words referring to people, and direct quotes, questions, "you"-sentences, and other sentences directly addressed to another person. The more of these personal elements, the more interesting for the average reader. My studies have shown that six per cent "personal words" and twelve per cent "personal sentences" make a good standard for news writing.[38]

The Dale-Chall formula, also promulgated in 1948, had only two elements — average sentence length and proportion of words falling outside Dr. Edgar Dale's list of three thousand words familiar to most fourth-grade school children. Dr. Flesch rejects all use of word lists (and that means virtually all formulas besides his own) because he says such use is impractical. "No newspaper man," he is quoted as saying, "can be expected to write with a word list at his elbow. If he were restricted to a list of three thousand words, he would go stark, staring mad."

That brings up the question of just what a working writer is expected to do with Dr. Flesch's own formula. At the end of *The AP Writing Handbook*, he says: "To sum up: Readability doesn't mean blindly following a formula. It means trying to write every story so that the average reader will read, understand, and remember it." And in the preface to that pamphlet, Executive Editor Alan Gould wrote: "There is no magic formula . . . The real benefit of any writing campaign is that it makes those who are putting words on paper *think* about what words to use and what combinations will be most effective."

There is really nothing inconsistent about this. Every good piece of writing is based upon rules, but the writer does not need a grammar or punctuation guide at his elbow. He has made these rules and principles his own, tucked them away somewhere in his cerebral cortex (how's that, Dr. Flesch?); and when he sits at his typewriter, he has them at his command but they do not bother or hamper the flow of his work. So it is with the principles of any kind of specialized writing. Any arbitrary formula too rigidly adhered to may endanger good writing, but a good set of principles used as a check and an aid may be very helpful.

The Flesch Associated Press drive, similar campaigns by the United Press and International News Service, and the work of Robert Gunning for the Scripps-Howard papers have done much more than introduce a formula. They have included emphasis on "sidebars" — short pieces to go along with the longer stories, commonly including "color," personalities, or human-interest features. They have emphasized "shorts," variation in leads, and smooth handling of the attribution of a story to its news sources. They have pointed up the value of terse, simple writing in a human-interest story — restrained writing, which does not overplay the point.

All this will remind the student of the history of American journalism of what Charles A. Dana's bright young men were writing for the *New York Sun* in the 1870's, and how Lincoln Steffens' staff on the *New York Commercial Advertiser* was handling the news in the 1890's. And it must also remind the realistic and catholic-minded student of literature that the best writing for the newspapers may possess qualities which we are wont to think of as distinctly literary.

Of course, those who think there is something sacrosanct about "literature," and that it has its mystic origins in the sacred fury of the Nine, will scoff at any literary pretentions of journalism. Indeed, few newspapermen will claim that even their best work is anything more than "good writing." But good writing, when it has an innate appeal to the emotions and a certain universality, may very well possess a clear title to the hallowed name of "literature."

Purposeful and informative writing has an aesthetic of its own.

"To really strenuous minds," says Walter Pater, "there is pleas-
urable stimulus in the challenge for a continuous effort on their
part, to be rewarded by securer and more intimate grasp of the
reader's sense." This writing with the double purpose of instruct-
ing the mind and pleasing the taste is precisely the best newspaper English. There is a functional beauty about it that is ab-
sent from lighter efforts in whatever field.

A fundamental requirement of style is that it should be suited
to its material and to the purpose of the particular piece of writing in question. The best reportorial style is singularly well
adapted to its aim. It has a sinewy movement; it is lean and well
trained; it is girt for speed and action. Matthew Arnold said
that "journalism is literature in a hurry." Its swift, unencumbered
movement is one of its chief beauties.

Such is the style of the best news writing. But we have much
slovenly prose in the newspapers, and in the past, at least, we
have had much that was florid. In the days when a more decorated style was fashionable in many quarters, bombast and ex-
travagance were common in the press. Perhaps the archetype of
such writing was a rhetorical piece in the *Ohio Statesman* of 1853,
entitled "A Great Old Sunset." [39] It was written by Editor S. S.
Cox, who was thereafter called, throughout a long career as Con-
gressman, diplomat, traveler, and lecturer, "Sunset" Cox. Though
the piece was much admired, and Cox was a popular man, there
was doubtless some good-natured derision in his nickname. By
the 1860's, writers of this kind of sophomoric balderdash were
being ridiculed by many critics. Who "Jenkins" was, and what
paper he worked for, are questions lost in the mazes of mid-
nineteenth-century journalism; but in the decade after the Civil
War, a reporter who overwrote his story, with exuberant images
and exaggerated figures, was called a "Jenkins." George William
Curtis, occupying the "Easy Chair" of *Harper's Magazine* in December, 1869, had some interesting things to say about this journalistic pest, who was rapidly becoming a comic figure. The essay
ended:

Meanwhile, as Mr. Jenkins is of a genial and humane temper, whose
purpose is to please his fellow-creatures, he ought to be satisfied with
the reflection that while Thucydides, and Sallust, and Gibbon, and

Grote, and Macaulay, and Motley may be read through without a
single smile, it is impossible to read Herodotus Jenkins without peals
of laughter at every line. "Small service is true service while it lasts."
Grimaldi, also, was a benefactor.

Jenkins gradually faded out of the journalistic picture. We
are reminded of him occasionally when an ambitious feature
writer "slops over," or when a city editor has to rebuke a cub
reporter for indulgence in purple passages. There is the classic
story of the young reporter sent to cover the Johnstown flood
in 1889, who began his dispatch to his paper: "God watches
tonight over the scene of disaster which was Johnstown . . ." His
editor interrupted with a rush wire: "Drop everything. Interview God."

Today there are two great reforms which are badly needed
in journalistic writing — one of them obvious and recognized, and
the other so fundamental that we often forget to insist upon it.

The better recognized need is for more freedom from the old
routine forms and more experimentation with fresh and attractive
writing. That the mainstay of the newspaper is the straightforward
workaday story is beyond question, and fancy antics with stories
that need only clear telling would be absurd; but there is wide
latitude for much more of the direct, vivid, and colorful writing
which our newspapers need to make them more attractive. Of
course, changes from any established system (in this case, especially changes in the order and organization of stories) require adjustments in editorial and mechanical processing which are not
easy to make. But as a writer in *Nieman Reports* pointed out in
April, 1950, "whenever we blame the peculiar mechanical conditions of the trade for a poor performance in our news columns,
such an 'out' is wasted on our readers. Readers expect miracles
from their newspapers, and should have them."

The less recognized need in the field of journalistic writing is
simply for more attention to the techniques and style of writing
itself. Reporters are too often looked upon as mere news-gatherers,
and "writing up" the story is merely "pounding it out" on the
"mill." The amazing excellence of some of the writing in our
newspapers excites our admiration, but the general level will
never be brought up to within hailing distance of the best until

individual reporters are led to study good writing and rewarded for achievement in that direction. Roy Roberts used to have a system for requiring the reading of a certain number of books regularly by members of his staff; perhaps that has something to do with the good writing on the *Kansas City Star*. Reporters ought to study good models. They ought to be interested in words, phrases, sentences. They ought to be encouraged, not in absurdities of writing indeed, but in honest experimentation in style and effectiveness.

But despite all the bad writing of which we have always had and always shall have far too much in our newspapers, the American press has provided throughout the years many stories which have been not only admirable as news reports but acceptable as literary performances. Collections of news stories between book covers invariably make good reading; the doubter should examine the fine Snyder and Morris *Treasury of Good Reporting*.[40] And in many newspaper pages consigned within twenty-four hours to wastepaper collection are stories which, judged both as to style and content, are comparable with the best writing in any field.

When we turn from printed news to the radio, we find the same diversity, the same appalling disparity between the best and the worst. James Bowen's description from Montevideo of the *Graf Spee* off the coast of Uruguay in 1939 was an early and memorable masterpiece. Edward R. Murrow's stories of the London blitz the next year were restrained emotionally but powerful and full of human interest, and his description of the Berlin air raid of December 2, 1943, made the day after he had been an observer in one of the bombers, was one of the high lights in the career of this master of radio news narrative. A newscast classic is the one recorded by George Hicks on board a landing craft moving toward the Normandy coast, and under attack by enemy bombers, on D-Day, June 6, 1944; after the recording had been "processed for security" in London, it was broadcast over all four networks on June 7. A great broadcast of the next year was H. R. Baukhage's story of President Roosevelt's funeral. Coverage of the national party conventions of 1948 called for the work of the country's leading radio newsmen. So did the re-

port of the election returns that year, as well as those of the conventions, campaign, and election of 1952.

The form of news over the air is less firmly fixed than that
of news in print. This is not only because radio is still more experimental than the newspaper, but also because its preparation
is much less tied in with large organizations and systems. The
form of the individual story in a radio news show still depends
a good deal on what the writer and the announcer think it ought
to be, and often the writer and announcer are the same person.
In other words, the radio story is more individualized. But this
statement must immediately be conditioned: radio has developed
some principles of presentation which are now generally observed.

The form of the radio news story was, of course, founded
upon, and developed from, that of the newspaper story. There
was, first, the matter of the lead. The summary lead as used in
newspapers makes difficult hearing; there is too much in it.
So the news writer deletes some of the details. The story is less
fully informative, but the radio has little responsibility for "the
record"; its time is limited anyway, and it must crowd in a large
number of items. It is useless to fire away with a lot of details
which do not register with the hearer. The rule is to "soften"
the lead and make it easier to grasp; the lead must "ease" the
story in. An opening like this would be a radio sin: "John Jones,
42, clerk at the Guarantee National Bank, was killed instantly
today at the corner of Main and Walnut sts., when he was struck
by a Cadillac driven by J. Wellington Smith, president of the
Tungsten Manufacturing company." Such a typical newspaper
lead would be transformed for the radio to something like this:
"Another fatal accident today at the corner of Main and Walnut
streets. John Jones, a bank clerk, was killed instantly this afternoon . . ." Short sentences, not too heavily loaded with details;
common and familiar words; a style which is conversational without being slangy or too colloquial. Simplicity, clarity, naturalness:
these are the keys to radio news style.

The story itself must be short. Even the fifteen-minute broadcast allows, with commercials, for only about two thousand
words — less than would fill two columns of an average news-

paper. Brevity is considered to be of the essence in any round-up newscast, though most of them would benefit by the elaboration of important items at the expense of some that could be thrown out.

The arrangement of stories for the show is, as a rule, a matter of departmentalization. In a typical round-up newscast, stories of international affairs are grouped together, governmental news forms another department, other national stories will make a third group, and local and regional events make a final budget. Often the newscaster will wind up his show with some bit of humor in the day's happenings. Some announcers give attention to transitions from one item to another, but most of them have little care for such refinements. There are not a few understaffed stations, moreover, on which the news announcer merely "rips and reads" the items that have come in most recently by teletype, with little or no attention to arrangement.

The disadvantages of radio as a news medium, in comparison with printed reports, are obvious enough: it offers the hearer far less variety and scope of news, more meager treatment of individual stories, and a more ephemeral presentation which does not permit rereading or checking. But when we survey the clear advantages of radio news, it becomes evident that listening and reading supplement each other and there is ample room for both. These advantages may be recapitulated in the following list.[41]

Radio news has greater speed. Its bulletins are continually and inevitably ahead of the newspaper stories; and radio has taken over the reporting of "flashes" and top bulletins ("We interrupt this program to announce —") which once made newspaper street extras necessary.

Radio and television can present special events, such as sports, great meetings, ceremonies, and sometimes even catastrophes, by eye-witnesses as they happen. Memorable examples have been the report of the Hindenburg disaster, the broadcasting of world series baseball, the story of the MacArthur return, and the reports of great political conventions.

Both radio and television can dramatize the news, as in the famous "March of Time" broadcasts.

Listening to radio news requires less effort than reading it.

The newscaster simply pours it into your ears, while you have to select what you read from the newspaper or magazine. Moreover, the shorter pieces, which radio offers, require less sustained attention.

Finally, the warmth and intimacy of the human voice give both radio and television an inestimable superiority over cold print. It must be noted, however, that the extent of this advantage depends on the skill with which the voice is employed. Good natural timbre and skill in inflections and enunciation are basic necessities in a radio voice, but they are not enough. Intelligent reading, with proper emphasis to bring out the full meaning of the phrases and sentences, is just as important.

The air seems to be full of the voices of bad readers of radio news scripts. Voices that emphasize all the unimportant prepositions in a sentence; voices that stumble and trip over proper names, and twist words that any high school freshman ought to know into almost unrecognizable vocables; smooth and mellifluous voices which seem to have no slightest adaptation to the content of the news; voices of bright young men who cannot read but who are now about to swallow their epiglottises in a brave effort to broadcast news by radio. The trouble is, of course, that modern grade schools do not teach reading aloud, and that too often young announcers have no practice in that art until they are placed before microphones with scripts in their hands.

The situation is better in the network offerings than in the station newscasts, though the hook-up shows are often bad enough in this respect. It is not that hearers demand the vocal arts and graces of trained actors; the idiosyncrasies of such men as Baukhage, Davis, and Kaltenborn are valuable as personal characteristics which endear them to their audiences. But what we do demand is something of the illusion of an intelligent man telling the people of an intelligent audience intelligibly about news in which he is interested and in which he thinks they will be interested. Such a newscast should be on a level only slightly more formal than the conversation of a cultivated man of affairs at a dinner party or in a living room — serious, but witty on occasion; richly informed, but never losing the common touch; easy and informal in delivery without being slipshod.

Doubtless the news-announcing situation will improve in the course of months and years; but it is like the careless style and poor typography of some newspapers — difficult to reform as long as the people do not complain too much about what they are getting. The stimulus of professional associations and the training of the schools should help, in the long run.

To our discussion of the forms of written news and news on the air, we should add some consideration of the form of reporting by pictures. With the growing realization that certain pictures are in themselves news has come an encouraging development of photo-journalism — which may be defined as the art of producing and editing pictures which report and comment upon the news.

Probably Confucius never said a picture was worth a thousand words; and if he did, it was one of the slips a wise man sometimes makes. A very good picture — like Joseph Rosenthal's "Flag Raising on Iwo Jima" — is worth a good many thousand words in the average newspaper, though not as much as the 265 words of the Gettysburg Address. On the other hand, a group picture captioned "Prominent Members of the State Dental Convention Now Meeting at the Grand Hotel. Left to right: James Whoosis, Charles Doke, and Frank Zilch," in which Whoosis looks as though his dentures were paining him, Doke looks like a pallbearer suffering from a hangover, and Zilch has his eyes shut, is not worth more than one noxious word — "lousy."

The key question is what makes a good picture. It must of course be good technically, with proper lighting, composition, exposure, and finishing. It must be well engraved, have an effective position in the paper and a good caption, and be well printed. But above all, it must have intelligent thinking behind it.

It seems only yesterday that the news photographer was looked upon as a queer fellow — half "roughneck" and half artist — who got in everybody's way at public events, invaded private homes, exploded stinking flashlight powder in enclosed rooms, and was notable for his big black box and his bad manners. There are still photographers of that type; and in some situations and some necessary fields of his activity, the cameraman has to be not only persistent but tough. But the modern news photographer, with his expensive equipment and his entree into important meetings, offices, and homes, is a great improvement over his prototype of a generation ago. The best of the guild today are intelligent professional gentlemen who know very well what they are doing.

They know that there is far more to shooting a good news picture than merely clicking a shutter. They know that the best photo-journalism is the result of thinking out problems of how best to make the news come alive before the eyes, as well as watchfulness for opportunities, quickness of reaction, and at least a modicum of good taste. And they have learned, too, that nothing can quite take the place of sound "picture sense" — a kind of instinctive judgment which is a gift from on high.

If pictures are to be accepted as news, they must come under the discipline of news. They must be timely; and today it is possible for photographs of events on the other side of the world to appear in a paper with telegraphic photo service and modern processing devices within less than hour of the actual happening. They must be accurate and honest; "faking" is taboo, and composite pictures, if used at all, must be conspicuously labeled as such. They must be fair; shots which misrepresent situations or personalities, even though they are actual photographs without "faking," are bad journalism.

What is the point of saturation in news pictures? When does a paper have too many, and when too few? The only answer seems to be that we always have too many poor pictures, and that we shall probably never have enough good ones.

The newsreel, originated by Pathé in France, was introduced in the United States in 1910. It underwent a great development in the twenties and had become so popular by the end of the thirties that small theaters showing only news films were set up in some large cities. The subjects were chiefly sports events and great public occurrences centering on famous national or international figures. Perhaps the most valuable were the "documentaries" — films built around some important situation, project, or problem. Of these the great "March of Time" shows were outstanding.

The newsreel show and its fortunes are tied up with the destiny of the entire motion picture industry, and what will come out of the struggle between moving pictures and television (whether in the home or the theater) is anyone's guess. TV already has some excellent network and station news shows. Whatever the issue, however, the problem of news on the screen is the same. That problem turns chiefly on questions of the value and the amount of the news screened. If the news is wisely chosen, so that it conveys significant information as well as entertainment, with a minimum of "rasslin'" shows and a maximum of great public events and personalities, the screen may become an increasingly important news medium.

In this whole matter of the patterns of news, we find ourselves looking often to the future. The newspapers are active in improving the form of their reports; the radio associations are much concerned with reforms in their field; a new generation of photojournalists have a new set of aims; and news on the screen may develop into we know not what new evolution. All we know is that the forms will always be many, and constantly changing.

CHAPTER SEVENTEEN

News Controls

A discussion of liberty of the press must begin with some observations concerning the nature of freedom. Absolute freedom in any field of activity exists only as a theoretical concept. When Jefferson wrote that the freedom of the press "cannot be limited without being lost," he was putting a philosophy of absolute ideas into a phrase which is practically misleading; or, more likely, he simply neglected to qualify his statement.[42]

Freedom is limited on every hand, from infancy to the grave. We are restrained, first, by mere physical inability to perform many acts. Our appetites, our desire to excel in sports, and our ability to perform labor are limited by such fundamental restrictions. We are restrained, second, by the rights of others. We exist in a civilized society the first rule of which is that we must live on terms with our families and our neighbors. There are many things we should like to do if we had not learned from early childhood to subdue our wills to what we fully recognize as the prerogatives of our fellows under the conventions of the society in which we live. And third, our freedom is limited by law, which is merely the governmental expression of certain of the limitations of the second class.

There is the classic story of the man who was arrested for swinging his arm in a crowd and hitting another man on the nose. Arraigned in court, the prisoner asked indignantly, "Why, Judge, haven't I got the right to swing my arm in a free country?" To which the Judge replied: "Your right to swing your arm, sir, ends where the other man's nose begins. Ten dollars."

We sometimes use the term "license" to express freedom from these accepted limitations, in order to tag with an unfavorable word the pursuit of human desires in that sector which we have given up. Thus we say it is a question of liberty versus license, when we might say, perhaps more realistically, that it is a matter of undisputed rights versus those which we have agreed to renounce, so that they are no longer "rights," but "wrongs." But it is precisely in the borderland between the area of undisputed rights and that of undisputed wrongs that all the great struggles for freedom have taken place. Just where shall we place the line between those acts which are to be forbidden for the sake of the public welfare, and those which are to be freely permitted? The conservatives and censors of our morals would enlarge the forbidden sector (always claiming that they do it for the general good), while the liberals and advocates of tolerance would enlarge that of free action. In what we call the free countries of the world, that boundary, which is always a battle-line, has been driven far to the right, into the censors' country; in autocracies it must always be far to the left.

That eternal vigilance is necessary along the frontier of freedom, even in democratic countries, is evident enough. When one reads ordered argument attacking certain guarantees in the First Amendment to the federal Constitution,[43] one becomes aware of how insidious the attack on this border line may be. Milton long ago pointed out in the *Areopagitica* how one yielding on the frontier leads to another: "If we think to regulate printing, thereby

to rectify manners, we must regulate all recreations and pas-
times, all that is delightful to man." Continually, in the past, in
the present, and in the future, there must be unrest and fighting
on the border between what is permitted to individual and group
action, on one hand, and what is forbidden in the name of the
public interest, on the other.

But our point is that such a border exists in this country and
in every country; and that in spite of the fighting along its whole
length, we must all admit that in any civilized society there
must always be two sectors. In other words, there must always
be not only an area in which freedom of action is sanctioned, but
also a sector in which individual human desires are checked and
limited for the good of all.

But let us come down to our special problem, which is the
freedom of the news. It should be obvious that there are many
clear limitations on printing, airing, and picturing the news. In
Chapter III we pointed out that the editor of a newspaper is
inevitably limited by three major elements in the situation: lack
of space in which to print all he would like to present, the non-
availability of much important news, and his knowledge of readers' demands. These limitations, though variable, are recognized
and indisputable. But they are only a beginning. They are, so
to speak, accepted conventions of the gathering and editing of
news. The limitations on freedom with which we are chiefly concerned come from outside the normal or proper functioning of
the news process.

There are two classes of invasions of the freedom of the press:
one proceeds from government, and the other consists of pressures from various groups and forces outside of government.

The classic, or historic, meaning and form of freedom of the
press is freedom from government control. That is what the term
originally meant, and that is its sole meaning in many parts of
the world today. The reason for this is clear: except where government is truly democratic, it is the natural enemy, and the
first and foremost enemy, of liberty of the press.

During the first century of the history of newspapers, there
was not a government in the world which did not look upon them
as a dangerous nuisance, to be abated if possible, and to be tol-

erated only under strict control. Roger L'Estrange, when he accepted his office as licenser of the English press in May, 1680, said: "A Newspaper makes the multitude too familiar with the actions and Councils of their Superiors, and gives them not only an itch, but a kind of colourable Right and Licence to be meddling with the Government."

The same ideas prevailed in the transatlantic frontiers of England. Sir William Berkeley, for thirty-eight years governor of Virginia, wrote to his home government in 1671:

> But, I thank God, we have not free Schools nor Printing; and I hope we shall not have these Hundred Years. For learning has brought Disobedience and Heresy and Sects into the world, and Printing has divulged them and libels against the Government, . . . God keep us from both.

This pious wish was fulfilled, so far as a permanent press in Virginia was concerned, until 1730. But slowly, decade by decade, in English-speaking lands and in Europe, the press was making its perilous way. Its progress was part of the advance of the common people, whose guide and weapon it was. No wonder arbitrary governments regarded it as "a dangerous engine"! The threat of Richard Brinsley Sheridan, uttered in the English House of Commons in 1810, still rings down the years:

> Give me but the liberty of the press, and I will give to the Minister a venal House of Peers — I will give him a corrupt and servile House of Commons — I will give him the full sway of the patronage of office . . . and yet I will go forth to meet him undismayed. I will attack the mighty fabric he has raised with that mightier engine; I will shake down from its height corruption, and bury it amidst the ruins of the abuses it was meant to shelter.

Slow though it was, the advance of the press against governmental opposition was sure and inevitable. In the American Colonies, the newspapers were a major instrumentality throughout the entire struggle for independence. When the new federal Constitution was submitted to the states in 1787, however, it contained no provision for liberty of the press. The reasoning of Alexander Hamilton, which was based on a clear perception of the uncertain boundary which exists between the liberties freely permitted to the press and the area in which there are bound to be limitations, had prevailed in the constitutional convention. Hamilton argued: "What signifies a declaration that 'the Liberty of the Press shall be inviolably preserved'? What is the Liberty of the Press? Who can give it any definition which does not leave the utmost latitude for evasion? I hold it to be impracticable . . ." [44]

Virginia, however, at the urging of Jefferson, and other states decided to condition their ratification of the Constitution upon the addition of a Bill of Rights which should include a declaration for liberty of the press. Accordingly, at its first session, the Congress voted favorably upon a set of amendments to the Constitution, later adopted by the states, which began: "Congress shall make no law respecting an establishment of religion, or prohibiting the free exercise thereof; or abridging the freedom of speech, or of the press . . ."

The wisdom of the inclusion of this provision in the Constitution has been demonstrated over and over again as the Supreme Court has used it as the basis for repeated decisions protecting freedom of utterance in newspapers and periodicals.

To be sure, the Sedition Act of 1798 constituted an infringement by Congress on freedom of the press. In later years, such a law would have been declared unconstitutional by the Supreme Court; but this was before John Marshall had announced, in the epochal Marbury v. Madison decision (1803), the right of the Court to set aside acts of Congress which were in conflict with the Constitution. So the Sedition Act ran its course until it expired with the Adams administration; but so widespread and so bitter was the opposition to this legislation designed to prevent press criticism of government, that it became one of the chief causes of the fall of the Federalist party. Congress later repaid many of the fines levied under the obnoxious law, and has never since been misled into the commission of a similar infringement on this basic freedom.

Meanwhile, the Supreme Court extended its watchfulness to enactments of State legislatures which threatened to deprive American citizens of rights guaranteed them under the federal Constitution. Jefferson and the advocates of States' rights were distressed, but nothing could stop this logical course of our jurisprudence. Outstanding cases related to the freedom of the press which have been decided under this development (as implemented by the Fourteenth Amendment) in recent years were those which went against the Minnesota "Gag Law" in 1931 and the Huey Long tax on newspaper advertising in Louisiana in 1936. The decision in the former case was written by Charles Evans Hughes, who pointed out that censorship by injunction — even that of "scandalous and defamatory" papers — is contrary to the Bill of Rights. Justice George Sutherland wrote the decision of a unanimous court in the Louisiana case, holding that Long's newspaper tax was "a deliberate and calculated device . . . to limit the circulation of information to which the public is entitled by virtue of the constitutional guarantees."

The Louisiana case suggests the question of how far newspapers can go in arguing that regulation of their business affairs is an infringement of freedom of the press. The Supreme Court has kept to the principle that what it is protecting under the First Amendment is the right of the people to a free flow of information rather than the right of publishers to make profits. This sometimes requires drawing a fine line, since anything affecting publishers' profits may — sometimes obliquely, and sometimes very directly — affect the free flow of information. But in general the doctrine is that newspapers are never to be specially favored in respect to regulations which control any type of business operation, or in regard to social legislation, or in matters of monopoly regulation. In 1946 the Supreme Court rejected the contention of the American Newspaper Publishers Association that newspapers should be exempted from the application of the "wage and hour law" on the basis of the First Amendment. Frederick S. Siebert, an authority on the law of the press, declares that "the courts are reluctant to extend the meaning of the constitutional guarantees of freedom of the press to cover social and economic regulations, or to grant any special immunities to publishers because of the nature of their service to the public." [45] Some publishers are far too prone to shout "Liberty of the press!" when their pocketbooks are touched, using that rallying-cry as a kind of caveat against interference with their business. This is bad policy for the publisher, since it obscures a fact which he should always insist upon — that liberty of the press is primarily the people's responsibility, based as it is on their right to know.

In the Minnesota "Gag Law" case, Chief Justice Hughes listed some of the limitations which government does place upon the press, thus indicating the area of restriction of liberty for the general good:

"When a nation is at war, many things that might be said in time of peace are such a hindrance to its effort that their utterance will not be endured so long as men fight, and no Court could regard them as protected by any constitutional right." (Schenck v. United States, 249 U.S. 47, 52.) No one would question that a government might prevent actual obstruction to its recruiting service, or the publication of the sailing dates of transports, or the number and location of troops. On similar grounds, the primary requirements of decency may be enforced against obscene publications. The security of the community life may be protected against incitements to acts of violence and the overthrow by force of orderly government . . ."[46]

War censorship is difficult and dangerous. In announcing the appointment of Byron Price as director of censorship a few days after the United States entered the Second World War, President Roosevelt wrote: "All Americans abhor censorship, just as they abhor war. But the experience of this and of all other nations has demonstrated that some degree of censorship is essential in war time, and we are at war." Mr. Price administered his duties well, with a minimum of complaint from press and people. Field censorship was a different matter, sometimes handled with reason and justice, sometimes unfair and unintelligent.

Antipathies between commanding officers and field correspondents are traditions of great wars. In the midst of the Civil War, which was more thoroughly covered by the newsmen than any war had ever been before, General W. T. Sherman wrote to his brother, Senator John Sherman, that the correspondents were "doing infinite harm." They revealed every plan for a surprise movement, he said. "The only really successful strokes out here," he wrote in the midst of the Vicksburg campaign, "have succeeded because of the absence of the newspapers, or by throwing them off the trail." One day when Sherman was informed that three correspondents had just been killed by enemy shells, he exclaimed,

"Good! Now we shall have news from hell before breakfast!" [47]
After the war, Sherman once refused to shake hands with Horace
Greeley because, he said, the *New York Tribune* had revealed certain details of his Carolina campaign of 1865, the publication of
which had resulted in heavy losses.

General Sherman is an extreme example, but many less out-
spoken commanders felt much as he did. Many years later, in the
Spanish-American War, General W. R. Shafter banished all Hearst
men from captured Santiago. In the Chino-Japanese War of 1894–
1895 efforts of news correspondents were severely curtailed on
both sides; English commanders kept a very strict control of newsmen during their 1900 war with the Boers; and the harassed reporters of the Russo-Japanese War of 1904–1905 had so much to
say of the persecution to which they had been subjected by the
commanding generals that many observers concluded that the
days of field reporting were over and the "war correspondent"
was a figure of the past.

But much better systems of war reporting from the field have
been evolved in recent wars. With great difficulty, after long
arguments and through the exertion of heavy pressures, the commanders of the military forces of western nations have generally
agreed to eyewitness reporting of military operations under codes
of field censorship which, though variable, have generally been
reasonable. The administration of such rules has sometimes been
incompetent and sometimes coöperative. The old antipathies
sometimes burst out, as in the denunciation of certain well-known
war correspondents by General Willoughby (endorsed by General MacArthur) in *Hearst's International Cosmopolitan* in December, 1951. On the other hand, many officers of the United
States Armed Forces have in recent years shown an active, intelligent, and helpful interest in the situation and the problems of war
reporting.

The great dangers of war censorship of the news, aside from
untrained and inept administration, are three. First, known and
accepted control of the news always encourages rumor; and
rumor, irresponsible and uncontrollable, is dangerous to public
morale and political action. Second, there is always a tendency
to withhold bad news, on the theory (often only an ill-judged

pretext) that the enemy will not otherwise be informed of our losses. In this case, the old familiar epigram of John Milton is reversed, and *good* news "rides post," while *evil* news "baits." The result is a distortion of the news picture which defeats the whole purpose to which our system is committed — that of full information within the limits of military security. Third, censorship, the basic phases of which must be in the hands of civil servants, is too apt a means of political manipulation to be unused for that purpose.

All this does not mean that, on the whole, the American people have not received a fairly adequate day-by-day report of the news of recent wars. It does mean that such news has been gathered under great difficulties and as the result of a constant struggle for open sources and clear channels.

There is one kind of censorship, however, which is not administered by any director or formulated in any code. This is censorship at the news source. In World War II there were many complaints about the difficulty of getting prompt news releases from the Navy Department. In Washington today there are certain offices and bureaus which the newsmen find "hard to crack," and many in which much information of public concern is suppressed. James S. Pope, of the *Louisville Courier-Journal*, is chairman of a committee of the American Society of Newspaper Editors which is trying "to educate the administrative offices of the government on what we consider a basic fact in our democracy: all the news of government belongs by right to the people." In a recent Kappa Tau Alpha lecture, Mr. Pope stated the matter well:

We recognize that certain activities and plans and decisions within the government should not be made public at a time when knowledge of them would clearly damage the public welfare — such as changes of policy by the Federal Reserve Board, affecting the stock market; military information affecting the national security, and diplomatic affairs linked to this security. But it is inevitable that secrecy breeds secrecy, and that for every piece of information justifiably concealed, tens and hundreds are submerged in the "system." And it is a fact that, whereas our national government swarms with officials empowered to hold back and shape information, there is literally no authority with the simple job of probing around and forcing open all the wells of information that should be open to us. Every employe of the government can build his own little dam, but nobody is employed to destroy them.

The cult of secrecy is not, of course, restricted to Washington. Our committee files are filled with cases of news suppression by state and local officials. It is heartening to discover two things about these new cases: (1) small-paper editors are fighting back promptly, and (2) small-time dictators are retreating promptly.

Reluctance of news sources, even when they are servants of the people, is nothing new; what is new is the present aggressive, organized campaign to smoke them out.

Thus far we have been discussing liberty of the press in its classic, or historic, sense — freedom of control by "authority." We must now consider the questions relating to the freedom of the modern press from other controls — political, economic, social — which, in one way or another, may exert sufficient pressure on the press to affect its news policy.

Nearly all groups, as well as many individuals, bring pressure on the newspapers. They want this or that movement promoted, or they want themselves publicized. The great minority classes of our society organize for the purpose of gaining publicity for the favorable activities of their groups. All this we call propaganda, and much of it is designed to be urged upon the press. We are not concerned here with the part of this promotional material which is acceptable to the newspaper and radio in due course, but we must consider as invasions of press freedom all that which is forced on them by stubborn insistence wearing away rejection, or by the impact of vocal groups compelling advocacy of reforms or counterreforms or more abstract ideologies.

Every newspaper editor is acquainted with such pressures. He is in the midst of them all the time. In general, they are a healthful influence. Wacky and troublesome though some of these "causes" are, it is as well that most of them should be heard. "Let the whole orchestra sound forth," discordant though it may sometimes be.

These pressures do not alarm us as much as those exerted on the financial side of the newspaper. Under the American press system of freedom from authority, there are no subsidies underwriting the publication of the news; and the newspapers must pay their own way. If we were to take newspapers out of the realm of "free enterprise," we should have to seek for them subsidies which would place them under the control and direction of the government, or of parties or organized groups which would finance them, thus shutting them off forever from other pressures and from the direct influence of the people. Without such drastic change in our press system, American journalism must remain both a business and a profession, as it has been from the very beginning. Newspapers, news-magazines, and radio and television stations must be going concerns financially, as well as agencies of service to the public, if they are to remain free from the control of government and parties.

But if they are business ventures, they must show profits; and this makes their news policies economically vulnerable. Since more than half a newspaper's revenue is derived from paid advertising, it is often asserted that advertisers exercise a sinister influence on its policies.

It is foolish to deny that influential advertisers sometimes keep something out of some newspapers and get other things in. The son of a department store owner gets into trouble, or there is an elevator accident in a certain store; and the newspaper may obligingly cut the item down to six lines and bury it on page seventeen. This is bad journalism, but it does no great harm. If the advertiser makes more sweeping demands — if, for example, he asks that the paper "lay off" an exposure of some local abuse, that is a different matter. It is fair to say that few newspapers would submit to that kind of dictation. Newspapers are continually making such exposures, and they almost never make them without stepping on the toes of some advertisers. There are always some venal publishers, of course; but on most newspapers such a demand as has been suggested is rarely made, and if made, would not be heeded.

It is rarely made because the advertiser himself (a) is usually not a scoundrel, and (b) is a businessman. As a businessman, he places his advertising not as a favor to the publisher but because he cannot do business without it. He may hate the very entrails of the publisher and come close to an apoplectic stroke every time he reads the paper; but if his business requires a full page of advertising in the despised sheet, he will place it and pay for it willingly. In fact, he is not likely to endanger his advertising by quarreling with the editor, for he knows that newspapers are quick to refuse advertisements submitted with threats and warnings. Most newspapers in these days are too well established to be easily frightened by a bellicose businessman.

Yet critics continue to regard advertising as the *bête noir* of free journalism. When the New York *PM* was launched as an adless daily, President F. D. Roosevelt sent his good wishes: "Your proposal to sustain your enterprise simply by merchandising information, with the public as your only customer, appeals to me as a new and promising formula for freedom of the press." But the promises of the formula were not fulfilled; nor would such advertising as its circulation might have attracted have affected the content of *PM's* news columns. Arthur Hays Sulzberger, publisher of the *New York Times*, writing in 1945, pointed out that about 20 per cent of his paper's revenue was obtained from retail advertising; then he added:

Only in the retail group . . . could you pick out, say, twenty-five merchants who might hope by economic pressure to influence the freedom of our editorial expression. Well, I admit they might try it, but I can tell you very definitely that they have not done so; and I would point out further that since these are advertisers who deal directly with a mass of consumers, every business instinct must suggest to them the avoidance of interference on matters on which their customers differ.

I have gone into this at length, for I should like to knock down once and for all the fallacious notion that advertisers are a venal influence upon editorial policies, and point out, conversely, that it isn't the advertising but the lack of advertising of which you should be fearful. When advertising revenue is non-existent or insufficient, as was conspicuously the case in France before the war, then watch out! [48]

There is, however, another and, on the whole, a more sinister angle to this matter of economic pressures upon American journalism. Publishers of newspapers and news-magazines and owners of radio stations are themselves businessmen, and their natural sympathies are with business and ownership and what President Roosevelt used to call "economic royalism." If they are conducting metropolitan dailies, they are indeed in "big business," for such papers are multi-million-dollar properties. Attitudes and sympa-

thies inhere within economic groups; and those of the businessman react unfavorably toward such modern phenomena as the
techniques of labor organization, the increasing socialization in
many fields, controls in trade and industry, and many social reforms. This does not mean that all publishers are opposed to such
things; certainly not all of them are. But a large majority of them
are faithful to their own guild and naturally espouse their own
causes.

We shall pursue the question of publishers' attitudes somewhat
further in connection with the ensuing discussion of "monopoly"
ownership of newspapers; but for the present our query is whether
or not the undoubtedly conservative leanings of the great majority
of owners and publishers, particularly on economic issues, actually
operate as controls in the publication of the news in American
papers. In the present state of content-analysis study, there can
be no comprehensive statistical answer to this question. What we
have to rely upon chiefly is a set of conclusions formed on the
basis of a careful and unprejudiced reading of large numbers of
newspapers over a considerable period of time. Most sincere and
informed critics, with such backgrounds of study, will agree that
there are some papers — not many, but a few — which, influenced
by ownership, print angled Washington letters and colored political news, mostly under by-lines, and provide such headline display and positioning of stories as to distort important parts of
the general news picture. They will agree, further, that many
papers, while they abstain from serious distortion of the news itself, do habitually "play" the news by position and headlining, in
such a fashion as to overemphasize the paper's position on current
issues. The responsibility for such a policy — as for all general
newspaper policies — rests on the publisher. It will also be agreed
that the reporting of some kinds of news of controversy is often
badly done. Labor and strike news is in this class, though it must
be admitted that reporting in this field has improved tremendously in the last two decades.[49]

But sincere and informed critics must also agree, upon survey-
ing the whole field of American news reporting and editing, that
in the great majority of our newspapers there is a full and reasonably "objective" coverage of events and situations. A genuine de-

votion to the ideal of the "objective" report is an outstanding characteristic of American news and newsmen today. The historical development of this concept as a controlling factor has been traced in earlier pages of the present volume (Chapter VIII). It is not necessary here to review again the progress of independence from partisan control, though we may once more point out a fact which will be clear in the minds of all readers — that in a national political campaign, when issues are hotly contested and prejudices are rife, speeches of candidates and pronouncements of leaders on both sides are fully and fairly presented even in highly partisan papers. This is a quadrennial test of a system of fair news presentation which works pretty well year in and year out. It is simply unrealistic to think that American publishers are accustomed to tailor their news to fit their personal opinions, prejudices, and whims. On the contrary, it may be said that generally, and in most newspapers, the owner, the publisher, the editors, and the reporters are united in defense of freedom of the news and against pressures for the distortion of "objective" reports.

This is precisely what the Russian critics of our papers deny. They choose to forget the whole matter of the classic liberty of the press from government control; and thus they claim that their own press is "free," being subject to none of the pressures that beset American and English papers simply because in a totalitarian dictatorship those pressures are not allowed to exist. Then, in speaking of our own papers, they are again blind to the freedom from state control which is so precious to us as one of the glories of our press system, but assert with fine abandon that American newspapers are the slaves of entrenched wealth, Wall Street, and economic warmongers. Their evaluation of our papers is not greatly different, indeed, from that of the more severe American critics, who, untroubled by too much knowledge or understanding of our news system, exaggerate the sinister influence of a kind of underworld of economic werewolves.

But there is another set of factors which, although perhaps outside the classification of infringements on the liberty of the press, are nevertheless closely related to the problems of free circulation of the news. We refer to the growth of "chain" ownership of news-

papers, and to the trend to consolidation of papers. These developments have been found alarming by many observers, and they are
constantly referred to by writers on contemporary problems. They
were the basis, for example, of the chief anxieties of the Luce-
Hutchins "Commission on Freedom of the Press." [50]

Newspaper "chains," or "groups," as they are more properly
called, differ greatly in size, distribution, and operation. There
were fifty-four of them in the American daily newspaper field in
1950, if we include all which owned, or partially owned, papers
in more than one city. They vary in size from two-paper groups
to one which includes twenty papers. Most of them are state or
regional in extent, but a few are national in scope. The total number of papers belonging to these groups, whether by majority or
minority control, is 316, comprising 17.8 per cent of the English-
language dailies of general circulation in the United States. Most
of the papers in these groups have small or medium-sized circulations; but four (the large Hearst and Scripps-Howard "chains"
and the small McCormick and Knight groups) include some papers with very large circulations. About one-eighth of the total
number of papers in group organizations are in the hundred-
thousand-circulation class, and the aggregate circulation of all
group papers amounts to about 40 per cent of the aggregate for
all the dailies in the country.[51]

While recent decades have shown a slight but steady increase
in group-ownership of smaller papers, that of larger papers has
declined since the thirties. The Hearst group, which comprised
twenty-five in 1937, now numbers sixteen; and the Scripps-Howard papers, which had twenty-five in 1929, now have nineteen.

There are great differences between the various groups in the
tightness of the control exercised by the overall management.
The chief values of such organization are supposed to be on the
business side, and there is much sharing of techniques and
the "know-how" of newspaper management. During the lifetime
of W. R. Hearst, his editors often received directives about the
handling of news, but that was exceptional; most groups expect
their papers to be "on their own" in respect to details of news
coverage. Some groups extend this laissez-faire to general news
policy; but in general, an emphasis on sensationalism, or on

"hard" news, or on local coverage will be found to characterize a whole group.

The question with which we are chiefly concerned here is whether such an organization of newspapers as has been described interferes with the free circulation of a full and fair news report to the people. In some cases it has made better papers and in some worse ones, but the inescapable fact is that the great majority of papers in these groups are good papers. The system makes for greater concentrations of wealth, and most of us will hold that against it. But the group organization principle itself, whatever other objections may be raised against it, cannot be said to have been generally injurious to the copious distribution of a good news report.

Similar in some respects to the "chain" development, but introducing many new elements, is the trend toward consolidation of newspapers. These mergers have been taking place ever since 1741, when the *New England Weekly Journal* and the *Boston Gazette* were consolidated; but in the last forty years an acceleration of the trend has brought us to the point where many of our cities and towns have only one paper each or two papers (morning and evening) under a single ownership.

The causes of these modern consolidations have been five in number.

(1) The wish to have opposition parties and cliques all represented in a given town or city had resulted in the establishment of more papers than were necessary to serve the public with either news or advertising; and with the decline of partisan feeling as a dominant motive in American journalism, it became possible to reduce the number of papers.

(2) Advertisers found it cheaper to buy space in one paper with a general circulation, even at increased rates, than in two with overlapping coverage.

(3) Combinaton of a morning with an evening paper, allowing for twenty-four-hour operation of a single plant, made for economy.

(4) Mounting costs, caused partly by the necessity of producing better modern papers, forced the elimination of unnecessary competition.

(5) This competition became increasingly "unnecessary" as readers, faced by a growing supply of news and entertainment from the radio, news-magazines, etc., tended to turn to one morning and one evening paper in each city, weakening the others.

Consolidations had been going on steadily for many years, when Frank A. Munsey dramatized the trend in 1916–1924 by his spectacular operations in New York. In this period, which included the years of America's participation in the First World War, and the decade of high costs which immediately followed, the fever for consolidations raged throughout the whole of the country. It had been working havoc among the weeklies since the turn of the century; now it struck the small dailies devastatingly, though it was more spectacular when it affected the great metropolitan papers.

During the ensuing decades the consolidations continued, steadily reducing the number of papers being published. In the depression thirties, the proportion of cities having two or more English-language daily papers fell from 21 per cent to 11.6 per cent; and that of cities having only one paper rose correspondingly from 79 per cent to 88.4 per cent.[52] It is even more striking to note what has happened to cities of 100,000 population or over in the last twenty years. In 1930 there were just nine such cities which did not have two or more English-language daily newspapers under separate ownership, and four of them (Cambridge and Somerville, Massachusetts; Elizabeth and Jersey City, New Jersey) adjoined great urban centers so closely that they were in the circulation territory of large metropolitan papers. Actually, there were only two one-newspaper cities of that size out of the range of great metropolitan purlieus — Des Moines, Iowa, and Duluth, Minnesota. But two decades later, in 1950, out of the 106 cities of 100,000 or over, an even fifty had single-management newspaper situations; that is, in nearly half of our large cities, there was either a single newspaper, or there were two papers owned and operated by the same corporation, or (in seven cases) two papers separately owned and edited but operated as a unit on the business side.[53]

In the smaller cities the reduction to single daily papers or single-ownership units has been even more general. Thus, while the country's population increased by about two-thirds between 1910 and 1950, and aggregate *circulation* of dailies more than doubled, the *number* of dailies decreased by about one-sixth. In the weekly field, where overcrowding of newspapers was more apparent than among the dailies, the consolidation movement gained headway somewhat earlier and seemed to reach a point of stabilization about the middle thirties; by that time the number of weeklies had been reduced from the 1910 figure by about one-fourth.

A corollary of this sharp reduction in the number of newspapers by consolidations and suspensions is the difficulty faced by anyone who wishes to start a new paper. It is safe to say that it would cost several million dollars to undertake a paper in any one of our fifty largest cities, and that even then the risk of failure would be very great in any one of them. Only Marshall Field's auditors know how much he put into the *Chicago Sun*. Even in small cities, considerable sums have to be risked to gain a foothold in competition with established dailies. In the weekly field the situation is somewhat different; a humble beginning may be made for ten or twenty thousand dollars, though the risks are always considerable.

There is nothing reprehensible, or even avoidable, about all this. It is a part of the universal trend of business and industry in the United States throughout the past generation. It is not the result of the machinations of monopolistic publishers, ruthless in their determination to kill off all competition; it is, rather, the effect of a struggle for survival in the face of rising costs. The effect of the Amendment to the Clayton Act, which became effective December 29, 1950, upon newspaper consolidations is still uncertain at this writing. Of course, antimonopoly legislation will not keep alive economically doomed newspapers. Herbert Brucker, editor of the *Hartford Courant*, makes the following suggestive comparison in his admirable book, *Freedom of Information*:

Standard-broadcast radio in the United States is limited to some two thousand stations because there is physically room for only that many in the spectrum. It may be that during the first half of the twentieth century a comparable economic spectrum has come into existence, and there is room in the United States for only a fixed, or perhaps even a shrinking, number of daily newspapers.

What does this mean in terms of free circulation of the news? Does it mean, as some would have us believe, that in hundreds of cities and thousands of smaller towns the community is permitted to receive only such one-sided news as an editorial dictator chooses to furnish it? John Stuart Mill declared in his essay on "Liberty" that "the only way in which a human being can make some approach to knowing the whole of a subject is by hearing what can be said about it by persons of every variety of opinion . . . No wise man ever acquired wisdom in any mode but this." Have our single-newspaper-ownership communities been forced to renounce this way to wisdom?

Such a conclusion is, of course, preposterous. In the first place, the single-ownership combinations which are so common in our cities are often so organized that there is sharp competition between the news staffs of the morning and evening papers. In the second place, papers in a monopoly situation are usually acutely conscious of the necessity of full and fair news service. When the *Des Moines Register* and *Tribune* bought out its last competitor, the *Capital*, a staff member remarked to Editor Harvey Ingham, "Now we can have our own way, can't we?" Ingham replied, "On the contrary. We must now be far more careful than ever before to give both sides of all questions; we are our own competition." A paper in such a situation is by no means invulnerable: it is subject to decreases of circulation if it grows lax in its service, followed by inevitable drops in revenue from both circulation and advertising. Such papers are continually aware that their security even in a comparatively noncompetitive and profitable situation depends on putting out a good paper every day.

The proper evidence on which to base a decision as to whether papers in a monopoly situation are doing a good job can be derived only from an examination of the papers themselves. It is believed that such an examination will demonstrate that such papers generally show a better grade of performance than those in competitive situations in comparable communities, and that they commonly maintain fair and many-sided coverage. The largest American city with a "monopoly" newspaper situation is Minneapolis, where the *Star* and *Tribune*, with independent news and editorial-page staffs, issue well-balanced papers. Executive Editor Gideon Seymour wrote not long ago, in "A Memo to a New Reporter": "We are jealously proud of the freedom of our news columns from slanted stories and biased selection of news." The second largest American city with single-ownership of its newspapers is Kansas City, where the famous *Star* and *Times* are published by a corporation composed of staff members. Few papers are regarded with so much affection by so many throughout any area. They certainly furnish a notably full coverage of local, regional and foreign news. The next city is Memphis, Tennessee, with its two great papers, the *Commercial Appeal* and the *Press-Scimitar*, under one management; and the next is Oakland, California, with Joseph R. Knowland's *Tribune*. Fifth in the list of single-management cities, according to size, is Louisville, Kentucky, where the *Courier-Journal* and *Times*, under the direction of Barry Bingham and Mark F. Ethridge, would rank high in any informed person's list of the great American newspapers.

In fact, we have just listed five of the foremost newspapers and newspaper combinations of the country. As we go on down the list, we are struck with the inescapable truth that nearly all the papers in single-ownership situations are very good papers. There are a few stumblers, but the level is high indeed. We are forced to listen with respect to the declaration of Publisher John Cowles, of the Minneapolis consolidated newspapers, which was made at the University of Missouri's Journalism Week exercises of 1951:

I say flatly that, with only a small number of exceptions, the best newspapers in America are those which do not have newspapers competing with them in their local fields. By "best" I mean the most responsibly edited, the fairest, the most complete, the most accurate, the best written, and the most objective.

This statement must be conditioned, as Mr. Cowles proceeded to condition it, by making exceptions of New York and Washington, each a unique journalistic field; and adding to the "best" papers, as he also suggested, a number which are published in uncontested morning or evening fields in our large cities. Mr. Cowles went on to say:

The reason why the newspapers that do not have local daily news-paper competition in their home field are superior, generally speaking, to those that do have competition are manifold.

In the first place, the publishers and editors have, I believe, a deeper feeling of responsibility because they are alone in their field.

Secondly, those newspapers that are not in hotly competitive fields are better able to resist the constant pressure to over-sensationalize the news, to play up the cheap crime or sex story, to headline the story that will sell the most copies instead of another story that is actually far more important. The daily that is alone in its field can be as free as it wants to be from the urge to magnify the tawdry and salacious out of its importance in the news of the day. The newspaper that is alone in its field can present the news in better perspective and can free the news of details which pander rather than inform.

Newspapers that don't have local newspaper competition are better able to resist the pressure of immediacy which makes for incomplete, shoddy and premature reporting. This pressure has become one of the worst enemies of responsible reporting. It breeds inaccuracies which can never be overtaken. It is responsible for distorted emphasis and lack of perspective. The newspaper in a single ownership city doesn't have to rush on to the streets with a bulletin rumor than Russian troops are invading Yugoslavia if it has reason to suspect that the un-confirmed report may not be true. It does not have to protect itself against a rival in case the story turns out by a long-shot chance to be accurate . . .

Moreover, it should not be forgotten that what we call "mo-nopoly newspaper situations" are by no means monopoly *news* situations. As we pointed out earlier in this volume (Chapter II), there are many channels of news in any American community besides that afforded by the local newspaper. Some of these cities with only one paper are near enough to other urban centers to get their news from outside papers if they prefer, or to supple-ment the local daily with one from nearby; such is the case in Oakland, across the bay from San Francisco, or indeed in Min-neapolis, adjoining St. Paul. In any case, there are the network and local news programs of the radio and television — not only those which may be owned by local publishers, but many others, up and down the dial. And there are the periodicals and papers on the newsstands or in the mails — *Time, Newsweek, Life,* and all the rest. And there are many other sources of news, oral and printed and pictured.

These considerations remove some of the bogies from the situation created by the declining number of newspapers. They tend to make such catchwords as "the vanishing marketplace of thought" thoroughly ridiculous.[54] Raymond B. Nixon has pointed out that "The readers of Horace Greeley's *Weekly Tribune*, most of whom probably received no other periodical of news and comment, suffered far more from a lack of diversification than do readers anywhere in America today." Perhaps such facts may cause us to wonder why so many watchful critics of our journalism and our democracy make so much fuss over the decline in the number of newspapers. It seems clear that there are two answers to such a question. First, effects of that decline have never been studied in sufficient detail, and most critics have been too impatient to observe even the general outlines of the actual result. Second, many sincere observers feel that in the present situation, too much depends upon the intelligent realization of responsibilities on the part of the publishers of "monopoly" papers. They feel that there is a little too much of the "benevolent dictator" in the picture. What will happen, they say, when such papers grow to feel too secure in their power? Or when new owners without newspaper backgrounds come into control?

After all, as Wilson Harris, editor of the London *Spectator*, points out in his book, *The Daily Press*, "everything depends on the reasons a publisher has for being a publisher. The motive may be simply an ambition for power; it may be a desire to acquire power for worthy ends; it may be merely political; it may be merely commercial; it may be a mixture." Basil Walters once observed to the present writer: "The two things that make a great newspaper are, first, an owner's honest heart, and, second, a faithful news report." In short, too much is being risked upon the backgrounds, the attitudes, and the motives of newspaper owners and publishers.

Power is a dangerous and often corrupting influence, and it is hard for most of us to overcome an almost instinctive mistrust of the rich and powerful publisher. If our mistrust were supported by an array of sound data showing that these wealthy publishers, or any considerable proportion of them, were in the habit of twisting and manipulating the news to suit their own purposes, the world would seem a little more ordered and logical. But apparently they are infected with much the same notions about "objective" news that have taken possession of their editors and reporters. We do not have to give them credit for any shred of altruism in this; they are smart businessmen selling news as their chief commodity, and much concerned to keep the product a good one so that sales will keep an upward curve. Of course, most great American publishers have come from newspaper families, and most great American papers are controlled by newspaper money — which is clearly an advantage to good journalism. Actually, it would be quite possible to name some very high-minded publishers, and we may get around to doing that in the next chapter. But it is hard, we repeat, to abandon the concept of the rich newspaper publisher as the villain in the play; and the least we can say is that he will bear watching.

While our discussion of liberty of the press has been concerned chiefly with the freedom of the newspaper to gather, print, and distribute the news, it must not be forgotten that the Bill of Rights forbids legislative invasion "of freedom of speech, or of the press," and that the liberty of speech guaranty is radio's palladium. Thus most of the philosophy, and even of the history, of freedom of the press reviewed in the preceding pages has equal application to newspaper and radio. But there is one great difference: the laws of physics limit the number of channels practically available for regular broadcasting in the United States to ninety-six, and the wisest possible use of them seems to allow for only about 2300 regular (or amplitude modulation) stations of varying power. If careful allocation of frequencies were not made and enforced within an overall pattern, there would be unlimited interference, and we should have no good broadcasting. Therefore we have set up a governmental agency to assign frequencies and grant licenses to broadcast. But there is no such natural limitation of activity in newspaper publishing; unless print paper some time becomes so extremely scarce as to require allocation by authority, there will never be a conceivable need to limit the number of papers published, and no "necessity of nature" to issue licenses for operation.

Licensing inevitably means control. Why grant a license to one applicant and not to another? Obviously, the licensing agency must erect a set of standards and then see that the operating stations meet those standards in order to keep their licenses. Such rigid but minimum control is a necessity to the system. The question which concerns us here is to what extent this system involves censorship of the content and extent of broadcast news.

A glance at the historical development of the licensing system is necessary. The first law for the regulation of radio was the Communications Act of 1912, which placed the Department of Commerce in charge of such operations, at that time conducted mainly by marine services. When commercial radio had its big development in the mid-twenties, and the Department of Commerce attempted to deny licenses to some applicants and enforce its frequency assignments, it met a check in the courts; and a kind of anarchy soon developed in the air waves, resulting in interference and jamming in all channels. This situation was met by the enactment of the Federal Radio Act of 1927, which established a Commission to assign frequencies and administer the provisions of the law. It was in this Act that the phrase "in the public interest, convenience, and necessity" was first used as a description of the proper services of radio. Further developments in the field in the next seven years required new legislation, and in 1934 Congress passed the Federal Communications Act, which established a seven-member Federal Communications Commission to have charge of the regulation of the telegraph, telephone, and radio facilities of the country.

The F.C.C. not only issues licenses under a set of standards based on "the public interest, convenience, and necessity," but it reëxamines these licenses every three years to see whether stations are observing its standards. Its decisions and pronouncements form a body of what may be loosely called "radio law." Two examples relating to newscasting may be cited.

In 1946 the Commission issued a "blue book" entitled *Public Service Responsibility of Broadcast Licensees*, in which it insisted that more than half the time in a news program should be directed to local news, and less than half to wire news. Outcry by the wire agencies resulted in some modification of definitions; it was decided that a "local live" program might consist of "substantially edited and rewritten" wire news.

In 1948 the Commission reviewed the famous "Mayflower decision" which had forbidden editorializing on the part of individual stations. The reasons given for that decision are worth quoting at length:

With the limitations in frequencies inherent in the nature of radio, the public interest can never be served by the dedication of any broadcast facility to the support of partisan ends. Radio can serve as an instrument of democracy only when devoted to the communication of information and the exchange of ideas fairly and objectively presented. A truly free radio cannot be used to advocate the causes of the licensee. It cannot be used to support the candidacies of his friends. It cannot be devoted to the support of principles he happens to regard most favorably. In brief, the broadcaster cannot be an advocate.

Freedom of speech on the radio must be broad enough to provide full and equal opportunity for the presentation to the public of all sides of public issues. Indeed, as one licensed to operate in a public domain, the licensee has assumed the obligation of presenting all sides of important questions, fairly, objectively, and without bias. The public interest — not the private — is paramount. These requirements are inherent in the conception of public interest set up by the Communications Act as the criterion of regulation.

This rule was accepted without much objection for four or five years, but after the end of World War II there was growing disapproval of it, partly because the advent of Frequency Modulation, with its new channels, and the use of directional broadcasting techniques had made it possible to increase the number of radio stations so greatly since the original ruling that the old "scarcity" was vanishing, and there seemed to be room for the expression of independent opinions by various stations. But the chief objection was that the regulation seemed to be too arbitrary a limitation on the freedom of speech, and even to be in contravention of Section 326 of the Communications Act, which denies the power of "censorship" to the Commission and forbids interference with "free speech." The National Association of

Broadcasters came out strongly against the regulation, and a poll of station managers by *Broadcasting* in 1947 showed a large majority favoring its abrogation. Accordingly, hearings were held, and in 1950 the Commission removed its objection to station editorializing, while still maintaining that such expression of views must be balanced by "a reasonable opportunity to hear different opposing positions." Thus far, however, stations have not taken advantage of their new freedom very widely.

These examples serve to illustrate attitudes of the F.C.C. It has not been despotic or uncompromising; on the other hand, it has been coöperative and sympathetic, listening to such complaints and suggestions as have obtained wide support in the "industry." It has had to steer its course between the Charybdis of political control and the Scylla of commercial influence. It is continually under criticism, as is proper; an agency wielding so much power must be watched carefully. But on the whole, the Federal Communications Commission seems thus far to have administered the regulation necessary under the physical limitations of the radio spectrum with judgment and restraint.

Thus it is seen that what we lightly call "freedom of speech" and "liberty of the press" are hedged about with many special conditions, limitations, and restrictions. And yet, when we regard the whole field of utterance and communication, we find that the sectors that are under strict controls are comparatively small, and that the borders between the free and controlled sectors are being actively and constantly contested. In the constitutions of many countries in the world the free press and free speech guarantees are no more than lip service; but the traditional American spirit of independent thinking and untrammeled action has maintained the declaration of our own Bill of Rights in all its dignity and clear significance.

The great gift of liberty of the press and of speech places heavy burdens of responsibility on newspapers, radio, and all agencies of communication in America. Those responsibilities have been discussed in the preceding pages, and they can never be too much emphasized.

But it must also be pointed out that the benefits of this gift accrue less to the agencies of communication themselves than to

the people — to readers and hearers and viewers. It is in behalf
of the people that the battles for liberty must always be fought,
and it is the people who should be chiefly concerned about any
infringements on that liberty. They cannot leave the struggles
against creeping invasions of those rights to the newspapers and
radio stations, which have indeed both financial and moral interests in such contests; but they must take their own part if they
are to preserve their freedoms. We must remember that liberty is
not merely a heritage from our ancestors which, like some valued
antique, we may store in the attic until we want it some day in
the living room; but it is something for which we have to struggle
constantly, day in and day out, if we want to preserve it. It is
continually under assault, and must continually be defended,

CHAPTER EIGHTEEN

To Lead or to Follow

There is one factor in this matter of control versus liberty
in the American news system which was not considered in the
last chapter. It is an element which has never been regarded as
a threat to press freedom because it is really a part of the news
process itself. This factor is the domination of the news by what
are believed to be the active interests of the readers themselves.

Why should readers' preferences be thought of as in any way
an invasion of freedom of the news? After all, is not news gathered and prepared and distributed for the benefit of the reader?
Is it not readers' news, so that domination by readers is self-
domination and protection from the readers' interests is protection from itself? So much, it seems, must be admitted; but
we have readers in great variety, and nobody knows with absolute certainty what they want, and it may be doubted whether
they themselves always know what they want. In such a complex situation, the simple solution for the editor appears to be
to choose a kind of common denominator of popular taste and
feeling, and shape the news report to fit. This may easily re-

sult in the domination of news by low intellectual and moral standards.

W. R. Hearst believed that this common denominator was excitement. In 1933, when he was seventy years old, he wrote a letter to the editors of his papers which contained the following eloquent paragraph:

I think *we* ought to be more interested in the news, more excited about it. In ancient time, McEwen said that he looked at the first page and remarked, "Gee whiz! " At the second page he said, "Holy Moses! " At the third page, "God Almighty! " Vibrate, respond to the news. Feature news more. Pick out news stories. Develop them. Write them well. Illustrate them. Make them better and more readable than any other paper. Make the paper distinctive by handling the news. A paper stands or falls by its news interest. Print all the news, but see more in the news than other editors do. To interest, be yourself interested. To excite, be yourself excited over the news. Get young people around you. Get rid of the *blasé* crowd. Then give them a chance. Let them get excited. Let them be young. Let them do things. Let them make a few mistakes. Maybe the public will like the mistakes. Maybe we are making the big mistake by not being vital enough.[55]

There are fine precepts in that paragraph. Its insistence on the news as the chief object of the newspaper, its doctrine that the editors themselves must be interested in the news, its suggestion of the values of youthful effort: these are fine principles. But is excitement, after all, the main element in a news report? It is the easiest kind of appeal — easy in editorial techniques, and easy in immediate popular response.

But it tends to debase news. Excitement, which is another word for sensationalism, in one paper calls out excitement in competing papers; and we soon have a rivalry in sensations, with all the cheap and whipped-up appeals to surface emotion and all the false emphasis on unsignificant details that such competition brings in its train. We have, in short, a tremendous overemphasis on "soft" news, in the course of which the really significant "hard" news is given an inconspicuous back seat.

Better than this undiscriminating reliance upon excitement as the common denominator of the news is the acceptance of reader interest surveys as guides for the news pattern. It is not necessary to review here the carefully devised and well-executed methods of the modern reader interest study which have been summarily described in Chapter III. It will suffice to repeat that such surveys inform us with much accuracy what proportions of readers actually look at what offerings in a newspaper or magazine. In the radio field, methods have been devised to inform us what broadcasts have the most hearers. The theory is that, having this detailed information, editors and station managers will then give the public more of what it seems to want; and everybody will be happy, because the readers and hearers are getting what they want and the newspapers and radio are getting what they want, which is customer-support.

The chief weakness in the system is that perhaps readers and listeners are not really being given an opportunity to vote on what they want most. The *non sequitur* in the reasoning lies in the assumption that the highest-rated items in the present offerings of newspaper and radio are what the public desires most deeply. Perhaps it really wants something it has not been offered at all — or at least not in such quantity as to give it a basis for judging.

It is true, of course, that these surveys will pick up novel and experimental offerings and rate them, which is a fine service. But it is also true that the public does not respond instantly to what is new and unaccustomed, and that the reports on such first attempts are commonly discouraging to a continuation of the experiments.

And yet it is well known that newspapers and the radio can, by bold educative effort, develop popular likings and preferences over a period of time. The reading and hearing public can be educated in things in which it is not now interested and of which, indeed, it is now scarcely aware. The newspapers have built our national interest in baseball, for example, to proportions which continually amaze foreign observers, and sometimes surprise thoughtful Americans. Many other cases of building popular interest by the newspapers could be adduced. Skillful handling, good writing, intelligent and imaginative editing by men who are convinced of the significance of the material they have determined to use can perform miracles in creating interest and building attention. It cannot be doubted that such techniques can displace sensational juvenility in newspapers and newscasts with mature thinking; and that, even in these days of fragmentary listening and impatient reading, press and radio, by sincere effort, can secure attention for important matters.

Hearst's advice to his editors to forget their *blasé* attitudes and get excited about the news sounds very well, and is indeed good counsel up to a certain point; but as a matter of fact intelligent editors are sure to be just a little contemptuous toward a continual striving after mere excitement. Such a standard of editing is, after all, an insult to the general public, which really has more sense than many papers give it credit for. Certainly anyone who thinks that what most readers really want is mere excitement has a far lower opinion of popular intelligence than the founding fathers of this nation had when they put its management into the hands of the people.

Fortunately, most American newspapers are not committed to an overemphasis on mere sensationalism in the news. But there is much to support the view that the newspapers and radio generally underestimate the capability of the general reader. We shall have some severe things to say about readers in the next chapter, but a faith in the basic mind and spirit of the people is essential to our belief in the democratic system. A journalist without such faith is miscast. A newsman who is contemptuous of the readers he serves must also be contemptuous of his profession: without a reasonably high concept of demos, no journalist can live up to the mark of his high calling. All workers in the communication field should agree profoundly with that fine dictum of Samuel Johnson's, found in his *Life of Addison*: "About things on which the public thinks long, it commonly attains to think right."

That statement points up the theory of long-term educational effort on the part of all communication media. Skill in the presentation of significant news is the first requisite. Edwin Lawrence Godkin, writing about the early numbers of the *Nation* in 1865, said: "It has been so far rather heavy . . . It is very difficult to get men of education in America to handle any subject with a light touch." It is no longer so difficult. The art of writing at once intelligently and entertainingly is not an easy one, but most good newspapermen today have mastered it. "Situationers" (as newsmen call the articles analyzing conditions and situations) often are colorful and vivid. Writers on science and economics have learned how to point up their stories with human-interest incidents and clever, bright writing. The second requisite in the presentation of "hard news" is keeping constantly at it — a persistent policy of publishing news of real significance. Not enough for a surfeit, but a generous plenty, and all of it good. And the third requisite is continuance over a long period, in accordance with the Johnsonian dictum.

Not a few editors resent as high-flown, impractical idealism any attempt to burden them with responsibilities for the education of readers. They say, very properly, that they have to produce a paper that the people will buy, or they and their reporters will be out of a job together. Emile Gauvreau, the famous tabloid editor, wrote in 1934: "After twenty-four years of experience in newspaper work, in almost every capacity, and watching many papers pass out of existence, I have come to the conclusion that the basic function of a newspaper is to make money, to pay its own way, and to pay its help adequate wages." [56] Such editors believe that the best way to make a successful paper is to study what people like best to read, build a simple formula on those preferences, and then go into production with that formula. "Leave education to the schoolteachers and professors," they say. And yet newspapers and radio definitely have the responsibility of conveying important information into the minds of the people. It is a responsibility that is laid upon them by their position in our democratic system as the informants of our rulers, the people. If they do not accept it, they will lose the respect of their readers, their influence, and, ultimately, the values derived from a free press system.

But the conflict between the necessities of the business of supplying the news on the one hand and professional responsibilities is, fortunately, not as sharp or as irreconcilable as it may appear when it is so baldly pointed out. In fact, it is probably more apparent than real. If you have a fairly good opinion of the public, you will agree that there is not a great difference between what it really wants in its newspapers and what the intelligent editor and publisher want to give it. In other words, subscribers and purchasers on most levels of readership are not going to resent the presentation of significant news in large quantities, if it is done skillfully; on the contrary, they are likely to feel the challenge of it, and a certain pride in being "intellectual." A paper is not inviting ruin by presenting plenty of "hard" news, if it does the job well.

It becomes, then, a question of editorial leading or following — leading readers to an appreciation of the significant matters in the news, or following reader-interest formulas. Following is probably simpler. Leading is the more difficult art; and when there are large investments at stake, it may even be dangerous unless it is done cleverly and with wise discrimination. But whatever difficulties there may be appear as the inescapable challenge of good editing in the modern world. With his professional skills, with the necessary faith in the democratic principle, and with determination and persistence, the "able editor" accepts his responsibility for leadership and makes his paper a real educative force in community and nation.

The whole history of American journalism is a history of the leadership of great editors and publishers. Greeley, often ridiculous, frequently inconsistent, exerted a profound influence on the thinking of a large section of the American people over many years. Pulitzer, when President Cleveland was leading the country full-tilt into a third war with England, was the chief influence in putting an end to that stupidity. Nelson, often the scolding schoolmaster of Kansas City, was its leader in a spectacular civic development. It would be easy to go on and on. Most great editors have been great leaders.

And it is wrong to assert, as some do, that the days of the great editors and publishers are past. That is an absurdity arising from lack of perspective. There are plenty of them whose names are widely known today, and whose personalities are as familiar in their own bailiwicks as were those of editors and publishers of the past in their times and places. Men like Sulzberger, Ethridge, Hoyt, Cowles, Knight — editors and publishers like Erwin Canham, of Boston; Sevellon Brown, of Providence;

Paul Smith, of San Francisco; Oveta Culp Hobby, of Houston; Helen Rogers Reid, of New York; Hodding Carter, of Greenville, Mississippi; Joseph Pulitzer II, of St. Louis; Frank Ahlgren, of Memphis; Grove Patterson, of Toledo; Dwight Marvin, of Troy, New York (though the list grows too long, it is hard to stop; why did we begin it?) — are not bound to the wheel of a reader-interest survey or frightened by the slightly leering face of a mythical "average reader." They find surveys useful — indispensable, indeed, for detailed knowledge of public tastes, — but no leader was ever satisfied with *status quo.*

Those who aim at the progression from Gee Whiz to Holy Moses to God Almighty as a kind of criterion, and who seek to form a journalism on that basis, are following what they conceive to be an emotional common denominator of the people. They concentrate on a policy which, once set, is easy to make and easy to take. But it is our conviction that their course, and the inevitably debasing results of it, represent a great and present danger to the American news system and to a free press.

On the other hand, the leadership that challenges the thinking of readers and hearers and provides skillfully, copiously, and persistently that information on crucial problems necessary to citizenship represents the highest professional duty in these times, as well as the greatest possible service to our democratic system.

CHAPTER NINETEEN

The Responsibilities of the Reader

That mythical person, "the average reader," has little to interest us. We may suspect that, on the whole, he is a pretty bad reader; but the questions that really concern us are what bad reading is and what its effects are and, on the other hand, what good reading can do for us.

Mr. Clifton Fadiman is anxious about "the decline of attention in our time," and particularly "the decline in the ability to read." He qualifies his terms, however, when he describes this modern phenomenon which justly disturbs him and so many other observers as a "paralysis" caused by various pressures, and as "a wholesale displacement" of the attention "away from ideas and abstractions toward things and techniques." [57] Probably there is no contemporary decline of the power of attention, which could result only from widespread physiological change among the people, but rather there are shifts in both interests and the manner of satisfying those interests. At any rate, the faults of modern methods of attention, as shown particularly in habits of reading and thinking, are very serious.

Two of these faults are fairly obvious. The first may be called "fragmentation." The modern American, to be sure, can concentrate his attention over a considerable period of time upon a matter which moves him deeply; but when his desires or curiosities are not strongly enlisted, the multiple pulls and lures of this our modern life divide his time and interest into small bits. Moreover, this fragmentation increases, and bits become smaller bits, so small that they tend to become useless and by their very multiplicity to destroy the effects of each other.

The second prominent fault in our reading and thinking is that we have not learned to fix our attention discriminatingly; we do not concentrate on the matters that are actually of the deepest import to our society and ourselves. This, too, is probably due largely to the whirling confusion of modern life, with its multiple pulls at our curiosities and its quick distribution of fads and popular fancies.

Against these great sins of our popular reading and thinking, against the common faults of attention, American media of communication should themselves lead reformatory crusades. They have responsibilities of leadership in such matters and, instead of catering to popular weaknesses and encouraging bad reading, ought of course to engage in a constant struggle to raise standards. But we cannot avoid the fact that, after all, the fundamental responsibility in these desperately important matters rests upon the reader, the hearer, and the viewer.

It is in the news and the way it is presented in America that we are chiefly interested here; and the newspaper is, historically as well as basically today, our main reliance for the presentation of the news. So let us look for a moment at the reader's relationship to his newspaper, keeping in mind that much of what is said about that medium applies also to the magazine, radio, television, the motion picture, and so forth.

The newspaper is primarily dependent on its readers for its very existence. Circulation is fundamental. It is not upon advertising but upon circulation that the life and prosperity of a newspaper depends. If it has readers, it is in a favorable position to get advertising; but it has to get readers first, and to keep them. Up to about 1890, circulation brought more revenue into most newspaper tills than advertising. Then, in a period of business expansion, advertising had an extraordinary growth in America until, by 1914, it provided two-thirds of the income of many dailies, and by the time of the financial crash of 1929, three-fourths. Thereafter that unreasonable proportion was steadily reduced, until it was back to two-thirds by about 1940. It continues to be reduced, under the influence of increases in subscription rates which are logical and necessary. Today there are many papers, especially outside the metropolitan fields, which receive as much revenue from circulation as from advertising; some receive more. But quite apart from this matter of proportional income, it has always been, and always must be, a fundamental fact that newspaper publication is founded on readership, and that the social, economic, and political functions of a newspaper are performed primarily for the benefit of readers.

That puts a great deal of power over a newspaper into the hands of its readers. They can make or break it. It cannot be said too often that the people as a whole can have very much the kind of newspapers they want. Even in a city with a non-competitive newspaper situation, editors and publishers are very sensitive to the results when readers begin to turn to the radio or out-of-town papers for their news. They know they are never secure, and that they do not dare to let circulation slip; they know that the paper's prosperity depends on reader acceptance.

This power of the people over their newspapers cannot exist

in a dictatorship, in which news as well as editorial policies are controlled by government. Nor is there need in such a state for the people to exercise any control over news policies, since they have no political powers which true information by newspaper would implement.

But in a democracy, the benefits which the people derive from their power over the newspapers are balanced, of course, by responsibilities. That is, the privilege which we enjoy in this country of being informed more fully than any other people in the world about events and situations at home and abroad is balanced by an obligation to maintain and improve our free press.

We take our responsibilities as members of a democratic society rather casually. Our forefathers were stirred by the sense of being part of a great experiment in the history of mankind; we have grown used to our democracy as to an old coat. There is much alarm expressed about the large proportion of qualified voters who do not go to the polls; but perhaps it is just as well that men and women who have failed to inform themselves adequately, and who have little care for the welfare of their information system, do not vote. Both property and literacy qualifications have been used in this country to limit the right to suffrage; but nobody has yet devised an acceptable information test for voters, and of course nobody ever will. We shall have to muddle along, supported by our enduring faith in the intelligence of the people as the best basis for government yet devised.

And we shall be aided and supported also by continuing efforts to make our information system, which is chiefly our news system, more and more effective. In that system — vast, multiform, tireless, efficient — there are many faults, shortcomings, and dangers. Some of them have been discussed in these chapters. For these failures as well as for the great successes of the system the people have a fundamental responsibility because the system is made and operated for them, and is answerable to them.

What can the people do about their news system? Well, to make a beginning, write letters to newspaper editors. Ask for more full texts of important speeches and documents, for more news behind the news, for more analyses by qualified experts of social and economic conditions in special fields. Ask for more foreign news. Complain of slanted presentations by specific by-liners. Complain of the "play" of news in a set political pattern. Similar complaints may be made to radio stations.

Do not despise this kind of direct action. It is your newspaper, your radio station, and the editors know it is. You would be surprised to find how sensitive editors actually are to such comments from readers and hearers. A dozen letters often seem to them to indicate an avalanche of reader reaction. Of course, they disregard what are patently crank letters, but reasonable remonstrances and suggestions have great weight. In these days of expensive and scarce paper, adding certain kinds of news means crowding something else out; but let the editor worry about that. It is his business. And your letters will not be unwelcome if they show some understanding of the news; intelligent coöperation on the part of readers and hearers is valuable, and is generally so recognized.

This direct action may often be carried a step farther. Especially in the smaller cities, readers may utilize personal contacts with editors. In general, they are the most approachable, most lively minded men in the world. They like to talk about newspapers, or radio, and they like to hear what their readers or hearers think about their product. They are used to criticism, which they may resent if it is malicious or hackneyed; but they are critical themselves, and they usually value constructive suggestions offered in good faith and friendly spirit. Few newspapermen would go as far as the publisher of the *Press Democrat*, of Santa Rosa, California, who set up an advisory panel representing chief elements in the community, with which he meets regularly; but readers' views, when well meant and sensible, are commonly welcomed and heeded in a newspaper office.

It is assumed that in such direct action, whether by letters to the editor or personal contacts with him, you are interested in the actual betterment of news service. Pulling wires for selfish ends, trying to get something into the paper for personal reasons, is a type of scheming against which newspapermen are always on guard. Only when it is on the high ground of public service can such direct action as is suggested be effective.

But after all, the chief contribution which readers can make to the cause of maintaining and improving our news system is to do a better job of reading. The "good reading" which was suggested at the beginning of this chapter is bound to have a double effect: it not only improves the general information of the reader, but in the long run it raises the level of the gathering and editing of the news. The former objective should furnish us with a compelling motive for good reading, but the latter is also an important consideration if we have the general welfare at heart. The more general result is a little like the "work of supererogation" of the old theologians — something not necessary to personal salvation, but a praiseworthy performance and not to be forgotten. It works after this fashion. Newspapers, dependent as they are upon readers for their prosperity, watch habits of reading through reader-interest studies and in other ways; then they adapt their offerings to what their audience seems to want. A change in the reading preferences of a single individual would, of course, have no effect, but any considerable shift would soon make itself felt. The individual who adopts a good reading pattern has the benefit of it himself, and the satisfaction of knowing that his weight is counting for the general good. In other words, he is voting right.

What is this "good reading" about which we have been talking?

In the first place, it is systematic. How much time do you devote each day to newspaper reading? Available studies show differences according to the age of the reader, but indicate that at forty years of age he spends forty minutes or more with his weekday paper, and more on Sunday.[58] Certainly forty minutes a day is little enough time for the newspaper; but whatever it is, is should be allocated regularly. It may be spent on a suburban train or a streetcar or bus, or in the living room after dinner, in an office or in a club or (Lord help us!) at the breakfast or luncheon table; but it should be as regular as sleeping or eating. Twenty minutes *every* day is better than an hour or two every second or third day, hit or miss, because without regularity the reader loses the connection and the sense of running events. Casual and cursory methods of "picking up the paper" lead to that fragmentation which is one of the great curses of newspaper reading.

This leads to the suggestion of a technique which is used, consciously or unconsciously, by all good readers — the "follow through" practice. Every series of events in the papers, from a campaign for a public swimming pool to a great war, is a serial story; and it is far more interesting and understandable if it is followed regularly. A young woman will sometimes complain: "Politics! Oh, I can't get interested in politics. It's just too confusing!" It is confusing, of course — until one gets into the current of the story. It is like a mystery novel in which a dozen characters are introduced in the first few pages: you have to read two or three chapters before you get them sorted out. But persistent reading day after day makes the figures of the great statesmen and political leaders emerge as personalities and as the spokesmen for ideologies which are very important to us.

One of the chief principles of good newspaper reading is that it should be comprehensive. What is your own habit on picking up your paper? Do you glance first at the top headlines on page one, and then turn quickly to the financial section? Or the sports pages? Or the women's pages? Or the comics? We shall always follow our special interests, to be sure; but to stop with such an interest or interests is a narrow and short-sighted policy. Explore the inside pages. Theodore M. Bernstein, an editor on the *New York Times*, remarked not long ago that "One of our national maladies might be described as a page-one fixation . . . the fallacious notion that all one need read to be well informed is the front page." Try reading in some field in which you do not now have an interest. Travel is broadening, even when made through the columns of a good newspaper.

Readers of the smaller papers often go through them from beginning to end, but many dwellers in large cities never have read a paper through. Large papers are made to be read much more thoroughly than many of us appreciate. The *Philadelphia Evening Bulletin* printed its issue for June 4, 1928, in the form of a cloth-bound book. It made 307 pages of highly diversified, entertaining, and instructive reading. This did not include the advertising, though readers certainly should not neglect that part of their newspapers.

But the Philadelphia reader of June 4, 1928, was by no means

limited to the *Evening Bulletin*, nor is he today. He can easily
pick up New York or Washington papers if he prefers them to
the local *Bulletin, Inquirer,* or *News*. The point is that a good
news reader should choose his newspapers with discrimination,
and should get some variety into his news fare. It is true that
many cities are now provided with only one paper, but it is an
exceptional situation in which out-of-town papers are not easily
available. Most good readers receive the local paper for local
news and supplement it with news from other sources.

The other sources ought by no means to be neglected. Shop
around among the various radio offerings and find the best. Read
the news-magazines. Try the Sunday *New York Times* or *Herald
Tribune*. Watch the news programs of your television station. In
these United States there is a rich and varied service of news and
information, it is inexpensive, and it is necessary for intelligent
living and citizenship.

And yet, with all these riches, it is easily possible to read in
such a casual and haphazard fashion that one may get very little
real information of any great importance from it all. This brings
us to the crux of the "good reading" problem.

A large part of our newspaper reading is done in situations of
relaxation. Father comes home from work tired. He washes up,
has a good dinner with his family, feels better. In the living room,
the children have turned on the radio, or perhaps the television
set. Father settles into his easy chair, takes off his shoes, lights his
pipe, picks up his paper. Who can begrudge him *enjoyment* of
his paper? He needs enjoyment, relaxation, escape from his day-
long worries. That is what comics, sports, and amusing features
are for; that is why picture pages, comics, and sports pages (in
that order) rank next to front pages in reader-notice surveys.

But good reading of newspapers does not stop with such diverting matters. A mind which is awake to the crucial problems on
which the fate of the world depends today wants far more than
the answer to such questions as what Stanley Musial's batting
average is at the moment, or how Alley Oop is faring in the
Roman amphitheater. A lively minded reader looks over the latest dispatches from European and Asiatic capitals; he reads the
correspondence from Washington; he must gather the views of

the columnists and editorial writers. In other words, a hard-headed reader will always spend a considerable amount of time on "hard" news, leaving concentration on "soft" news to soft heads.

The serious reader will also want enough of a given story to get his teeth into. If the President of the United States or a returned General of the Army or a Nobel prize winner makes a major pronouncement, he will read, if not the whole of it, at least a sizable portion. The newspaper serves all classes of readers and must always be a highly composite miscellany, with thousands of brevities; but a good reader wants significant events, situations, and pronouncements set forth with fullness and detail, and he is willing to give time and effort to reading and studying such stories.

In these days when there is more leisure than ever before, there should be more time for serious reading. If our people will not read seriously, they will not deserve a mature press and radio.

Schools and colleges can do something about it. High school courses in current events which emphasize techniques of newspaper reading and radio-news listening (and now television viewing) are now part of the curricula of all good modern high schools and preparatory schools. In colleges and universities, specialized training of this kind, outside schools of journalism, is likely to be neglected on the theory that the student will keep abreast of the news anyway — perhaps in connection with courses in the social sciences. But neither schools nor colleges should dare to neglect this essential training.

Schools may help, and the press and radio may do much toward the end of the proper reception and appreciation of the news — an important patriotic duty — but we must remember that, after all, the final verdict on good reading and therefore on a good news system rests with us, the people — the readers, hearers, and viewers themselves.

CHAPTER TWENTY

Looking toward the Future

Horace Walpole wrote cynically in one of his letters, "The wisest prophet makes sure of the event first." Perhaps the wisest man never ventures upon prophecy at all. Certainly we shall not offer, in this brief postscript to our essay on the news in America, a set of prognostications in the "I predict" vein, but rather a collection of the intelligent anticipations which seem to be current among workers in the news field today.

Many contemporary observers believe that a realignment of news media — the daily and weekly newspaper, the weekly and monthly magazine, the topical book, the radio, television, and the newsreel — is imminent, or at least inevitable in the course of time. In this change, television is the catalyst.

As this is written, television is the great newcomer in the field of the news report. This medium, whose growth has been one of the wonders of the midcentury years, made its first great debut in the presentation of the news by its special events shows. Frequent demands are now heard that sessions of the houses of Congress should be televised. The joint session addressed by Mac-Arthur has already been on the screen. TV men are a very optimistic breed; most of them think it is only a question of time until all important sessions of both House and Senate are fully televised. It is interesting to speculate on what changes in procedure and attitudes would occur if a United States senator, instead of talking to an empty Chamber, were to find himself addressing a million voters.

A warm debate is in progress over the ethical and legal questions involved in "hippodroming" examinations of persons accused of wrong-doing, as was done in the crime hearings. Similar questions are bound to arise all along the line, as the people's right to know is pitted against traditions of orderly procedure in television's coming struggle to invade council rooms of all kinds, legislative halls, churches, and even courtrooms.

Meantime, TV general news programs are being developed rapidly. The stereotyped station shows in which a man sat at a desk and read a script, with pictures interspersed, tends to give way to more original presentations. The great current successes in TV news are the panel interviews with persons actually prominent in the affairs discussed as participants. The great news agencies, with reporter-photographer news teams at all important spots, are now furnishing wire-photos and news films to television stations.

Color, which will make the video screen far more attractive, is postponed only by the exigencies of a military-preparedness industrial program. The progress of frequency modulation, of which so much was expected a few years ago, has been stopped by the tremendous growth of TV. It seems obvious that regular radio news will be supplanted more and more by television; why merely listen to a national convention when you can both see and hear it? Newspapers, while they are jittery over television as they were over radio when it first reached gianthood, are generally hopeful that they may not suffer greatly from the incursions of the new medium. If viewers follow the pattern set by listeners, and want to read in print fuller reports than they can glimpse on the screen or hear in limited radio time, newspaper readership will not suffer.

Facsimile, which was said to be "just around the corner" fifteen years ago, is still there. It does not seem to be a present candidate for a position as an important medium of news dissemination, though the idea of a newspaper unrolling from a receiver in one's own living room is an attractive and well-demonstrated possibility. But facsimile seems actually to be a losing competitor with TV.

The electronic age in the dissemination of news will develop new problems, and furnish variations of the old ones. The effect of a crisis on the people is bound to be more immediate and intimate and therefore more exciting when the news of it comes by television. The dangers of public hysteria are much greater in such situations. This points to the newspaper's function of interpretation and explanation as likely to assume a greater importance as the various media supplement each other in the proper integration of a news system.

Such a reintegration, such new adjustments of the alignment along the news front, such recognitions of new duties and relinquishments of old customs, seem to be indicated for the future. Erwin Canham predicts daily news magazines. It seems likely that the newspaper of the future will be more and more concerned with interpretation. As it yields the "flash" news and bulletins to radio and television, it will give more attention to orderly, departmentalized news for the record.

Moreover, we are already seeing a tendency toward obliteration of the lines between different news media, experimentation in new types of publication, and many new trends in affiliation and new kinds of competition. Thus, there is the talk about "daily magazines," the noticeable prosperity of suburban papers (to which Basil Walters has often called our attention in recent years), and the growth of the newspaper-like urban weekly magazines in all our cities. We now have magazine-like newspapers, newspaper-like magazines, magazine-like books, and book-like magazines. It will indeed be strange if the quarter-book does not eventually become important in the news field.

Some technological changes already operative are interesting — even exciting — and some others "just around the corner" seem fantastic. One of the leading changes in news handling being effected by newspapers at the moment is that which comes from the installation of teletypesetter circuits. This device represents the extension of the teletype to the linotype. An operator at a wire service bureau punches a tape which is transmitted by leased wire to the various newspapers on the circuit; that is, the holes on the bureau tape are reproduced on the tape made in the newspaper office. This tape is then fed into a composing-casting machine (linotype or intertype), causing it to cast lines of type (slugs) for the forms of the newspaper. The tape may be edited in the newspaper office before it goes to the machine, though more commonly the editing is done on galley proofs after the type is set; but the point is that it may be edited by each newspaper. All the general wire services are furnishing teletypesetter service, which is practicable only when several newspapers in a given region join in a circuit to receive it. Over six hundred daily papers are on such circuits in 1952, with more to come.

Though fears have been expressed that the teletypesetter circuits might give us a "carbon copy journalism," an examination of papers using the service seems to show that the editing of tape and the exercise of independent news evaluation preserve the identity of the papers and their variety in the use of their wire news. This "carbon copy" threat is real, however, and the new process will bear watching.

Automatic casting, which has been greatly stimulated by labor troubles, is also in use in some offices which punch their own tapes. Linotypes are now on the market for automatic operation which are much faster than those which are run from a keyboard by hand. Also there are reports of a composing machine which will eliminate slug-casting entirely by a photographic process involving the engraving of lines on a plate. Other marvels are said to be in process of development.

Chief effects of all of this, so far as the reader of news is concerned, are increases in speed of production and in ease of reading. Perhaps patterns of hope guide prophecy in this instance, but it seems probable that the newspaper of the future will be handsomer typographically and more easy and comfortable to read than the papers of the present. This would only continue a course of progress in that direction which has continued for many years and has been much accelerated in our times.

That newspapers will be made more attractive by increased use of color seems also inevitable. No decrease in the use of pictures seems probable, but we surely shall have an increase in the effectiveness, the significance, and the technical excellence of pictures.

Newspapers, radio, and television will surely benefit in the years to come from a growing sense of professionalism in the field of communication. Journalists are far better educated than they were a generation or two ago; they have better backgrounds in the social sciences and in the knowledge necessary to anyone working with news. Schools of journalism, at first misunderstood, sometimes stumbling, are now generally accepted by the better minds in both educational and journalistic circles. Many of them have been working away faithfully for years, so that thousands of their graduates are now prominent in practical communication work. The new generation of journalists give us encouragement for the progress and improvement of our news system in the ensuing decades.

It is on this kind of personnel and on the essential rightness of the American public that we must depend for a more mature press and radio in the future. If and when the American character deteriorates, the communication agencies will follow it down; but most of us believe pretty thoroughly in the soundness of our national spirit and people.

As far as freedom of speech and press is concerned — the preservation of the people's right to know — we need have no expectation of disaster so long as the people as well as the press and radio are on guard. The vigilance of the people will be the price of their liberty in the future as in the past.

But all our thinking about the years immediately before us is shadowed by fears of world conflict. All our "intelligent anticipations" are necessarily conditioned by an international situation which is, at this writing, precarious and uncertain. War, if it comes, we shall face and follow through to what we shall be determined to make an ordered world at last; but that such an objective may be reached, more slowly perhaps but no less surely, without the appalling destruction of a third world war is the hope of every sane person. We can end our little series of thoughts about the future only with a prayer for peace on earth.

NOTES

Notes

[1] See R. A. Scott-James, *The Influence of the Press* (London, 1913), pp. 37–40.

[2] Controversy probably will always rage around certain questions connected with the *acta*. For example, was Caesar's deed important as a new departure, or was it merely a continuation of *acta populi* already familiar? It has been common to regard a possibly ambiguous statement of Suetonius, in his history of Caesar, as establishing a claim to priority; but there are arguments on both sides. Inquiry into the whole matter of the Roman posted journals is full of interest, and may be pursued in (1) Gaston Boissier's "The Roman Journal," a charming and learned essay included in the author's *Tacitus and Other Roman Studies* (New York, 1906), translation by W. G. Hutchinson; in (2) *Des Journaux chez les Romains* (Paris, 1838), a comprehensive treatment of the subject by J.-Vict. Le Clerc; and in (3) a learned work in Latin by the German scholar Emil Hübner, *De Senatus Populique Romani Actis* (Leipzig, 1859). In both (2) and (3) references to the *acta* in extant Latin literature are accumulated.

[3] *Editor & Publisher International Year Book*, 1951 (data for 1950), furnishes the data for this count. I have omitted a few suburban and specialized dailies of under 50,000 circulation. *Editor & Publisher* lists only English-language dailies of general circulation. Of course, even when a morning and an evening paper are under a single ownership, they are counted as two papers.

[4] Paul F. Lazarsfeld and others, *Radio and the Printed Page* (New York, 1940), *The People Look at Radio* (Chapel Hill, 1946), and *Radio Listening in America* (New York, 1948).

[5] It may be helpful to place here a summary outline of the common, or popular, media of news communication:

    I. Informal
        1. Oral rumor, gossip, chatter
        2. Personal letters
    II. Printed
        1. Newspapers
            a. Metropolitan dailies
            b. Suburban dailies
            c. Small-city dailies
            d. Community weeklies
            e. Specialized papers
        2. Periodicals
            a. Weekly news magazines
            b. Picture weeklies and biweeklies

        c. Journals of comment
        d. General and weekly monthly magazines
        e. Specialized periodicals
        f. "Confidential" reports
     3. Pamphlets and broadsides
     4. Topical books
  III. Broadcast
     1. Radio news, commentators, special events
        a. Networks
        b. Local programs
     2. Television
        a. Networks
        b. Local programs
  IV. Projected
     1. Newsreels
     2. Documentary and educational films

[6] Wilbur Schramm, "The Nature of News," *Journalism Quarterly* (September 1949), reprinted in a volume edited by Schramm, *Mass Communications* (Urbana, Ill., 1949). See E. L. Thorndike, *The Psychology of Wants, Interests and Attitudes* (New York, 1935); C. S. Sherrington, *The Integrative Action of the Nervous System* (New Haven, 1906).

[7] We are inevitably reminded of the distinction which W. R. Hearst is said to have made between "interesting" and "merely important" news. See Helen MacGill Hughes, *News and the Human Interest Story* (Chicago, 1940), pp. 57, 265.

[8] For Parton, *N.A.R.*, CII (April 1866), 378; for the Baptist clergyman anecdote, *Southern Quarterly Review*, I (January 1842), 11; for Dana, *The Art of Newspaper Making* (New York, 1895), p. 12.

[9] For W. R. Hearst's ideas about excitement in the news formula, see p. 200.

[10] Susan M. Kingsbury, Hornell Hart, and Associates, *Newspapers and the News* (New York, 1937). Chapters I, II, III, IV, and VII were published in the *Journalism Quarterly*, 1933–1934.

[11] *Commonweal*, November 11, 1925. Copyright 1925 by Calvert Publishing Corp. Reprinted by permission. The quotation regarding the *Christian Science Monitor's* news policy is from an article in the *Independent* (April 1925) by Willis J. Abbot, then editor of that paper.

[12] These three human-interest stories were reprinted in collections of news stories edited by the author of the present volume. "Apple Annie" was in *News Stories of 1934* (Iowa City, 1935), "Florio and His Sewing-Machine" in *Headlining America 1937* (Boston, 1937), and "The Story of Joe Doakes" in *Headlining America 1938–1939* (New York, 1940).

[13] See *News, Its Scope and Limitations*: Addresses Delivered at the Twentieth Annual Journalism Week at the University of Missouri, May 5–11, 1929. Journalism Series, No. 57.

[14] Frederic Hudson, *Journalism in the United States* (New York, 1873), p. xxiii.

[15] George Santayana, *Obiter Scripta* (New York, 1936), p. 132. By permission of Charles Scribner's Sons, publishers.

[16] Alfred Korzybski, *Science and Sanity* (Lancaster, Pa., 1933), p. 470. Irving J. Lee, *Language Habits in Human Affairs* (New York, 1941), p. 187. I am indebted to Lee for the suggestion of the quotations from Hudson and Santayana above.

[17] Irving Dilliard, "The Role of the Press in Congressional Investigations," in *University of Chicago Law Review*, 18 (Spring, 1951), 585–590.

[18] Elmer Davis, *Must We Mislead the Public?* Fifth Annual Memorial Lecture sponsored by Twin Cities Local, American Newspaper Guild, C.I.O., and School of Journalism, University of Minnesota, Minneapolis, November 3, 1951.

[19] Clarence K. Streit, "The Problem of False News," Report to the League of Nations for the International Association of Journalists Accredited to the League of Nations (Conf. D. 143, November 1, 1932, Geneva). Translated into French as *Comment combattre fausses nouvelles*. Mr. Streit was Geneva correspondent of the *New York Times*.

[20] Charles F. Wingate, ed., *Views and Interviews on Journalism* (New York, 1875), p. 27.

[21] Stanley Walker, *City Editor* (New York, 1934), pp. 46, 87.

[22] This computation is based on listings in *Editor & Publisher Year Book*, 1951.

[23] Louis Stark, "The Press and Labor News," in *Annals of the American Academy of Political and Social Science*, 219 (January 1942), 112. This number of *Annals* was devoted to a symposium entitled "The Press in the Contemporary Scene," edited by Malcolm M. Willey and Ralph D. Casey. Note, in addition to Stark's article, William A. Sumner, "The Press and Agricultural News"; and Watson Davis, "Science and the Press."

[24] These figures and those following are based on the lists of Press Gallery seats in *Editor & Publisher Year Book*, 1951. Some Press Gallery seats are assigned to men not on constant duty at Washington.

[25] Cabell Phillips and others, ed., *Dateline: Washington* (Garden City, N. Y., 1949), p. 269. Quoted by permission of Doubleday & Company, Inc.

[26] Merriman Smith, *Thank You, Mr. President* (New York, 1946). Until 1951 press conferences were held in the President's office.

[27] See Bruce Caton, "Handouts," in *Dateline: Washington*, p. 167. Civil Service figures in 1947 showed 2818 persons employed by the

federal government in the "Information and Editorial Series." See also *Problems of Journalism, 1951* (Proceedings of the American Society of Newspaper Editors), p. 65.

[28] See John Hersey's "Conference in Room 474," *New Yorker*, December 16, 1950.

[29] In the first place, the proportions are based on total non-advertising space rather than on total news space; secondly, the sample is too small to insure a representative quality in the results, especially since no effort was made to select variant types of papers. The counts for 1910–1940, from which the above figures are extracted, were made merely to give a broad indication of trends in the proportions of various types of newspaper content in large metropolitan papers. See F. L. Mott, "Trends in Newspaper Content," in *Annals of the American Academy of Political and Social Science*, 219 (January 1942), 60–65; reprinted in Wilbur Schramm, ed., *Mass Communications* (Urbana, 1949), pp. 337–345. The 1950 measurements were for this volume.

[30] For an excellent and extensive survey of such coverage, as it existed before World War II, see Robert W. Desmond, *The Press and World Affairs* (New York, 1937).

[31] Russell F. Anderson, "The Disappearing Foreign Correspondent," in *Michigan Alumnus Quarterly Review* LVII (December 9, 1950), 1–12. This article, somewhat revised, was printed in the *Saturday Review of Literature*, November 17, 1951, under the title, "News from Nowhere."

[32] See Anderson, *op. cit.*, for contemporary figures; F. L. Mott, *American Journalism*, rev. ed. (New York, 1950), p. 742, for war figures.

[33] See the *Journalist* (New York) through February–March 1890. For the Maverick quotation, see his *Henry J. Raymond and the New York Press for Thirty Years* (Hartford, 1870), p. 250.

[34] A zestful account of this episode in Chicago journalism may be found in Vincent Starrett's "The Old Newspaper Gang," *Plain Talk*, January, 1928, pp. 92–98.

[35] This composite description is based on observations in various newsrooms, but particularly in those of the *Chicago Daily News*, the *Des Moines Tribune*, and the late lamented *St. Louis Star-Times*.

[36] This composite description is based chiefly on the operations of WHO, Des Moines, and KGO, San Francisco.

[37] See Rudolph Flesch, *The Art of Plain Talk* (New York, 1946). Available in a cheap series is I. A. Richards, *Pocket Book of Basic English*.

[38] *Reports of the Continuing Study Committees, Associated Press Managing Editors Association* (Fort Worth, 1949), p. 31.

[39] It may be read in Allan Nevins' excellent anthology, *American Press Opinion, 1785–1927* (New York, 1928), pp. 189–190.

[40] The publishers are Simon & Schuster, New York, 1949; the editors are Louis L. Snyder, associate professor of history in the College of the City of New York, and Richard B. Morris, professor of history in Columbia University.

[41] There is an excellent discussion of the differences between radio and newspaper news in Chapter III of Mitchell V. Charnley, *News by Radio* (New York, 1948).

[42] Letter to James Currie, January 18, 1786. P. L. Ford, ed., *The Writings of Thomas Jefferson* (New York, 1898), IV, 132. Jefferson wrote many letters, some of them no doubt hurriedly.

[43] Charles A. Siepmann, *Radio, Television, and Society* (New York, 1950), pp. 225–233.

[44] *The Federalist*, LXXXIV.

[45] See Siebert's "Legal Developments Affecting the Press" in *Annals of the American Academy of Political and Social Science*, vol. 219 (January 1942).

[46] Chief Justice Hughes did not mention in his list the matter of press interference with "the orderly course of the administration of justice," which has resulted in various contempt cases against newspapers and reporters. This question may be studied in J. Edward Gerald, *The Press and the Constitution, 1931–1947* (Minneapolis, 1948), a volume which is valuable, within its period, for this whole discussion.

[47] But they had not been killed — only captured — and all three lived to escape and rejoin their papers. See Junius Henri Browne, *Four Years in Secessia* (Detroit, 1866), p. 238 *et passim*; cf. W. E. Woodward, *Meet General Grant* (New York, 1928), p. 260.

[48] Members of the Staff of the New York Times, *The Newspaper: Its Making and Its Meaning* (New York, 1945), p. 180.

[49] See pp. 104–105.

[50] Commission on Freedom of the Press, *A Free and Responsible Press* (Chicago, 1947). On p. 1 growth of monopoly is given as the first reason press freedom is believed to be in danger. This idea is emphasized throughout, and five of the thirteen "recommendations" with which the book closes are designed to correct such "monopoly."

[51] The data on which these calculations are based are found in *Editor & Publisher Year Book*, 1951. Our list of group ownerships is also that of this standard manual, with the addition of the McCormick papers, which we can find no good reason for omitting.

[52] Herbert Brucker, *Freedom of Information* (New York, 1949), p. 67. Figures were compiled by Office of Radio Research, Columbia University, for Newspaper Radio Committee in 1941.

[53] These counts are based on the lists in *Editor & Publisher Year Books* for 1931 and 1951. See also Raymond B. Nixon's excellent essay on "The Problem of Newspaper Monopoly" in Wilbur Schramm, ed., *Mass Communications* (Chicago, 1949), pp. 158–167; and the

same author's "Concentration and Absenteeism in Daily Newspaper Ownership," *Journalism Quarterly*, 22 (June 1945), 97–114.

[54] The phrase is used as a chapter heading in Morris L. Ernst, *The First Freedom* (New York, 1946).

[55] Quoted from Mrs. Fremont Older, *William Randolph Hearst* (New York, 1936), by permission of Appleton-Century-Crofts, publishers.

[56] Letter to the author, dated March 26, 1934.

[57] Clifton Fadiman, "The Decline of Attention," in *Saturday Review of Literature*, 32 (August 6, 1949), 20.

[58] Henry C. Link, on the basis of 4000 interviews, found that readers in the 15–19 years group spent 22 minutes daily with newspapers; at 40–49 years, 44 minutes. Eugene Liner, in a University of Illinois thesis, found readers in the 20–30 years group spend 38.5 minutes; at 40–50 years, 51 minutes. See Schramm, ed., *Mass Communication* (Urbana, 1949), p. 405. Note also that results of a survey of the National Panel of Consumer Opinion (4412 responses) show 43 minutes spent with an evening newspaper in homes provided with television, and 48 in those without TV. *Editor & Publisher* (March 31, 1951), p. 5.

INDEX

Index

Abbot, Willis John, 222
Acheson, Dean, 84, 118
Acme Newspictures, 102
Acta, 2–3, 221
Adams, Henry, 9
Ade, George, 65
Advertisers, Pressures by, 183–185
Advertising, News in, 11–12
Advertising Compared with Circulation, 207
Agricultural News, 105
Ahlgren, Frank, 205
Alexander the Great, 44
American Association for the Advancement of Science, 90, 103
American Magazine, or A Monthly View, 36–37
American Newspaper Publishers Association, 178
American Society of Newspaper Editors, 117, 181
Americus Times-Recorder, 136
Ames, Fisher, 50–51
Amsterdam Recorder, 136
Anderson, Paul Y., 73–74, 88, 118
Anderson, Russell F., 127, 224
Archer, William, 23
Areopagitica, 174
Associated Negro Press, 101
Associated Press, History of, 98–100; New York Bureau of (description), 131–139; readability of report of, 161–164; 72–73, 78–79, 90, 103, 109–110, 125, 129
Atlanta Constitution, 91
Atlanta Journal, 91
Atlantic Monthly, 16, 81
Atree, William, 60
Attention, Decline of, 206
Automatic Casting, 217

Baillie, Hugh, 79
Baltimore Sun, 109, 121, 123, 126, 129
Barnett, Lincoln, 66

Barth, Alan, 73, 84, 88
Baukhage, Hilmar Robert, 167, 170
"Beats." *See* "Scoops"
Bennett, James Gordon, 51–52, 61, 89
Berkeley, Sir William, 176
Berkson, Seymour, 79
Bernstein, Theodore M., 211
Bickel, Karl, 79
Biddle, Nicholas, 73
Bingham, Barry, 192
Bohemianism, 140–142
Boissier, Gaston, 221
Bonfils, Fred G., 90
Books, Topical, 17, 216
Boston Gazette, 188
Boston Globe, 90
Boston News-Letter, 34–35, 49, 69
Boston Rehearsal, 59
Bourne, Nicholas, 23
Bovard, Oliver K., 85
Bowen, James, 167
Bradford, Andrew, 36–37
Brevity in the News Story, 159–161, 168–169, 206
Broadcasting, 16, 198
Brooklyn Eagle, 55
Brown, Sevellon, 204
Browne, Charles Farrar, 92
Browne, Junius Henri, 225
Brucker, Herbert, 74, 190–191, 225
Bryant, William Cullen, 92
Burke, Edmund, 7
Burnham, Samuel, 91–92
Business Papers, 15
Business Week, 16–17
Butter, Nathaniel, 23
By-lined News, 83, 93

Cables, Undersea, 43
Caesar, Julius, 2–3
Cahan, Abraham, 44–45
Campbell, John, 34–35, 49, 69
Canham, Erwin Dain, 80, 204, 216
Carey, Mathew, 24

Carlyle, Thomas, 7, 9, 38
Carrington, Edward, 5
Carter, Hodding, 205
Casey, Ralph Droz, 94–95, 223
Caton, Bruce, 223
Censorship, 24, 25, 119, 175–182
Chains. *See* Group Ownership
Charnley, Mitchell Vaughn, 95, 225
Chicago Daily News, 66, 102, 123, 126, 224
Chicago Daily Tribune, 91, 102, 109, 126, 140, 157
Chicago Record, 65
Chicago Sun-Times, 126, 189
Christian Science Monitor, 12, 45, 52, 53, 80, 123, 126, 222
Church News. *See* Religious News
Cicero, Marcus Tullius, 2
Cincinnati Gazette, 46
Circulation Basis of Newspaper, 207
City Editor, 93, 144–146
Clark, Delbert, 118–119, 121
Clarke, Joseph I. C., 62
Clayton Act Amendment, 190
Clemens, Samuel Langhorne, 92
Cleveland Plain Dealer, 92
Coleman, William, 91–92
Collier's, 16, 26
Color. In television, 215; in newspapers, 217
Columbian Centinel, 70
Columnists, 82, 93
Commentators, 18, 82, 150
Commission on Freedom of the Press, 20–21, 187, 225
Community Newspapers. *See* Weekly Newspapers; Newspapers, Small-City; Suburban Papers
"Confidential" Newsletters, 17, 81
Conflict as Element of Interest, 28–31
Confucius, 171
Congress of Industrial Organizations, 104
Consolidation of Newspapers, 187–195
Contempt Actions against Newspapers, 225
Continuing Studies of Newspaper Reading, 25, 91
Coolidge, Calvin, 113

Cooney, Celia, 55
Cooper, Kent, 78–79
Corante, 23
Coray, M., 6
Corbett, James J., Story of, 158
Cowles, John, 192–193, 204
Cox, Samuel Sullivan, 165
Creation Story, 161
Creelman, James, 47
Crime News, 18, 52–56
Criteria of News Importance, 26–32, 123
"Crusades," 54, 106
Curtis, George William, 165–166

Daily Magazines, 216
Daily Sports News Service, 101
Dale-Chall Formula, 163
Dana, Charles Anderson, 34, 46, 62, 64, 164
Davis, Elmer, 86–87, 88, 170, 223
Davis, Watson, 104, 223
Definitions of News, 22–26, 29
Demosthenes, 2
Denver Post, 90, 91
Des Moines Capital, 26, 191
Des Moines Register, 13, 102, 191
Des Moines Tribune, 141, 191, 224
Detroit News, 102
Dilliard, Irving, 84–85, 223
Diplomatic Correspondents, 115–116
Documentary Films, 19–20
Domestic News, 97–98
Dunne, Finley Peter, 66
Dunning, John P., 73

Early, Stephen T., 113, 118
Editor & Publisher, 16, 55, 221, 223, 226
Editorials, News in, 11, 83
Education for Journalism, 217–218
Education of Readers as Editorial Aim, 202–205, 206
Educational Newsfeatures, 101
Egyptian Papyrus Tales, 1, 49
Elements of Interest, 28–31
Eliot, Charles William, 141
Engineering News-Record, 16
Ernst, Morris Leopold, 194, 226
Essary, Jesse Frederick, 121
Ethridge, Mark Foster, 192, 204

"Exchanges" as News Sources, 97–98

Facsimile, 215
Facts on File, 15
Fadiman, Clifton, 206, 226
Faribault Daily News, 94
Faris, Barry, 79
Farm News. *See* Agricultural News
Features, News in, 11
Federal Communications Commission, 196–198
Field, Marshall, 190
Fisher, Paul, 66
Fleet, Thomas, 59
Flesch, Rudolph, 162–164, 224
Flynn, Errol, 54
Foreign-Language Press, 15
Foreign News, 122–131, 134
Foreign News Service, 129
Fortune, 21
Fourdrinier Papermaking Machine, 98
Fourth Estate, 6–7
"Fragmentation." *See* Brevity in the News Story
Frank Leslie's Illustrated Newspaper, 15
Franklin, Benjamin, 36–37
Freedom of the Press. *See* Liberty of the Press
Frequency Modulation, 197, 215
Front Page, The, 141
Fugger Brothers, 3

Gallup, George Horace, 25
Gammack, Gordon, 141
Gannett News Service, 109
Gauvreau, Emile, 203
General Magazine, 36–37
Gerald, J. Edward, 225
German News Pamphlets, 3, 49
Godkin, Edwin Lawrence, 202
Gossip, 82. *See* Rumor
Gould, Alan, 163
Government News, 105–122
Government Press Agents, 116–119
Governmental Controls, 175–182
Graf Spee, 167
Grant, Ulysses Simpson, Nomination of, 158, 159

Grasty, Charles Henry, 71
Gray-Leary Formula, 162
Greeks and News, 2
Greeley, Horace, 72, 93, 180, 204
Green, Bartholomew, 35
Green, Thomas, 97
Group Ownership, 186–188
Guarantee of Press Freedom, 174, 176–178
Gunning, Robert, 164

Hamilton, Alexander, 91–92, 176–177
"Handouts," 116–118
"Hard News," 32, 40–41, 48, 199–205. *See* "Significant Importance"
Harding, Warren Gamaliel, 113, 119
Harper's Magazine, 16, 165
Harper's Weekly, 15
Harris, Benjamin, 23, 33–34, 68, 69, 157
Harris, Wilson, 194
Hartford Courant, 74, 97, 190
Hart, Hornell, 52, 222
Harvey, George Brinton McClellan, 39
Headlines, 157, 158
Headlining America, 222
Hearst, William Randolph, 26, 47, 100, 104, 187, 200, 222
Hearst Newspapers, 100, 109, 180, 187
Heliography, Communication by, 42
Hersey, John, 224
Hicks, George, 167
Hindenburg Disaster, 169
"Hippodroming," 51, 214
History and News, 33–41
Hobby, Oveta Culp, 205
Hoe Presses, 98
Holmes, Oliver Wendell, 4
Hoover, Herbert, 113, 119
Hoover, John Edgar, 56
"Hot Corn" Stories, 61–62, 65
Hoyt, Edwin Palmer, 204
Hudson, Frederic, 76, 223
Hübner, Emil, 221
Hughes, Charles Evans, 178, 179
Hughes, Helen MacGill, 58, 222
Human-Interest Story, 4, 28, 58–66
Hutchins, Robert M. *See* Commission on Freedom of the Press

Ickes, Harold, 82
Independence of Party Control, 71–72, 108
Ingham, Harvey, 191
International News Photos, 102
International News Service, 72, 79, 100–101, 103, 109–110, 125, 138–139, 161, 164
Interpretive Reporting, 78–87
Irwin, Will, 73
Isolationism, 95–96
Iwo Jima Flag-Raising, 171

Jarnagin, William Claude, 26
Jefferson, Thomas, 5–6, 177, 225
"Jenkins," 165–166
Johnson, Gerald W., 26
Johnson, Samuel, 202
Johnstown Flood, 166
Jonson, Ben, 45
Jonson, Broer, 23
Journal of Commerce, 99

KDKA Radio Station, 102–103
KGO Radio Station, 224
KMPC Radio Station, 95
Kaltenborn, Hans V., 170
Kansas City Star, 13, 26, 63–64, 66, 91, 167
Katz, Daniel, 18
Kemsley Foreign News Service, 125
King Features, 102
Kingsbury, Susan Myra, 52, 222
Knight Newspapers, 187
Knowland, Joseph Russell, 192
Kobre, Sidney, 55
Korzybski, Alfred, 77–78, 223

Labor News, 104–105
Labor papers, 15
Lazarsfeld, Paul F., 18, 221
"Lead" of News Story, 158–159, 161
Le Clerc, Jean-Victor, 221
Lee, Irving J., 223
L'Estrange, Sir Roger, 68, 176
Liberty of the Press, 173–199, 218
Licensing Radio Stations, 196–198
Lies in the News, 84–87
Life, 16, 126, 193
Lincoln, Abraham, Assassination of, 157–158

Liner, Eugene, 226
Link, Henry C., 226
Lippmann, Walter, 31, 79
Literary Digest, 15
Literature and Journalism, 164–165, 167
Living Church, 17
Local News, 88–96, 105–106, 134
Long, Huey, 178
Look, 16
Lorge, Irving, 162
Louisiana Tax on Advertising, 178
Louisville Courier-Journal, 21, 192

MacArthur, General Douglas, 137–138, 152, 169, 180, 214
Macaulay, Thomas Babington, 6–7
McCarthy, Joseph R., 84
McCormick Newspapers, 187
MacDougall, Curtis Daniel, 53, 79
MacEwen, Arthur, 26, 200
McIntyre, Oscar Odd, 64
McKinley, William, 113
McMaster, John Bach, 38–39
Magazines and the News, 15–17, 36–37, 81, 216
Managing Editor, 92
"March of Time," 19, 169, 172
Marshall, John, 177
Marshall Plan, 118
Marvin, Dwight, 205
Mather, Increase, 33
Maverick, Augustus, 141, 224
"Mayflower Decision," 197–198
Media of News Distribution, 9–21
Memphis Commercial Appeal and *Press-Scimitar*, 192
Mill, John Stuart, 191
Milton, John, 174, 181
Minneapolis Star and *Tribune*, 192–193
Minnesota "Gag" Law, 178, 179
Money as Element of Interest, 28–31
Monopoly in News, 20–21, 191–194. *See* Consolidation of Newspapers
Morris, Richard B., 167, 225
Morse Telegraph, 98–99
Motion Pictures, Reporters in, 142
"Mugwumps," 71
Munsey, Frank Andrew, 189

Murger, Henri, 140
Murrow, Edward R., 167

Nation, 16
National Association of Radio News Directors, 149
National Association of Science Writers, 104
National Broadcasting Company, 109, 149
National Intelligencer, 35
National Negro Press Association, 101
National Police Gazette, 57
National Press Association, 100
National Press Club, 117
National Recovery Administration, 104, 110-111
Negro Press, 15
Nelson, William Rockhill, 40, 204
Nevins, Allan, 92, 224
New England Courant, 88
New England Palladium, 50
New England Weekly Journal, 188
New-London Gazette, 69
New Republic, 16
New York Commercial Advertiser, 44-45, 164
New York Courier and Enquirer, 99
New York Evening Post, 91-92
New York Express, 99
New York Herald, 51-52, 61, 99, 140
New York Herald Tribune, 66, 102, 109, 123, 126, 212
New York Mirror, 52
New York Sun, 20, 46, 60, 62-63, 99, 140, 164
New York Times, 12, 23, 32, 35-36, 45, 46, 99, 102, 104, 109, 118, 123, 126, 158, 159, 184, 211, 212, 225
New York Transcript, 60
New York Tribune, 46, 61, 72, 99, 158, 180
New York World, 64, 65
New Yorker, 16
News Editor, 145
News Magazines, 15-16, 37, 81
News of the World, 57
News Release. See "Handout"
News Services, 99-102. See Associ-

ated Press, United Press Associations, International News Service, Reuters, etc.
Newsletters, 2-3
Newspaper Enterprise Association, 102, 125
"Newspaper Game," 29-30
Newspapers, Metropolitan Daily, 12-13, 140-148
Newspapers, Small-City Daily, 13-14, 93-95
Newspapers, Weekly. See Weekly Newspapers
Newspapers in General, 10-11, 216
Newsreels, 19-20, 172-173
Newsweek, 15, 37, 126, 193
Nieman Reports, 79-80, 166
Niles' Register, 15, 41
Nixon, Raymond Blalock, 194, 225-226
North American Newspaper Alliance, 102, 125

Oakland Tribune, 192
Oatis, William N., 127
"Objective" News, 75-80, 150, 185-186, 195
Ohio Statesman, 167
Older, Mrs. Fremont, 226
O'Malley, Frank Ward, 73
Oregon Journal, 91
Oregonian, 91
Origins of News, 1-4
Overseas News Agency, 125
Overstreet, Harry Allen, 29
"Overt News," 31

PM, 184
Paducah Survey, 21
Pamphlets, 6, 17
Parks, William, 97
Partisan Press, 70-72, 108
Parton, James, 33
Pater, Walter, 165
Pathfinder, 15
Patterson, Grove, 205
Pegler, Westbrook, 82
Pennsylvania Evening Herald, 24
Penny Press, 51, 59-61, 72, 89-90
Personal Journalism, 92-93
Petrie, W. Flinders, 1

Pew, Marlen Edwin, 55
Philadelphia Evening Bulletin, 211–212
Philadelphia Public Ledger, 61, 140
Phillips, Cabell, 223
Photo-Journalism, 171–172
Picture Weeklies and the News, 16
Pictures and News, 171–172
Pigeon Post, 42
"Play" of News. See "Hippodroming"
Police Court Reports, 60–61
Pony Express, 43, 98
Pope, James Soule, 181–182
Pravda, 129
Prediction, 5, 37–38, 214
Presbyterian Life, 17
Presidential News Conferences, 113–114, 119–120
Press Association, 103
Press Gallery of Congress, 109–112
Press Secretary of President, 113
Pressures as Censorship, 182–186
Price, Byron, 179
Printer's Ink, 16
Probable Consequence as News Test, 27
Prominence in the News, 27–28
Prophecy. *See* Prediction
"Providences" and News, 33–34, 50
Proximity as News Test, 27
Public Affairs Pamphlets, 17
Publick Occurrences, 23, 33–34, 49, 68, 69, 157
Publishers' Attitudes, 184–186, 194–195
Publishers' Weekly, 16
Pulitzer, Joseph, 104, 204
Pulitzer, Joseph, II, 205
Pyle, Ernest Taylor, 64, 66, 96

Quick, 15

Radio News. Description of station handling of, 148–156; form of, 167–171; general and historical discussion of, 17–19; liberty of speech in, 195–198; opinion in, 81–82, 100, 103, 109, 135
Radio Style, 161, 167–171
Ralph, Julian, 73

Raymond, Henry Jarvis, 46
Reader Complaints, 208–209
Reader Interest, 24–25, 91, 199–205
Readers, Power and Responsibilities of, 205–213
Reading Techniques, 210–213
Reading Time, 210, 226
Reid, Helen Rogers, 205
Reid, Whitelaw, 46, 90
Reliability of News, Basis of, 39–40
Religious News, 105
Religious News Service, 101
Religious press, 15, 17
Reporter, 16
Repplier, Agnes, 53–54
Reston, James Barrett, 118
Reuters Limited, 125
Rice, Thomas Stevens, 55
Richards, Ivor Armstrong, 224
Riis, Jacob August, 65
Ritter, Dr. William Emerson, 104
Roberts, Roy Allison, 167
Robinson, Solon, 61–62, 65
Romans and News, 2–3
Roosevelt, Franklin Delano, 113, 167, 184
Roosevelt, Theodore, 112
Rosenthal, Joseph, 171
Ross, Charles Griffith, 113
Rumor, 10, 34, 67–68, 88, 156–157
Russia. *See* Soviet Union
Ryan, William L., 129

St. *Louis Post-Dispatch*, 55–56, 73–74, 85, 123, 126
St. *Louis Star-Times*, 224
St. *Paul Dispatch*, 26
San Francisco Chronicle, 123, 126
San Francisco Examiner, 26
Sandusky Register-Star-News, 13
Santa Rosa Press Democrat, 209
Santayana, George, 76, 223
Saturday Evening Post, 16
Schindler, Jacob John, 26
Schools and Newspaper Reading, 213
Schools of Journalism, 216–217
Schramm, Wilbur, 30, 222, 224, 225, 226
Science News, 103–104

Science Service, 101, 104
"Scoops," 44–47
Scott-James, R. A., 221
Scripps, Edward Wyllis, 100, 104
Scripps-Howard Group, 100, 109, 187
Sedition Act, 177
Semantics of News Reporting, 77–78
Semaphore Communication, 42
Sensation, 4, 48–57, 200, 202
Sex as Element of Interest, 28–31, 49
Seymour, Gideon, 192
Shafter, Gen. William Rufus, 180
Sheridan, Richard Brinsley, 176
Sherman, Gen. William Tecumseh, 179–180
Sherrington, C. S., 222
Short, Joseph, 137
Shuman, Edwin Llewellyn, 158
Siebert, Frederick Seaton, 178, 225
Siepmann, Charles A., 225
"Significant Importance" in the News, 30–32, 122, 123
Slosson, Edwin Emery, 104
Smith, Henry Justin, 66, 148
Smith, Merriman, 223
Smith, Paul, 205
Snyder, Louis L., 167, 225
Society News, 89–90
"Soft News," 32, 41, 48, 199–205
Soviet Union, 47, 128–129, 186
Stark, Louis, 104–105, 223
Starrett, Vincent, 224
Starzel, Frank J., 72–73, 75, 79
State Department News Conferences, 115
State Government, News of, 106–108
Steffens, Lincoln, 44–45, 164
Stokes, Thomas Lunsford, 110–111, 121
Streit, Clarence K., 87–88, 223
Suburban Papers, 13, 216
Sullivan, John L., Story of, 158
Sulzberger, Arthur Hays, 32, 184, 204
Summaries of News, 81
Sumner, William A., 223
Sutherland, George, 178
Swanson, Neil Harmon, 121

Tabloids, War of the, 54–55
Tacitus, Cornelius, 2
Tacoma News-Tribune, 66
Taft, William Howard, 113
Taft-Hartley Act, 104
Taylor, Gen. Charles Henry, 90
Telegraph, 42–43, 98–100
Telephoto, 43, 135
Teletype, 98
Teletypesetter Circuits, 216–217
Television, 19, 95, 173, 214–215
Tests of News Importance. *See* Criteria
Thorndike, Edward Lee, 30, 222
Time, 15, 37, 126, 161, 193
Timeliness of News, 22–23, 27, 41–48
Transradio Press Service, 103
Treasury of Good Reporting, 167
Truman, Harry S., 114, 119, 120, 137–138
Twain, Mark, 92

United Nations Assembly Correspondents, 116
United Press Associations, 72, 79, 100, 102, 103, 109–110, 125, 138–139, 161, 164
United States News and World Report, 15, 126
Universal Service, 101
Universal Trade Press Syndicate, 101

Veseler, George, 23
Villard, Oswald Garrison, 54
Virginia City Enterprise, 92
Virginia Gazette, 97
Voltaire, 67

WHO Radio Station, 224
WWJ Radio Station, 102
Wagner Act, 104
Walker, Stanley, 90, 223
Wall Street Journal, 109
Walters, Basil L., 194, 216
War News, 3–4, 50, 179–181
Ward, Artemus, 92
Ward, Paul William, 129
Washington, George, 119

Washington Correspondence, 83, 108–122

Washington Globe, 35

Waterloo, News of Battle of, 76

Weekly Newspapers, 14–15, 93–95, 189

Welch, Stuart, 66

Wells, Herbert George, 38

Westchester County Newspaper Service, 101

Western Union Telegraph Company, 99–100

White, Horace, 71

White, Paul, 82

White House Correspondents, 112–114

Wide World Photos, 102, 135

Wight, John, 60

Willey, Malcolm Macdonald, 223

Willoughby, Gen. Charles A., 180

Wilson, Woodrow, 113, 119

Wingate, Charles F., 223

Wire Services. *See* News Services

Wireless Systems, 43

Wirephoto. *See* Telephoto

Wisner, George W., 60

World News, 126

Wyden, Peter, 55–56